Jesus and the Reign of God in John

Jesus and the Reign of God in John

MARK C. KILEY

◆PICKWICK *Publications* · Eugene, Oregon

JESUS AND THE REIGN OF GOD IN JOHN

Copyright © 2025 Mark C. Kiley. All rights reserved. Except for brief quotations in critical publications or reviews, no part of this book may be reproduced in any manner without prior written permission from the publisher. Write: Permissions, Wipf and Stock Publishers, 199 W. 8th Ave., Suite 3, Eugene, OR 97401.

Pickwick Publications
An Imprint of Wipf and Stock Publishers
199 W. 8th Ave., Suite 3
Eugene, OR 97401

www.wipfandstock.com

PAPERBACK ISBN: 979-8-3852-2292-6
HARDCOVER ISBN: 979-8-3852-2293-3
EBOOK ISBN: 979-8-3852-2294-0

Cataloguing-in-Publication data:

Names: Kiley, Mark Christopher [author].

Title: Jesus and the reign of God in John / by Mark C. Kiley.

Description: Eugene, OR: Pickwick Publications, 2025 | Includes bibliographical references and index.

Identifiers: ISBN 979-8-3852-2292-6 (paperback) | ISBN 979-8-3852-2293-3 (hardcover) | ISBN 979-8-3852-2294-0 (ebook)

Subjects: LCSH: Bible.—John—Criticism, interpretation, etc. | Bible.—John—Theology. | Jesus Christ—Teachings. | Kingdom of God—Biblical teaching.

Classification: BS2615.52 K57 2025 (paperback) | BS2615.52 (ebook)

VERSION NUMBER 10/16/25

PERMISSIONS AND SCRIPTURE ATTRIBUTIONS

The author gratefully acknowledges permission from Hebrew Union College Press to reproduce the chart of Dan 5:26–28 from John Wolters, "The Riddle of the Scales in Daniel 5," *HUCA* 62 (1991) 155–77.

Unless otherwise specified, Scripture quotations are the author's translation.

Scripture quotations marked NAB are from the *New American Bible, revised edition, copyright* © 2010 Confraternity of Christian Doctrine, Washington, DC, and are used by permission of the copyright owner. All rights reserved.

Scripture quotations marked NRSV are from the New Revised Standard Version, copyright © 1989, Division of Christian Education of the National Council of the Churches of Christ in the United States of America. Used by permission. All rights reserved.

Scripture quotations marked NRSVA are from the New Revised Standard Version Bible: Anglicised Edition, copyright © 1989, 1995 the Division of Christian Education of the National Council of the Churches of Christ in the United States of America. Used by permission. All rights reserved.

Scripture quotations marked NRSVCE are from the New Revised Standard Version Bible: Catholic Edition, copyright © 1993 National Council of the Churches of Christ in the United States of America. Used by permission. All rights reserved worldwide.

Scripture quotations marked NRSVue are from the New Revised Standard Version, Updated Edition, copyright © 2021 National Council of Churches of Christ in the United States of America. Used by permission. All rights reserved worldwide.

In chapter three of this study, Sophia, the title κυριος is rendered "Sovereign", not "Lord."

Cover: Piero della Francesca (Italian, ca. 1415–1492), *St. John the Evangelist*, 1454–69. Tempera on panel, 52 3/4 x 24 1/2 in. (134 x 62.2 cm). The Frick Collection, New York. Image ©The Frick Collection.

Contents

Acknowledgments | ix
Abbreviations | xi

Introduction | 1

Chapter One: Sayings | 8
Chapter Two: Servant | 40
Chapter Three: Sophia | 64
Chapter Four: Stories | 103
Chapter Five: Seeing | 142

Bibliography | 163
Ancient Document Index | 169

Acknowledgments

I THANK THE EDITORIAL team at Wipf & Stock for their thorough attention to detail. Grateful for all those who share with me the grace of participating in the post–Vatican II Catholic biblical renewal, I dedicate these pages to tomorrow's researchers in New Testament and Christian origins.

MARK C. KILEY
SEPT. 30, 2025

Abbreviations

AB	Anchor Bible
Ant.	*Jewish Antiquities*
APOT	*The Apocrypha and Pseudepigrapha of the Old Testament.* Edited by Robert H. Charles. 2 vols. Oxford: Clarendon, 1913
AYBRL	Anchor Yale Bible Reference Library
Bib	*Biblica*
BibInt	Biblical Interpretation Series
BD	Beloved Disciple
BTB	*Biblical Theology Bulletin*
CBET	Contributions to Biblical Exegesis and Theology
CBQ	*Catholic Biblical Quarterly*
CBQMS	Catholic Biblical Quarterly Monograph Series
CCTC	Cambridge Classical Texts and Commentaries
DCLS	Deuterocanonical and Cognate Literature Studies
ECL	Early Christianity and Its Literature
ExpTim	*Expository Times*
HUCA	Hebrew Union College Annual
JBL	Journal of Biblical Literature
J.W.	*Jewish War*
LCL	Loeb Classical Library
NewDocs	*New Documents Illustrating Early Christianity.* Edited by Greg H. R. Horsley and Stephen Llewelyn. North Ryde, NSW: The Ancient History Documentary Research Centre, Macquarie University, 1981–

Abbreviations

Od.	*The Odyssey.* By Homer. Edited and translated by A .T. Murray and George E. Dimock. 2 vols. LCL 104–5. Rev. ed. Cambridge, MA: Harvard University Press, 1998
OG	Old Greek
OGIS	*Orientis Graeci Inscriptiones Selectae.* Edited by Wilhelm Dittenberger. 2 vols. Hildesheim: Olms, 1960
OTL	The Old Testament Library
OTP	*Old Testament Pseudepigrapha.* Edited by James H. Charlesworth. 2 vols. New York: Doubleday, 1983, 1985
OtSt	*Oudtestamentische Studien*
Resp.	*Respublica.* Plato. *The Republic: Books 1–5.* Translated by Paul Shorey. Rev. ed. LCL 237. Cambridge, MA: Harvard University Press, 1937.
RThom	*Revue thomiste*
SBLDS	Society of Biblical Literature Dissertation Series
SBLSP	Society of Biblical Literature Seminar Papers
SEG	Supplementum epigraphicum graecum
SFSHJ	South Florida Studies in the History of Judaism
VTSup	Supplements to Vetus Testamentum
WW	*Word and World*

Introduction

THE REIGN OF GOD cannot be strictly defined any more than "God" or "love" or "beauty" can be strictly defined.[1] Nevertheless, even as the hope for definition fades, so the reality of describing some of the tensive contours of kingdom symbolism in John, that is, a poetic history/historicized poetics, offers another kind of hope. For example, when the Prologue eschews the usual *ktiz-* root to describe creation and speaks instead of the Word's making the world as a "becoming" (1:3, 10), we have moved into a kind of poetics. This study of portions of the Fourth Gospel as historicized, perhaps philosophical, poetics offers its own winsome pleasure. For example, the text is not, strictly speaking, a Gospel; the word occurs nowhere in the text, either as noun or verb. There is a reason for that having to do in part with its Hebraic background. But the sheer idiosyncrasy of the fact exemplifies the allure of this text, offering to the hungry more than enough food for thought.

Our study explores aspects of God's reign in relation to the person of Jesus in John. At first glance, this reading is counterintuitive in that the phrase "reign of God" is mentioned in only two verses in the text (John 3:3, 5); indeed, only once in synagogal Scripture and that in a Greek-only text not even recognized as authoritative canonical literature by Jewish believers or Protestant Christians (Wis 10:10). There is no canonical consideration that restricts Catholic Christians from pursuing this verse cluster, but studies have tended to accord the verses only the amount of space commensurate with their integral presence in the Greek text of the Gospel. This dearth of attention to reign-of-God language in John stands in sharp contrast to the quite-frequent occurrence of reign-of-God diction in the Gospels of Matthew, Mark, and Luke. Hence, a first glance may turn out

1. Robinette, "Christology," 109.

to be shortsighted and unnecessarily narrow. When attention is given to the *transformation* of themes however, the logjam breaks, and the reader begins to reap the reward inherent in detecting the author's move from tradition to tradition renewed. The transformation of water to wine in John 2 is one of the first and most obvious clues regarding the author's agenda at large. If the Johannine author is inviting the reader to a game of Name That Tune, he does so as an outlier to the synoptic tradition of God's reign but, I would argue, as a faithful explorer of the depths of this central theme of the Gospel. For those moreover who do not find that the synoptic claim concerning God's reign is credible or even intelligible, this reading amounts to a fresh invitation to rethink the reign of God, this time as it appears in John.

Our study will include attention to resources both inside and outside the biblical canon, including both Testaments, what are referred to as either apocrypha or deuterocanonical texts, and Greek, Hebrew, Aramaic and Latin terms. Before describing the basic content of the upcoming chapters, let me draw the reader's attention to one of my favorite instantiations of John's rendering of the reign of God, the hypothetical one in Latin terms residing behind the Greek:

Greek εξουσια (authority) and αληθεια (truth) are present together in both John 1:12, 17 and again in 17:2, 17.[2] Therein resides another example of the Johannine expression of God's reign.

Their Latin equivalents (Latin is named, uniquely among the canonical Gospels, at the Johannine cross in John 19:20) are

- *Auctoritas*
- *Veritas*

Their component parts are

- *Actor*
- *Auctor*
- *Auctoritas*
- *Via*

---

2. A 1964 document of the Pontifical Biblical Commission, "On the Historical Truth of the Gospels," cited both of these terms in its fourth paragraph: "In order to shed full light on the perennial *truth and authority* of the Gospels, he [the Catholic exegete] will adhere to the norms of scholarly, Catholic hermeneutics; and he will make appropriate use of the new exegetical techniques, particularly those advocated by the historical method taken as a whole" (emphasis added).

Introduction

- *Vita*
- *Veritas*

In the following combinations, they are the building blocks of what may be called the Johannine Trinity:

1. *Auctor Vita* (Author of life)—The Father
   As the Father raises from the dead and gives life, so also the Son enlivens those whom he wishes. (5:21)

2. *Actor Veritas* (Enactor of truth)—The Son
   The Word became flesh. (1:14)
   Your word is truth. (17:17)

3. *Via Auctoritas* (Way of authority)—The Spirit
   No one takes my life from me. I lay it down from myself. I have authority to lay it down and authority to take it up again. (10:18)[3]

In texts that do not explicitly name Son and Spirit, those personal terms are intercalated.

The letters of υιος (Son) are present immediately prior to the word αληθεια (truth) in John 17:17:

αὐτοὺς . . . ἀληθείᾳ· ὁ λόγος . . . ἀλήθειά

Sanctify them in the truth. Your word is truth.

The letters of πνευμα (Spirit) are present prior to εξουσια (authority) in John 10:18:

διὰ τοῦτό με ὁ πατὴρ ἀγαπᾷ ὅτι ἐγὼ τίθημι τὴν ψυχήν μου, ἵνα πάλιν λάβω αὐτήν.¹⁸ οὐδεὶς αἴρει αὐτὴν ἀπ' ἐμοῦ, ἀλλ' ἐγὼ τίθημι αὐτὴν ἀπ' ἐμαυτοῦ. ἐξουσίαν ἔχω θεῖναι αὐτήν, καὶ ἐξουσίαν ἔχω πάλιν λαβεῖν αὐτήν· ταύτην τὴν ἐντολὴν ἔλαβον παρὰ τοῦ πατρός μου.

---

3. One may make a reasoned case for the notion that John 10 presents the *way of authority* in the presentation of Jesus as the door of the sheep, allowing them access to pasture (v. 7), as well as in the explicit naming of the εξουσια (authority) of Jesus exercised in his laying down his life and taking it up again (v. 18). This theme is overlaid on a schema showing distinct points of similarity with the narrative of Naboth in 1 Kgs 21: a place willed by God and threatened by a thief using false accusations of blasphemy and stoning to attempt the robbery. In fact, the single instance of *auctoritas* in the Vulgate Bible occurs at 1 Kgs 21:7.

> No one takes it [my life] from me, but I lay it down of myself. I have authority to lay it down and I have authority to take it up again. This command I have received from my Father.

Nor is this an isolated instance. John 5:27–28 also makes explicit mention of ἐξουσία in a cluster of verses that intercalate the letters of πνευμα (Spirit).

> καὶ <u>ἐξουσίαν</u> ἔδωκεν αὐτῷ κρίσιν <u>ποιεῖν</u>, ὅτι υἱὸς <u>ἀνθρώπου ἐστίν</u>. 28 μὴ θα<u>υμά</u>ζετε τοῦτο, ὅτι ἔρχεται ὥρα ἐν ᾗ πάντες οἱ ἐν τοῖς μνημείοις ἀκούσουσιν τῆς φωνῆς αὐτοῦ.

> And he has given him authority to do judgment because he is Son of Man, and do not wonder about this.

Wonderful indeed the intercalation of πνευμα within a span of seven words, beginning at <u>ποιεῖν</u>, and the last of which, θα<u>υμά</u>ζετε (wonder), contains υμα at its heart (similar to the diction in 5:20, where the echo of the Johannine Trinity is quite compressed).[4]

Of course, Christic theists who see the presence of these assertions percolating within the Johannine text would perhaps be likely to affirm that such intimate give-and-take among the persons of the one God happens seamlessly in ways infinitely beyond the linguistic limits of the word bundles here. Those in the United States who might be given to interpreting mundane created reality in view of this theological construct could entertain a correlation between these phrases and the branches of government as described in the US Constitution:

- *Auctor Vita*—Legislature
- *Actor Veritas*—Executive
- *Via Auctoritas*—Judiciary

A brief word about the suggested correlations between these two aspects of reality, theological and legal. The Latinate doublets are tied in John to language of Father, Son, and Spirit, not an invention of the author but a new iteration of what is present in the opening verses of the earliest letter in the New Testament canon, Paul's First Letter to the Thessalonians. As such,

---

4. Since Saint Thomas Aquinas would insist that abstract nouns are real only insofar as they are present in existent being(s), John's agenda of linking authority and truth to Father, Son, and Spirit is noteworthy. For a sustained treatment of a portion of the tripersonal terms in John, see Attridge, "Trinitarian Theology and Fourth Gospel."

Introduction

it is a narrative development of a paraenetic assertion regarding the presence of God in Christ who cannot be fully understood without reference to the I AM of the Jewish Scriptures. And I would add that I read those data as stages on the way to the later conciliar definitions at Nicea/Constantinople regarding the Trinitarian mystery, and Chalcedon regarding the person of Jesus. However, the US Constitution belongs to all citizens, people of faith or no faith. The Latinate building blocks are of potential interest to that believing subset of the populace who self-identify as Christic theists. And when these building blocks are thought of in relation to created reality as described in the US Constitution, some obvious distinctions must be made. The legislature authors life only in the limited legal sense of preserving values at the heart of the American experiment. These values include life, liberty, and other human rights, separation of powers, the rule of law, and equality of persons before the law. The truth enacted by the chief executive is that of the law issuing from Congress under ever-changing circumstances. The presidential task exists by law for a prescribed amount of time to be followed by the peaceful transfer of power to the next exercitant of this public service. The way of authority is exercised by the judiciary in saying what the law is in a case of disputed enactment. In the words of a former Associate Justice of the Supreme Court, such adjudication is crafted in dialogue regarding the text of the Constitution, yes, but also with due regard for the purpose and consequences of law in a particular case, and the workability of any anticipated ruling.[5]

As of this writing, the decision of the Supreme Court's majority in Trump v. United States (on July 1, 2024) is judged by many to give almost unlimited authority to the president of the United States in what the majority describes as core powers, official acts, and involves immunity from prosecution even for actions that would be deemed unlawful when done by any other citizen. While the six-to-three majority of the court rests its judgment on the importance of avoiding an exponential increase in litigation surrounding action taken by the chief executive, some critics have voiced grave concerns that the majority's ruling provides a theoretical blueprint for autocracy.[6] Such a severe difference of opinion has the potential to rend irreparably the fabric of the republic that is at this writing approaching the

---

5. Breyer, *Reading the Constitution*.

6. Ryan illustrates the danger apparent when one branch of government allows another to dominate by citing the example of the Supreme Court failing to control the anticommunist hysteria of the 1950s (*On Politics*, 608).

250th anniversary of its Declaration of Independence. Will the six majority members of the court remain unmoved by the claim that nothing in the Constitution grounds their recent stance? This study makes no pretensions about how that discussion will turn out and is content merely to name John as a potential theological resource for those in the ongoing political debate.

With greater certainty, we can anticipate the contours of the data examined in this volume.

CHAPTER 1—"SAYINGS"

I examine some examples of trilingual dynamics as such, Hebrew, Greek and Latin, followed by several traditional synoptic samples of reign-of-God sayings as they contribute in transformed skein to a portrait of John's Jesus.

CHAPTER 2—"SERVANT"

The ruling arm of the Lord is complemented by the servant of Yhwh in Isa 42, 49, 50, and 52–53. The letters of the name are successively utilized to structure the four Servant Poems in Isaiah, which in turn serve as a model for the presentation of Jesus in both Matthew and John. The pertinent Johannine texts involve Jesus interacting with women in chapters 2, 4, 11, and 12.

CHAPTER 3—"SOPHIA"

Wisdom of Solomon (esp. chs. 8 and 10) presents the βασιλεια (reign) and related ονομα (name) of God. Through that lens, John presents Jesus as Sophia/Wisdom, the female representation of the Sovereign. This chapter at the center of the present study is also the lengthiest.

CHAPTER 4—"STORIES"

Parables of the reign of God. Most of these citations of John's parabolic Jesus draw on the parables of the Synoptic Gospels but also include the contribution of a mysterious text at a royal court in Dan 5.

Introduction

CHAPTER 5—"SEEING"

The reign of God is both seen and entered in John 3:3, 5. In seeing the reign of God, primary attention devolves on the τεχνοπαιγνια (picture puzzles) of Hellenism, which paint pictures by the physical placement of words. Images include that of Jesus crucified/glorified as well as the letter *M*.

Chapter One

Sayings

THIS CHAPTER FOCUSES PRIMARILY on some of the ways in which Jesus and God's reign in Synoptic Gospel sayings appear transformed in the Fourth Gospel. Most of the arguments presented here rely on the standard Greek text in its most recent critical instantiation while not neglecting aspects of Hebrew and Latin in that cultural context. And because it has received relatively little critical attention, I begin with variants of intercalation as practiced by the Fourth Evangelist.

The abecedarian psalms, whose verses are formally shaped by the successive letters of the Hebrew alphabet, have their analogue in the Greek and Latin literature of the period prior to the writing of John.

What follows are two texts about the crescent moon, both antedating the first century CE:

Aratus's *Phaenomena*, lines 783–87, employs the letters of the adjective <u>λεπτή</u> in each of the successive lines of the poem:

> <u>λ</u>επτὴ μὲν καθαρή τε περὶ τρίτον ἦμαρ ἐοῦσα
> <u>ε</u>ὔδιός κ' εἴη· λεπτὴ δὲ καὶ εὖ μάλ' ἐρευθὴς
> <u>π</u>νευματίη· παχίων δὲ καὶ ἀμβλείῃσι κεραίαις
> <u>τ</u>έτρατον ἐκ τριτάτοιο φόως ἀμενηνὸν ἔχουσα
> <u>ἢ</u> νότῳ ἀμβλύνται ἢ ὕδατος ἐγγὺς ἐόντος.

> If she is
> slender and clear about the third day, she heralds

calm: if slender and very ruddy,
wind; but if thick and with blunted horns she displays but a feeble
   light on the third and
fourth night, her beams are blunted
by the South wind or imminent rain.¹

Note that the acrostic proceeds in the direction of the text. Virgil (*Georgics*, 1.429–30) effects a variation of this procedure, this time by hinting at his name in the first two letters of successive lines of the poem:

> <u>ma</u>ximus agricolis pelagoque parabitur imber: ⁴³⁰ at si virgineum suffuderit ore ruborem, <u>ve</u>ntus erit; vento semper rubet aurea Phoebe. sin ortu quarto (namque is certissimus auctor) <u>pu</u>ra neque obtunsis per caelum cornibus ibit

> A heavy rain is awaiting farmers and seamen. But if over her face she spreads a maiden blush, there will be wind; as wind rises, golden Phoebe ever blushes. But if at her fourth rising—for that is our surest guide—she traverses the sky clear and with un-dimmed horns

Note that the acrostic proceeds in the opposite direction to the flow of text: <u>P</u>ublius <u>V</u>ergilius <u>Ma</u>ro.²

A proximate Johannine analogue to these intercalary processes begins by hearing the statement about the kingdom of heaven likened to a treasure (θησαυρος) in Matt 13:44. The underlined letters for treasure are made to reside in the uniquely Johannine tradition at John 6:68.

> ἀπεκρί<u>θη</u> αὐτῷ Σίμων Πέτρος· Κύριε, πρὸς τίν<u>α</u> ἀπελε<u>υ</u>σόμεθα; ῥήματα ζωῆς αἰωνί<u>ου</u> ἔχεις.

> Simon Peter answered him, "Lord, to whom shall we go? You have the words of everlasting life."

I suggest that this verse also works together with John 21:15–19, the discourse of Peter and Jesus at breakfast, to instantiate the principle of the

---

1. Aratus, *Phenomena*, 30. Aratus was the subject of approximately twenty-seven commentaries in antiquity, in both Greek and Latin. In various places, John's intercalations may be seen to reflect the diction of *Phaenomena*: lines 783–87 and the καθαρ- root for cleansing in John 2; πνευμα in John 3; southerly water under darkening conditions in John 4 and 5; line 833 and observation of implicit sun imagery in John 6:15–21; lines 977–81 and explicit wintertime setting in John 10:22 and implicit rays of the sun in John 10:40–42.

2. Ross, *Backgrounds to Augustan Poetry*, 28–29.

reign of God in Matt 6:21: "Where your treasure is, there will your heart be also."

MORE ON JOHN'S TRILINGUAL MIND

The Johannine text is not limited only to such intercalation, however. It is swimming in these trilingual waters. For example, at least three points in John 13 replicate a tight cluster of root words in the Hebrew lexicon: דד (breast), דוד (beloved), and דוח (wash, cleanse). John 13, where we first encounter the Beloved Disciple under that title, is also working in a linguistic world bearing the impress of Aratus's Greek and Virgil's Latin. Aratus's καθαρη (clear) and υδωρ (water) also appear together in John 13:5, 11. Students in bilingual schools like those advocated by Quintilian at the close of the first century CE would have been asked to identify the single Latin term that resides behind the Greek of John 13:13, διδασκαλος και κυριος (teacher and master), and would have been congratulated when they answered, *magister*. Sometimes the text will ask us to attend to special arrangements of letters in one language pool that point toward the reign of God. Sometimes the text will point us toward the convergent influences of these languages in articulating the author's vision of the reign of God.

GREEK

There are only five instances of the word reign (βασιλεια) in the Johannine text. The first two (at 3:3, 5) contain within them the Greek letters, in correct order, for dunking (βάπτισμα), a word not explicitly present otherwise in John:

v. 3 Βασιλείαν
v. 5 ἀπεκρίθη ... τις ... πνεύματος

In between these verses, in v. 4, we find the intercalation of the Greek letters of cross (σταυρος):

Πῶς ... δύναται ... δύναται ... μητρὸς

The latter three instances of βασιλεια in John all occur in 18:36:

ἀπεκρίθη Ἰησοῦς· Ἡ βασιλεία ἡ ἐμὴ οὐκ ἔστιν ἐκ τοῦ κόσμου τούτου· εἰ ἐκ τοῦ κόσμου τούτου ἦν ἡ βασιλεία ἡ ἐμή, οἱ ὑπηρέται οἱ ἐμοὶ

Sayings

ἠγωνίζοντο ἄν, ἵνα μὴ παραδοθῶ τοῖς Ἰουδαίοις· νῦν δὲ ἡ βασιλεία ἡ ἐμὴ οὐκ ἔστιν ἐντεῦθεν.

Here again we find the Greek letters for cross (σταυρὸς) sprinkled in the correct order throughout the text:

ἔ<u>στ</u>ιν ... β<u>α</u>σιλεία ... <u>ὑ</u>πηρέται ... ο<u>ἱ</u> ... τοῖ<u>ς</u>

This sketch of βασιλεια in chapters 3 and 18 displays a careful assertion of the intricate bond between the cross of Jesus and the reign (of God).

Other Greek dynamics include the fact that the usual word for prayer (προσευχ-) is missing from the text. Instead, what we have is a presentation of Jesus as "Word whom the Father always hears" (11:42; see also 1:1). What is that?

In addition, Jesus is never said to suffer (πασχειν) in this text. Before the reader cries "gnostic heresy," allow me to ask about an aspect of what suffering involves. It is an imposition of pain of various kinds experienced against one's will. However, the Johannine text goes out of its way in 12:27–28 to insist that the lifting up of Jesus on the cross and into the Father's glory is something with which Jesus is in total agreement. Insofar as one considers Jesus' will as such, Jesus does not *suffer*; he *acts*. One can further gauge the emphasis of the text through this lens by noting that, though πασχειν is absent from the text, Πασχα (Pesach-Passover) is present ten times, three of them indicating the spring festival (2:13; 6:4; 13:1). This trait of the text represents a more frequent attention to Pascha than in the Synoptic Gospels and indicates the text's greater focus on Jesus' work at that season, his action. As articulated in the lifting-up sayings, these acts dwell on:

- Eternal life given to others (an aspect of the birth from above in the Spirit) (John 3:14)
- People coming to know I AM, and Jesus' speech from the Father (John 8:38)
- Jesus drawing others to himself (John 12:32)

These lifted-up loci, emphasizing as they do Spirit, Father, and Jesus, demonstrate both the continuity with the three synoptic passion and resurrection traditions of Mark and parallels (Mark 8:31; 9:30; 10:32) as well as the profound progress made by the Johannine sensibility.

In each of these instances, the net shift is toward one or another thoughtful recalibration of an earlier assertion about the person of Jesus.

HEBREW

One way of understanding the coherence of the chapters to follow concerns the interplay of three Hebrew words: מָשַׁל (*māshal*, reign); שֵׁם (*shēm*, name); מָשָׁל (*māshāl*, parable). The interchange of *shin*- and *mem*- approximates deliberate literary metatheses in the Hebrew Bible, as presented in the study of Isaac Kalimi.[3] Chapter 2 in this study explores the presence of the reign and name in Isaiah and John, and chapter 3 examines God's reign in Wisdom of Solomon and John. The alternate meaning of *mashal* as parable is the subject of chapter 4 of this study, tracing the transformation of themes in and reasons for parabolics in the Fourth Gospel.

In addition, John never uses the word "gospel," either as noun or verb. That does not mean that the evangelist has never known or simply forgotten the term. Rather, the Hebrew root בשר can mean either good news/gospel (*bāsar*) or flesh (*bāsār*). John emphasizes flesh, particularly in John 6. The gist of that makeover is that Jesus does not simply preach good news; he *is* the good news enfleshed.

I think that it remains an open question whether the intercalated letters for "parable" in John 13:1–2 are intentional and to what extent that category serves to describe the nature of the Johannine text:

> Πρὸ δὲ τῆς ἑορτῆς τοῦ πάσχα εἰδὼς ὁ Ἰησοῦς ὅτι ἦλθεν αὐτοῦ ἡ ὥρα ἵνα μεταβῇ ἐκ τοῦ κόσμου τούτου πρὸς τὸν πατέρα ἀγαπήσας τοὺς ἰδίους τοὺς ἐν τῷ κόσμῳ εἰς τέλος ἠγάπησεν αὐτούς. ² καὶ δείπνου γινομένου, τοῦ διαβόλου ἤδη βεβληκότος εἰς τὴν καρδίαν ἵνα παραδοῖ αὐτὸν Ἰούδας Σίμωνος Ἰσκαριώτου

> Now before the festival of the Passover, Jesus knew that his hour had come to depart from this world and go to the Father. Having loved his own who were in the world, he loved them to the end. ² The devil had already put it into the heart of Judas son of Simon Iscariot . . . (NRSV)

I have argued elsewhere that the Beloved Disciple of this text is Judas Iscariot and that this portrait may well be grasped, at least in part, as parabolic.[4]

---

3. Kalimi, *Metathesis in Hebrew Bible*.
4. Kiley, "Beloved Disciple, Judas Iscariot."

Sayings

One more interaction serves to introduce our focus on Jesus and the reign of God in John. In the Shema we hear, "Hear, O Israel, the Lord our God, the Lord is one" (Deut 6:4). The word for "one" employs the consonantal roots אחד. It is readily apparent that these letters are also the first letters of Hebrew אמת (truth), חיים (life), דרך (way). Might Hebraic "one" have influenced, at least in part, the choice of Jesus' self-identification in John 14:6, "I am the Way, the Truth, and the Life"? That is one option. Further aspects of the Latinate alternative that already appeared in the introduction will be discussed below.

LATIN

At least two lexical neighbors of Latin *regnum* (kingdom) adorn John 3 where the reign of God is announced. Latin *regeneratio* (being born again) is the literal sense understood by Nicodemus when Jesus speaks of γεννηθῇ ἄνωθεν (John 3:3). "How can someone being old be born again? Can he really enter the womb of his mother a second time to be born?" (John 3:4). Not far from *regnum* in the Latin lexicon is *reglesco* (to increase). That is at the heart of the baptizer's words in John 3:30, "He must increase." Similarly, Latin *rex* (king) may generate John's attention to the open palm slaps inflicted on Jesus in 18:22 and 19:3. Mark 14:65 uses ῥάπισμα also but in the discussion with the high priest when there is no discussion of kingship. John 19:3 may suggest that the status of ῥάπισμα in John is a lexical satellite of *rex*: "[The soldiers] came to him and said, 'Hail, king of the Jews,' and gave him open palm slaps."

Latin *veritas* (truth) contains within itself both *via* (way) and *vita* (life). The three terms coinhere. Is the evangelist presenting Jesus as a Latinate point of entry into life in the God of Israel? The aesthetic power of the suggestion is grounded in the available languages of the period, named as such in John 19:20.

In addition to the foregoing, the evangelist has drawn on and rendered in Greek some of the words that reside between—that are, so to speak, *contained within*—the span of words between those indicating sovereignty in both Latin and Hebrew. Among the canonical Gospels, these exercises are unique to the Fourth Gospel.

Between Latin *regnum* (reign) and *rex* (king) we find the evangelist employing the Greek equivalent of *rescribo* (write anew), for example, an imperial edict in John 19:19–22 regarding the *titulus* on the cross. In John

20:22, we find Jesus glorified, exercising *respiratio* (exhalation). In John 21:7–11, there is a rendering of *reno* (swim back) at the Sea of Tiberias.

Between Hebrew מלך (king) and משל (reign), we find Johannine equivalents of מעט (become small) in John 3:30.[5] In John 4:7, we find משה (draw [water]).

In sum, the Latinate and lexical delving into what is contained in sovereignty occurs soon after the several occurrences of the word for "king" in John 19. The Hebraic and lexical delving into what is contained in sovereignty occurs soon after the only occurrences of the phrase "reign of God" in John 3:3, 5.

I have cited these various linguistic underpinnings of the text to invite the reader to think carefully about the language used of a given Johannine event. A difference from a presumed base of earlier material may sometimes represent a development rather than a simple difference. The text invites, one could readily say, insists on, a certain level of nimble footwork, an openness to a sort of lyricism. No heavy boots allowed on most of this trek through the Johannine woods.

THE JOHANNINE JESUS AND THE REIGN OF GOD AS PERMUTATIONS OF SYNOPTIC SAYINGS

The Reign of God as Subject in Mark and Believing In . . .

At first glance, there is an aura of plausibility in the claim of Chrys Caragounis that the Fourth Gospel has transmuted the "reign of God" language in the Synoptic Gospels into that of "eternal life."[6] However, much evidence suggests that such an approach is adequate only as prolegomenon. The opening of the ministry in Mark depicts the reign of God as the grammatical subject of a sentence: "The reign of God has drawn near, repent and believe in the good news [ἐν τῷ εὐαγγελίῳ]" (Mark 1:15). The particle *en* also occurs in the unique notice in the Fourth Gospel "that everyone believing in him [ἐν αὐτῷ] may have eternal life" (John 3:15). Elsewhere in John, the uniform practice is to talk about believing *eis Iesous* (6:40; 11:25). It is no accident, I think, that the only occurrence in John of believing *en*

---

5. John 10 is the shortest of a handful of passages concerning the baptizer (John 1:19–37; 3:22–30, 31–35; 10:40, 41). These narratives grow successively smaller, illustrating the claim of the baptizer in 3:30 that he—Jesus—must grow greater, while I diminish.

6. Caragounis, "Kingdom of God."

Sayings

Iesou occurs near the only Johannine verses announcing the reign of God. This expression *en Iesou* is part and parcel of the portrayal of Jesus as the good news enfleshed, as mentioned at the outset of the Gospel.

The first sign of Jesus in John concerns his turning water to wine. What if we were also treated in that scene to a transformed rendition of Jesus' inaugural proclamation of the reign of God in Mark 1:15? John has no exact equivalent for the Markan Jesus' opening proclamation in Mark 1:15:

> καὶ λέγων ὅτι Πεπλήρωται ὁ <u>καιρὸς</u> καὶ <u>ἤγγικεν</u> ἡ βασιλεία τοῦ θεοῦ· μετανοεῖτε καὶ πιστεύετε ἐν τῷ εὐαγγελίῳ.

> The opportune moment [<u>καιρὸς</u>] is fulfilled. The reign of God has drawn near [<u>ἤγγικεν</u>].

Reform your mind and believe in the good news.

Johannine commentaries of varying sizes largely ignore this Markan verse because it is not quoted or even paraphrased in the usual manner within John. However, that may be to miss one of the most interesting dynamics of the text, a carefully plotted sprinkling of the letters underlined in the correct order in John 2:1.

Following the acclamation of Jesus as king of Israel in 1:49, John 2:1 may be read as indeed gesturing toward the initial proclamation of Jesus in Mark 1:15. I reproduce the Greek text, underlining the letters κ-α-ι-ρ-ὀ-ς:

> <u>Καὶ</u> τῇ ἡμέρᾳ τῇ τρίτῃ γά<u>μος</u> ἐγένετο ἐν Κανὰ τῆς Γαλιλαίας, καὶ ἦν ἡ μήτηρ τοῦ Ἰησοῦ ἐκεῖ·

> And on the third day there was a wedding in Cana of Galilee, and the mother of Jesus was there. (John 2:1)

Furthermore, John 2:1–2 allows a reading emphasizing yet another of the words in Mark 1:15, ἤ-γ-γ-ι-κ-ε-ν:

> Καὶ τῇ ἡμέρᾳ τῇ τρίτῃ γάμος ἐ<u>γ</u>ένετο ἐν Κανὰ τῆς Γαλιλαίας, <u>κ</u>αὶ ἦν ἡ μήτηρ τοῦ Ἰησοῦ ἐκεῖ· ² ἐκλήθη δὲ καὶ ὁ Ἰησοῦς καὶ οἱ μαθηταὶ αὐτοῦ εἰς τὸν γάμο<u>ν</u>.

> And on the third day there was a wedding in Cana of Galilee, and the mother of Jesus was there. And Jesus and his disciples were invited to the wedding. (John 2:1–2)

Various other aspects of the Cana wedding narrative may be read as renditions of elements of Mark 1:15. The Markan Jesus' call to reform your mind and believe the good news becomes in John:

- The chief steward's astonishment at the change in wedding banquet custom
- The disciples' beginning to believe in Jesus

What we have in John 2:1–12 is nothing less than a transformed version of the inaugural announcement of the Markan Jesus regarding the reign of God.

The Reign of God as Subject in Luke 17:20

On being asked by the Pharisees when the reign of God comes, Jesus answered them and said (that) the reign of God does not come with close inspection. "Neither will they say, 'Behold, look here or there,'

> ἰδοὺ γὰρ ἡ βασιλεία τοῦ θεοῦ ἐντὸς ὑμῶν ἐστιν.

for behold, the reign of God is among you."

Compare John 20:19c–20a:

> ἦλθεν ὁ Ἰησοῦς καὶ ἔστη εἰς τὸ μέσον, καὶ λέγει αὐτοῖς· Εἰρήνη ὑμῖν καὶ τοῦτο εἰπὼν

Jesus came and stood in their midst and said to them, "Peace be with you," and saying this . . .

Here I underline the relevant phrase about God's reign:

> ἦλθ<u>εν</u> ὁ Ἰησοῦς καὶ ἔστη εἰς <u>τὸ</u> μέ<u>σ</u>ον, καὶ λέγει αὐτοῖς· Εἰρήνη ὑ<u>μῖν</u> καὶ
>
> τοῦτο εἰπ<u>ὼν</u>

In this case, the Lukan phrase ἐντὸς ὑμῶν, present implicitly in the underlined intercalation, is also delineated by the explicit Johannine phrase εἰς τὸ μέσον. This coming of Jesus to the gathered disciples limns, at one level, the coming of the reign of God.

Sayings

Luke's Surrogate for the Reign of God (Luke 4:16–30) in John 20:19–23

Luke has no verbatim equivalent to the first spoken words of Jesus' public ministry as reported in Mark 1:15:

> The time is fulfilled, and the reign of God has drawn near; repent and believe the good news.

Instead, by reason of its placement as the first spoken words of Jesus' public ministry, Luke 4:16–30 may be read as a stand-in for the reign-of-God theme. The letters of the phrase βασιλεια του θεου (reign of God) occur here:

> καὶ πτύξας τὸ βιβλίον ἀποδοὺς τῷ ὑπηρέτῃ ἐκάθισεν· καὶ πάντων οἱ ὀφθαλμοὶ ἐν τῇ συναγωγῇ ἦσαν ἀτενίζοντες αὐτῷ. ²¹ ἤρξατο δὲ λέγειν πρὸς αὐτοὺς ὅτι Σήμερον πεπλήρωται ἡ γραφὴ αὕτη ἐν τοῖς ὠσὶν ὑμῶν. ²² καὶ πάντες ἐμαρτύρουν αὐτῷ καὶ ἐθαύμαζον ἐπὶ τοῖς λόγοις τῆς χάριτος τοῖς ἐκπορευομένοις ἐκ τοῦ στόματος αὐτοῦ, καὶ ἔλεγον· Οὐχὶ υἱός ἐστιν Ἰωσὴφ οὗτος. (Luke 4:20–22)

Note that, as in Mark 1, the announcement follows a quote from the prophet Isaiah.

In addition, John 20:21–23 reveals a stunning transformation of Luke's effort. Together, they assert that the reign of God is announced, albeit indirectly, not only at the beginning of the public ministry of Jesus but also in the words and actions of the crucified in glory.

In the following Greek renderings of the Lukan and Johannine texts, the similar diction is underlined.

Luke 4:16–30

> Καὶ ἦλθεν εἰς Ναζαρά, οὗ ἦν τεθραμμένος, καὶ εἰσῆλθεν κατὰ τὸ εἰωθὸς αὐτῷ ἐν τῇ ἡμέρᾳ τῶν σαββάτων εἰς τὴν συναγωγήν, καὶ ἀνέστη ἀναγνῶναι. ¹⁷ καὶ ἐπεδόθη αὐτῷ βιβλίον τοῦ προφήτου Ἡσαΐου καὶ ἀναπτύξας τὸ βιβλίον εὗρεν τὸν τόπον οὗ ἦν γεγραμμένον· ¹⁸ Πνεῦμα κυρίου ἐπ' ἐμέ, οὗ εἵνεκεν ἔχρισέν με εὐαγγελίσασθαι πτωχοῖς, ἀπέσταλκέν με κηρύξαι αἰχμαλώτοις ἄφεσιν καὶ τυφλοῖς ἀνάβλεψιν, ἀποστεῖλαι τεθραυσμένους ἐν ἀφέσει, ¹⁹ κηρύξαι ἐνιαυτὸν κυρίου δεκτόν. ²⁰ καὶ πτύξας τὸ βιβλίον ἀποδοὺς τῷ ὑπηρέτῃ ἐκάθισεν· καὶ πάντων οἱ ὀφθαλμοὶ ἐν τῇ συναγωγῇ ἦσαν ἀτενίζοντες αὐτῷ. ²¹ ἤρξατο δὲ λέγειν πρὸς αὐτοὺς ὅτι Σήμερον πεπλήρωται ἡ γραφὴ αὕτη

ἐν τοῖς ὠσὶν ὑμῶν. ²² καὶ πάντες ἐμαρτύρουν αὐτῷ καὶ ἐθαύμαζον ἐπὶ τοῖς λόγοις τῆς χάριτος τοῖς ἐκπορευομένοις ἐκ τοῦ στόματος αὐτοῦ, καὶ ἔλεγον· Οὐχὶ υἱός ἐστιν Ἰωσὴφ οὗτος; ²³ καὶ εἶπεν πρὸς αὐτούς· Πάντως ἐρεῖτέ μοι τὴν παραβολὴν ταύτην· Ἰατρέ, θεράπευσον σεαυτόν· ὅσα ἠκούσαμεν γενόμενα εἰς τὴν Καφαρναοὺμ ποίησον καὶ ὧδε ἐν τῇ πατρίδι σου. ²⁴ εἶπεν δέ· Ἀμὴν λέγω ὑμῖν ὅτι οὐδεὶς προφήτης δεκτός ἐστιν ἐν τῇ πατρίδι αὐτοῦ. ²⁵ ἐπ' ἀληθείας δὲ λέγω ὑμῖν, πολλαὶ χῆραι ἦσαν ἐν ταῖς ἡμέραις Ἠλίου ἐν τῷ Ἰσραήλ, ὅτε <u>ἐκλείσθη</u> ὁ οὐρανὸς ἐπὶ ἔτη τρία καὶ μῆνας ἕξ, ὡς ἐγένετο λιμὸς μέγας ἐπὶ πᾶσαν τὴν γῆν, ²⁶ καὶ πρὸς οὐδεμίαν αὐτῶν <u>ἐπέμφθη</u> Ἠλίας εἰ μὴ εἰς Σάρεπτα τῆς Σιδωνίας πρὸς γυναῖκα χήραν. ²⁷ καὶ πολλοὶ λεπροὶ ἦσαν ἐν τῷ Ἰσραὴλ ἐπὶ Ἐλισαίου τοῦ προφήτου, καὶ οὐδεὶς αὐτῶν ἐκαθαρίσθη, εἰ μὴ Ναιμὰν ὁ Σύρος. ²⁸ καὶ ἐπλήσθησαν πάντες θυμοῦ ἐν τῇ συναγωγῇ ἀκούοντες ταῦτα, ²⁹ καὶ ἀναστάντες ἐξέβαλον αὐτὸν ἔξω τῆς πόλεως, καὶ ἤγαγον αὐτὸν ἕως ὀφρύος τοῦ ὄρους ἐφ' οὗ ἡ πόλις ᾠκοδόμητο αὐτῶν, ὥστε κατακρημνίσαι αὐτόν· ³⁰ αὐτὸς δὲ διελθὼν διὰ <u>μέσου</u> αὐτῶν ἐπορεύετο.

When he came to Nazareth, where he had been brought up, he went to the synagogue on the Sabbath *day*, as was his custom. He *stood up* to read ¹⁷ and the scroll of the prophet Isaiah was given to him. He unrolled the scroll and found the place where it was written:

¹⁸ "The *Spirit* of the Lord is upon me,
because he has anointed me
to bring *good news* to the poor.
He has sent me to proclaim release to the captives
and recovery of sight to the blind,
to let the oppressed *go free*,
¹⁹ to proclaim the year of the Lord's favor."

²⁰ And he rolled up the scroll, gave it back to the attendant, and sat down. The eyes of all in the synagogue were fixed on him. ²¹ Then he began to say to them, "Today this Scripture has been fulfilled in your hearing." ²² All spoke well of him and were amazed at the gracious words that came from his mouth. They said, "Is not this Joseph's son?" ²³ He said to them, "Doubtless you will quote to me this proverb, 'Doctor, cure yourself!' And you will say, 'Do here also in your hometown the things that we have heard you did at Capernaum.'" ²⁴ And he said, "Truly I tell you, no prophet is accepted in the prophet's hometown. ²⁵ But the truth is, there were many widows in Israel in the time of Elijah, when the heaven was *shut up* three years and six months, and there was a severe famine over all the land; ²⁶ yet Elijah was *sent* to none of them except to

a widow at Zarephath in Sidon. [27] There were also many lepers in Israel in the time of the prophet Elisha, and none of them was cleansed except Naaman the Syrian." [28] When they heard this, all in the synagogue were filled with rage. [29] They got up, drove him out of the town, and led him to the brow of the hill on which their town was built, so that they might hurl him off the cliff. [30] But he passed through *the midst* of them and went on his way. (NRSV)

John 20:19–23

Οὔσης οὖν ὀψίας τῇ ἡμέρᾳ ἐκείνῃ τῇ μιᾷ σαββάτων, καὶ τῶν θυρῶν κεκλεισμένων ὅπου ἦσαν οἱ μαθηταὶ διὰ τὸν φόβον τῶν Ἰουδαίων, ἦλθεν ὁ Ἰησοῦς καὶ ἔστη εἰς τὸ μέσον, καὶ λέγει αὐτοῖς· Εἰρήνη ὑμῖν. [20] καὶ τοῦτο εἰπὼν ἔδειξεν τὰς χεῖρας καὶ τὴν πλευρὰν αὐτοῖς. ἐχάρησαν οὖν οἱ μαθηταὶ ἰδόντες τὸν κύριον. [21] εἶπεν οὖν αὐτοῖς ὁ Ἰησοῦς πάλιν· Εἰρήνη ὑμῖν· καθὼς ἀπέσταλκέν με ὁ πατήρ, κἀγὼ πέμπω ὑμᾶς. [22] καὶ τοῦτο εἰπὼν ἐνεφύσησεν καὶ λέγει αὐτοῖς· Λάβετε πνεῦμα ἅγιον· [23] ἄν τινων ἀφῆτε τὰς ἁμαρτίας ἀφέωνται αὐτοῖς· ἄν τινων κρατῆτε κεκράτηνται.

When it was evening on that *day*, the first day of the week, and the doors of the house where the disciples had met were *locked* for fear of the Jews, Jesus came and *stood among* them and said, "Peace be with you." [20] After he said this, he showed them his *hands* and his *side*. Then the disciples rejoiced when they saw the Lord. [21] Jesus said to them again, "Peace be with you. As the Father has *sent* me, so I *send* you." [22] When he had said this, he breathed on them and said to them, "Receive the Holy *Spirit*. [23] If you *forgive* the sins of any, they are forgiven them; if you retain any, they are retained."

Note that in the vocabulary of the Johannine narrative world, εὐαγγελίσασθαι (share good news) does not occur as either noun or verb. Instead, John displays one sense of Hebrew *b-s-r* that can mean either good news or flesh, emphasizing the flesh. The Fourth Evangelist provides testimony to the flesh of the crucified in glory by drawing attention to his χεῖρας (hands) and πλευρὰν (side). John has taken a cue from Luke's sotto voce rendering of the reign of God and placed a similarly whispered reign-of-God theme in his text where it will furnish, together with Luke, a frame to the entire public ministry of Jesus.

It will also be of interest to some readers that the exact equivalent of εἰς τὸ μέσον in John 20:19 occurs in the immediately ensuing Lukan pericope of exorcism. Whereas the demon casts down the tormented man "in their midst" (Luke 4:35) before Jesus raises him up, John's Jesus has laid down his life and taken it up, giving evidence of the same "in their midst."

The Johannine Reign of God as Direct Object

A variety of Johannine linguistic expressions and concepts, most of them already in Paul and the Synoptic Gospels, portray God's reign as inaugurated in Jesus, those concerning

- Seeking
- Inheriting
- Suffering violence in
- Seeing
- Entering

the reign of God. A few basic things may be said about their presence in John. Except for the reign as subject of the intransitive verb "to suffer violence," here we deal with instances in which the reign of God functions grammatically as the direct object of various verbs.

Seeking the Reign of God

"Seek [ζητειτε] first [πρωτος] the reign of God and his righteousness [δικαιοσυνη], and all these things will be added to you" (Matt 6:33–34). This verse and its Matthean environs have left their imprint on John 1:29–51 as well as on John 2:13—3:21.

The intercalated presence of the phrase "reign of God . . . seek . . . justice" in John 1:36–39 looks like this:

> καὶ ἐμβλέψας τῷ Ἰησοῦ περιπατοῦντι λέγει· Ἴδε ὁ ἀμνὸς τοῦ θεοῦ. ³⁷ καὶ ἤκουσαν οἱ δύο μαθηταὶ αὐτοῦ λαλοῦντος καὶ ἠκολούθησαν τῷ Ἰησοῦ. ³⁸ στραφεὶς δὲ ὁ Ἰησοῦς καὶ θεασάμενος αὐτοὺς ἀκολουθοῦντας λέγει αὐτοῖς. Τί ζητεῖτε; οἱ δὲ εἶπαν αὐτῷ· Ῥαββί (ὃ λέγεται μεθερμηνευόμενον Διδάσκαλε), ποῦ μένεις; ³⁹ λέγει αὐτοῖς· Ἔρχεσθε καὶ ὄψεσθε. ἦλθαν οὖν καὶ εἶδαν ποῦ μένει, καὶ παρ' αὐτῷ ἔμειναν τὴν ἡμέραν ἐκείνην· ὥρα ἦν ὡς δεκάτη.

And he looked at Jesus as he walked, and said, "Behold, the Lamb of God!" [37] The two disciples heard him say this, and they followed Jesus. [38] Jesus turned, and saw them following, and said to them, "What do you seek?" And they said to him, "Rabbi" (which means Teacher), "where are you staying?" [39] He said to them, "Come and see." They came and saw where he was staying; and they stayed with him that day, for it was about the tenth hour. (RSV)

John has placed in John 1:30 the word πρωτον (first) that functions adverbially in the Matthean reign-of-God statement. In John, it is part of an assertion about the priority of Jesus vis-à-vis John.

οὗτός ἐστιν ὑπὲρ οὗ ἐγὼ εἶπον· Ὀπίσω μου ἔρχεται ἀνὴρ ὃς ἔμπροσθέν μου γέγονεν, ὅτι <u>πρῶτός</u> μου ἦν·

This is he of whom I said, "After me comes a man who ranks before me, for he was *before* me."

Notice also what John has done with the Matthean Jesus' counsel "Do not worry about tomorrow [την αυριον]" (Matt 6:34), which follows the saying about seeking the reign of God first. This first chapter of John is punctuated by a threefold repetition of the phrase "on the morrow [επαυριον]" (John 1:29, 35, 43). Three questions in Matt 6:31 introduce the reign-of-God saying, "What are we to eat? What are we to drink? What are we to wear?" Their Johannine analogues, distinctive in the tradition, include extensive attention to eating in the bread of life discourse (John 6), the furnishing of wine (2:1–11), and the uniquely Johannine emphasis on the tunic of Jesus that goes to one of the soldiers at the cross (19:23–24).

The Johannine bloc from John 2:13—3:21 is also thoroughly imbued with reign-of-God emphases like those in Matt 6. Aspects of Matt 6:22–24 and 7:6 are integrated into John 2:13—3:21. The sayings precede and follow Matt 6:33 about seeking first the βασιλεια of God.

Matthew 6:22–24 reads:

Ὁ λύχνος τοῦ σώματός ἐστιν ὁ ὀφθαλμός. ἐὰν οὖν ᾖ ὁ ὀφθαλμός σου ἁπλοῦς, ὅλον τὸ σῶμά σου φωτεινὸν ἔσται. [23] ἐὰν δὲ ὁ ὀφθαλμός σου πονηρὸς ᾖ, ὅλον τὸ σῶμά σου σκοτεινὸν ἔσται. εἰ οὖν τὸ φῶς τὸ ἐν σοὶ σκότος ἐστίν, τὸ σκότος πόσον. [24] Οὐδεὶς δύναται δυσὶ κυρίοις δουλεύειν· ἢ γὰρ τὸν ἕνα μισήσει καὶ τὸν ἕτερον ἀγαπήσει, ἢ ἑνὸς ἀνθέξεται καὶ τοῦ ἑτέρου καταφρονήσει. οὐ δύνασθε θεῷ δουλεύειν καὶ μαμωνᾷ.

The eye is the lamp of the body. So, if your eye is healthy, your whole body will be full of light; [23] but if your eye is unhealthy, your whole body will be full of darkness. If then the light in you is darkness, how great is the darkness. [24] No one can serve two masters; for a slave will either hate the one and love the other or be devoted to the one and despise the other. You cannot serve God and wealth. (RSV)

Consider the display of μαμώνας (wealth) in John 2:14–15:

καὶ εὗρεν ἐν τῷ ἱερῷ τοὺς πωλοῦντας βόας καὶ πρόβατα καὶ περιστερὰς καὶ τοὺς κερματιστὰς καθημένους, [15] καὶ ποιήσας φραγέλλιον ἐκ σχοινίων πάντας ἐξέβαλεν ἐκ τοῦ ἱεροῦ τά τε πρόβατα καὶ τοὺς βόας, καὶ τῶν κολλυβιστῶν ἐξέχεεν τὰ κέρματα καὶ τὰς τραπέζας ἀνέστρεψεν,

The oblique presence of "wealth" is integrated into the verses dealing in part with money as such. Note also that Jesus' complaint in 2:16 concerns the "house of commerce" there.

The two kinds of eyes, απλους (simple) and πονηρος (evil), transmitting light and darkness (Matt 6:22–23), shape aspects of John 3:16–21:

Οὕτως γὰρ ἠγάπησεν ὁ θεὸς τὸν κόσμον ὥστε τὸν υἱὸν τὸν μονογενῆ ἔδωκεν, ἵνα πᾶς ὁ πιστεύων εἰς αὐτὸν μὴ ἀπόληται ἀλλὰ ἔχῃ ζωὴν αἰώνιον. [17] οὐ γὰρ ἀπέστειλεν ὁ θεὸς τὸν υἱὸν εἰς τὸν κόσμον ἵνα κρίνῃ τὸν κόσμον, ἀλλ' ἵνα σωθῇ ὁ κόσμος δι' αὐτοῦ. [18] ὁ πιστεύων εἰς αὐτὸν οὐ κρίνεται· ὁ δὲ μὴ πιστεύων ἤδη κέκριται, ὅτι μὴ πεπίστευκεν εἰς τὸ ὄνομα τοῦ μονογενοῦς υἱοῦ τοῦ θεοῦ. [19] αὕτη δέ ἐστιν ἡ κρίσις ὅτι τὸ φῶς ἐλήλυθεν εἰς τὸν κόσμον καὶ ἠγάπησαν οἱ ἄνθρωποι μᾶλλον τὸ σκότος ἢ τὸ φῶς, ἦν γὰρ αὐτῶν πονηρὰ τὰ ἔργα. [20] πᾶς γὰρ ὁ φαῦλα πράσσων μισεῖ τὸ φῶς καὶ οὐκ ἔρχεται πρὸς τὸ φῶς, ἵνα μὴ ἐλεγχθῇ τὰ ἔργα αὐτοῦ· [21] ὁ δὲ ποιῶν τὴν ἀλήθειαν ἔρχεται πρὸς τὸ φῶς, ἵνα φανερωθῇ αὐτοῦ τὰ ἔργα ὅτι ἐν θεῷ ἐστιν εἰργασμένα.

For God so loved the world that he gave his only Son, so that everyone who believes in him may not perish but may have eternal life. [17] Indeed, God did not send the Son into the world to condemn the world, but in order that the world might be saved through him. [18] Those who believe in him are not condemned; but those who do not believe are condemned already, because they have not believed in the name of the only Son of God. [19] And this is the judgment, that the light has come into the world, and people loved darkness rather than light because their deeds were evil. [20] For all who do evil hate the light and do not come to the light, so that their deeds may not be exposed. [21] But those who do what is true come to the light, so that it may be clearly seen that their deeds have been done in God. (NAB)

The light informs a suitable body (Matt 6:22c), which body is a central emphasis of John 2:21:

ἐκεῖνος δὲ ἔλεγεν περὶ τοῦ ναοῦ τοῦ σώματος αὐτοῦ

And this may prepare for the advent of Nicodemus visiting Jesus at night (John 3:2).

On the far end of the reign-of-God saying in Matt 6:33 (ζητεῖτε δὲ πρῶτον τὴν βασιλείαν καὶ τὴν δικαιοσύνην αὐτοῦ, καὶ ταῦτα πάντα προστεθήσεται ὑμῖν [Seek first the reign of God and his justice, and all these things will be given you besides]), we find a warning:

Μὴ δῶτε τὸ ἅγιον τοῖς κυσίν, μηδὲ βάλητε τοὺς μαργαρίτας ὑμῶν ἔμπροσθεν τῶν χοίρων, μήποτε καταπατήσουσιν αὐτοὺς ἐν τοῖς ποσὶν αὐτῶν καὶ στραφέντες ῥήξωσιν ὑμᾶς.

Do not give what is holy to dogs, nor throw your pearls before swine, lest they trample them and rip you apart. (Matt 7:6)

Note the intercalation of one of Matthew's key terms, the holy, in John's term for the whip as well as the presence of the βαλ root in his word for "eject":

καὶ ποιήσας φραγέλλιον ἐκ σχοινίων πάντας ἐξέβαλεν ἐκ τοῦ ἱεροῦ τά τε πρόβατα καὶ τοὺς βόας, καὶ τῶν κολλυβιστῶν ἐξέχεεν τὰ κέρματα καὶ τὰς τραπέζας ἀνέστρεψεν. (John 2:15)

Drawing on the material on either side of the reign-of-God saying in Matt 6:33, the Johannine author has fashioned aspects of John 2:13—3:21. One need only remove from one's eye the plank occluding the Matthean center to know that these Johannine chapters implicitly, as well as explicitly, are discussing the reign of God.[7] It is, I think, no exaggeration to say that, in John 2:13—3:21, Jesus who has gone up to the Temple Mount in Jerusalem

---

7. I do not at the moment have the stomach for reporting in their entirety the intercalated presence of the Greek words for "dog" and "swine" in the description of Nicodemus (John 3:1–2), but they are there; as are the more palatable *margaritas* in John 2:15–18 and John 3:11–13. These features suggest that the Jesus event elicited a differing interpretation of some aspects of Judaism with which the author(s) were familiar. The historicity of such a divergence is an ongoing question in Johannine studies.

in John 2:13 is engaged in a variation on a central portion of the Matthean Sermon on the Mount.[8]

Inheriting the Reign of God (1 Cor 6:9,10; 15:50; Gal 5:21)

John contains no language about inheriting the reign of God as such. However, it has been perhaps too easy to overlook the fact that κληρονομησουσιν (will inherit) contains the same *onom-* sequence as in the Greek word *onoma* (name). The present study will focus in part on John's exploration of the name Yhwh. For example, the only two psalms that begin with the phrase "The Lord is my . . ." (Pss 23 and 27) may be seen as a substructure of the Johannine endeavor: Ps 23 ("The Lord is my shepherd") in the minor signs of John 1–11, and Ps 27 ("The Lord is my light and salvation") in John 9 particularly, again in 12, and in counterpoint to darkness in 13–21.

A particularly pervasive extension of this theme resides in the fifty occurrences of Αμην sprinkled throughout the text. The consistently double expression Αμην Αμην, unique to this Gospel, allows for the relatively easy detection of the *m-n* sequence present in the name εγω ειμι ο ων. As a stylistic device, the double Amen that *echoes* points to the voice of the one speaking as the one manifested at the burning bush of Exod 3.

The Reign of God Suffering Violence

"Blessed are those persecuted for the sake of justice; the reign of heaven is theirs" (Matt 5:10).

The first two letters of δικαιοσυνη (justice/righteousness) are present in the Διψω (I thirst) at the cross of Jesus and are followed by the remaining letters of the word in John 19:28–30:

> Μετὰ τοῦτο εἰδὼς ὁ Ἰησοῦς ὅτι ἤδη πάντα τετέλεσται ἵνα τελειωθῇ ἡ γραφὴ λέγει· Διψῶ. ²⁹ σκεῦος ἔκειτο ὄξους μεστόν· σπόγγον οὖν μεστὸν τοῦ ὄξους ὑσσώπῳ περιθέντες προσήνεγκαν αὐτοῦ τῷ στόματι. ³⁰ ὅτε οὖν ἔλαβεν τὸ ὄξος ὁ Ἰησοῦς εἶπεν· Τετέλεσται, καὶ κλίνας τὴν κεφαλὴν παρέδωκεν τὸ πνεῦμα.

The letters βασιλεια του θεου (reign of God) follow thereafter in John 19:31–32:

---

8. Note that Matt 6:33 is the approximate center of what follows the Our Father in Matt 6:9–13.

Οἱ οὖν Ἰουδαῖοι, ἐπεὶ παρασκευὴ ἦν, ἵνα μὴ μείνῃ ἐπὶ τοῦ σταυροῦ τὰ σώματα ἐν τῷ σαββάτῳ, ἦν γὰρ μεγάλη ἡ ἡμέρα ἐκείνου τοῦ σαββάτου, ἠρώτησαν τὸν Πιλᾶτον ἵνα κατεαγῶσιν αὐτῶν τὰ σκέλη καὶ ἀρθῶσιν. ³² ἦλθον οὖν οἱ στρατιῶται, καὶ τοῦ μὲν πρώτου κατέαξαν τὰ σκέλη καὶ τοῦ ἄλλου τοῦ συσταυρωθέντος αὐτῷ·

Then the Jews, since it was Passover, in order that the bodies might not remain on the cross on the Sabbath—for the day of that Sabbath was great—asked Pilate that they might break their legs and so be lifted [off the cross]. So the soldiers came and broke the legs of the one and then the other crucified with him.

The closely related beatitude in Matt 5:6 says, "Blessed are those who hunger and thirst for justice; they will be satisfied."

If thirst for justice is an intentional echo in John, we would expect a narrative rendition of χορτασθησονται (be filled/satisfied). We have those letters at the breakfast of John 21:13–15:

ἔρχεται ὁ Ἰησοῦς καὶ λαμβάνει τὸν ἄρτον καὶ δίδωσιν αὐτοῖς, καὶ τὸ ὀψάριον ὁμοίως. ¹⁴ τοῦτο ἤδη τρίτον ἐφανερώθη ὁ Ἰησοῦς τοῖς μαθηταῖς ἐγερθεὶς ἐκ νεκρῶν. ¹⁵ Ὅτε οὖν ἠρίστησαν λέγει . . .

Jesus comes and takes bread and gives it to them, and the fish likewise. This was now the third time Jesus was manifested to the disciples after being raised from the dead. When they had finished breakfast, says . . .

In this reading, the lifting up of Jesus constitutes the desired justice, this meal being a celebration thereof.

John furthers the interpretation of God's reign as suffering violence from Matt 11. The Matthean *basileia* (kingdom), following the scene of John the Baptist in prison, balances verbs of force (*biaz-*) and seizure (*harpaz-*): "From the days of John the Baptizer until now the reign of heaven suffers violence, and the violent seize it" (Matt 11:12).

The Lukan statement distributes the letters of *basileia* throughout the description of evangelizing and force: "The reign of God is announced, and everyone is brought by force into it" (Luke 16:16). Any preaching of the reign of God is based in part on the violent deaths of John and Jesus.

John explores seizure; the wolf's seizure of sheep in the flock of the hired hand and the implied power of the Father and Son's seizure and retention of their own sheep (John 6:15; 10:12, 27–30).

In all three Gospels, violence surrounds Jesus and anticipates the cross as part of the mystery effected through him. In no case does an evangelist promote violence as ingredient to the act of preaching as such, much less catechesis, or means of retaining believers in Jesus.

Jesus perceives that the crowd is about to seize (αρπαζ-) him and make him king (John 6:15).[9] This "seizure" is mentioned again three times in John 10, making it the most numerous concatenation of the verb in any one document of the NT canon. The details of its instantiation are worth our attention.[10]

John 10:12 tells us about sheep and a wolf, but in so doing intercalates a reference to the βασιλεια (reign).

> ὁ μισθωτὸς καὶ οὐκ ὢν ποιμήν, οὗ οὐκ ἔστιν τὰ πρόβατα ἴδια, θεωρεῖ τὸν λύκον ἐρχόμενον καὶ ἀφίησιν τὰ πρόβατα καὶ φεύγει—καὶ ὁ λύκος ἁρπάζει αὐτὰ καὶ σκορπίζει.

The hired hand and not the one who is shepherd, whose own sheep these are not, sees the wolf coming and leaves the sheep and flees, and the wolf seizes them and scatters them.

John 10:27–30 speaks of the unity of Father and Son in keeping their sheep. It speaks as well of the wolf unsuccessfully attempting to seize them, and in so doing intercalates a statement about the usual Matthean expression for God's reign, βασιλεια των ουρανων (reign of the heavens):

> τὰ πρόβατα τὰ ἐμὰ τῆς φωνῆς μου ἀκούουσιν, κἀγὼ γινώσκω αὐτά, καὶ ἀκολουθοῦσίν μοι, [28] κἀγὼ δίδωμι αὐτοῖς ζωὴν αἰώνιον, καὶ οὐ μὴ ἀπόλωνται εἰς τὸν αἰῶνα, καὶ οὐχ ἁρπάσει τις αὐτὰ ἐκ τῆς χειρός μου. [29] ὁ πατήρ μου ὃ δέδωκέν μοι πάντων μεῖζων ἐστιν, καὶ οὐδεὶς δύναται ἁρπάζειν ἐκ τῆς χειρὸς τοῦ πατρός. [30] ἐγὼ καὶ ὁ πατὴρ ἕν ἐσμεν.

---

9. Barrett suggests that this notice, unique to John, intends to instantiate the saying in Matt 11:12 (*Gospel According to St. John*, 278).

10. The name Yhwh may have something to do with these four instances of the verb αρπαζ- in John 6:15 and 10:12, 28, 29. I AM, an unambiguous allusion to the name, occurs at John 6:20. The large gap between this instance of the name in John 6 and the cluster of other instances of αρπαζ- in John 10 approximates the spacing of the letters that constitute the name Yhwh. Yod is the tenth letter of the Hebrew alphabet, while heh-vav-heh are the fifth and sixth letters of the alphabet respectively.

Sayings

John's intercalation of the letters of the Matthean expression "reign of heaven" suggests that he is commenting on the same Matthean verse as is Luke but placing the emphasis differently than does Luke.[11]

John's Seeing and Entering the Reign of God as Informed by Exodus 3 and Other Parallels in the Synoptic Gospels

Indeed, there is a tight symmetry between the see-enter combination in Exod 3 and that in John 3, even as regards their location in the respective texts:

> And Moses said: "I will turn aside and *see*
> this great sight, why the bush is not burnt." . . .
> Then he said, "*Do not come near.* Put off
> your shoes from your feet, for the place on which
> you stand is holy ground." (Exod 3:3, 5 RSV)

> Jesus answered him: "Truly, truly I say to you,
> unless one is born anew, s/he cannot *see* the reign of God. . . .
> Jesus answered, "Truly, truly I say to you, unless one
> is born of water and the Spirit, s/he *cannot enter*
> the reign of God." (John 3:3, 5 RSV)

Furthermore, the Exod 3 background of see-enter has implications for the content and structure of John 14:

- You have seen him. (John 14:7; compare to Exod 3:2-3, containing three verbs of seeing)

- I will reveal myself to him. (John 14:21; compare to "I AM WHO AM" [Exod 3:14])

- The prince of this world comes; he has nothing on me. (John 14:30; compare to "Pharaoh king of Egypt . . . I will strike the Egyptians with all my wonders" [Exod 3:18-19])[12]

---

11. See the discussion of Matt 11:12 in Davies and Allison, *Gospel According to Saint Matthew*, 2:252-56.

12. The disciples' names at these three points are presented amid dynamics of the three languages named by this evangelist in 19:20, i.e., Latin, Greek, and Hebrew. The juxtaposition of Θωμας κυριε in John 14:4 contains each of the letters in Italic *Roma* and precede a Latinate exploration of Αληθεια Truth according to the constituent parts of *Veritas*: Way (*Via*), Truth (*Veritas*), Life (*Vita*). Φιλιππος contains all of the letters in Greek ΠΙΠΙ, a term that visually resembles and so was used in some LXX manuscripts to represent the letters in יהוה, the tetragrammaton. This section of John 14 contains many

Jesus and the Reign of God in John

When individually considered, John's use of see-enter suggests that they were framed in part by synoptic parallels.

Seeing the Reign of God

"Some here will not taste death until they see the reign of God" (Luke 9:27).

One might readily understand the crowd who sees the raising of Lazarus (John 11:45) through this optic. In addition, there is a heavy concentration of "see" and "heaven" language in John 3:3, 36; 6:19, 30, 62. Chapter 5 of the present study will examine the visual schematic of the glorified Jesus present in the structure of the text.

Entering the Reign of God

We may identify four sets of sayings here and their transformed presence in John:

1. *Greater righteousness* and entry to the reign (Matt 5:20). Righteousness is mentioned only in John 16:8, 10. It is something taught by the Spirit and concerns Jesus' going to the Father. In that reality, Jesus will make it possible for his disciples to effect "greater works" than he (John 14:12).

2. *Unless one becomes like a child* and entry to the reign (Matt 18:3). In John, there is a dearth of chronological children, probably because of the vision articulated in John 1:12, "become children of God." That is, everyone in the text influenced by Jesus toward discipleship is being formed as a child of God.

3. *"If your eye ... remove it ... to enter"* (Mark 9:47). A discourse about spiritual blindness, following the healing of sight in John 9:35–41, is likely to be a recrafting of the synoptic saying.

4. *The difficulties of a rich person* to enter (Matt 19:23–24; Mark 10:23–25; Luke 18:24–25). A fable circulating under Aesop's name depicted

---

words ending in -ι and also features some repetition of themes, mirroring the structure of ΠΙΠΙ. Finally, Ιουδας in John 14:22 is followed by the word γεγονεν (become), thereby alluding to the Hebraic rendering of the name in Exod 3 as concerns begetting. The next verse, in John 14:23, uses the phrase "answered and said," a particularly Hebraic expression for "reply." These names prepare for discussion of the climactic glorification of the name in John 17.

a miser who sold all his possessions, then melted down and buried the proceeds as a single gold ingot, only to have it stolen. In commenting on the fable, the pre-Socratic orator Antiphon said, "The value of money resides not in its possession but in its use." We may surmise that Nicodemus, who in John 19 provides extensive and expensive materials for the burial of Jesus (John 19:39–42), has thereby experienced some of the parabolic difficulties of a rich person in entering God's reign. His earlier difficulties in dialogue with Jesus about the reign of God as such are chronicled in John 3.

Seeing the reign of God is linked to birth "from above" (ανωθεν) in John 3:3. That vertical dimension of the event is explicitly developed in John 3:14, "Just as Moses lifted up the serpent in the desert, so the Son of Man must be lifted up." The cross of Jesus is in view here. So too, John 3:5 links entering the reign of God with water and Spirit. The phrase in the Greek carries the letters for blood (αιμα) here underlined:

> ἀπεκρίθη Ἰησοῦς· Ἀμὴν ἀμὴν λέγω σοι, ἐὰν μή τις γεννηθῇ ἐξ ὕδατος καὶ πνεύματος, οὐ δύναται εἰσελθεῖν εἰς τὴν βασιλείαν τοῦ θεοῦ.

The blood at the cross of Jesus is in view in John 3:5.

Both seeing and entering the reign of God are expressed succinctly in the Beloved Disciple who is present to Jesus lifted up and his blood at the cross (John 19:34). When the Beloved Disciple enters the empty tomb, sees, and believes (John 20:8), we have another instantiation of the reign of God.

The Reign of God as Indirect Object in Mark 12 and John 21

The conjunction of Mark 12:34 and John 21:12 almost jumps off the page (or out of the boat, whichever you prefer). After the Markan interaction of Jesus and the perceptive scribe, we hear Jesus say, "You are not far [ου μακραν] from the reign of God." Then the narrator intones, "And no one dared [ετολμα] question him any further." After the narrator in John 21:8 notes that the disciples were not far (ου μακραν) from land, John 21:12 yields, "And Jesus said to them 'Come, have breakfast.' And not one of the disciples dared [etolma] to inquire of him 'Who are you?' for they knew it was the Lord." The central commands of love are the focus of the Markan passage; Jesus' interrogation of Simon Peter "Do you love me?" is the ensuing focus in John.

Jesus and the Reign of God in John

The Keys of the Kingdom and John 21:15–19

Matthew 16:19 makes this promise to Peter:

> I will give you the keys of the kingdom of heaven.

> δώσω σοι τὰς κλεῖδας τῆς βασιλείας τῶν οὐρανῶν.

Intercalated keys appear in a Johannine narrative particularly focused on Peter in John 21:15–19.

> When they had finished breakfast, Jesus said to Simon Peter, "Simon son of John, do you love me more than these?" He said to him, "Yes, Lord; you know that I love you." Jesus said to him, "Feed my lambs." ¹⁶ A second time he said to him, "Simon son of John, do you love me?" He said to him, "Yes, Lord; you know that I love you." Jesus said to him, "Tend my sheep." ¹⁷ He said to him the third time, "Simon son of John, do you love me?" Peter felt hurt because he said to him the third time, "Do you love me?" And he said to him, "Lord, you know everything; you know that I love you." Jesus said to him, "Feed my sheep. ¹⁸ Very truly, I tell you, when you were younger, you used to fasten your own belt and to go wherever you wished. But when you grow old, you will stretch out your hands, and someone else will fasten a belt around you and take you where you do not wish to go." ¹⁹ (He said this to indicate the kind of death by which he would glorify God.) After this he said to him, "Follow me." (RSV)

In a story given to threefold repetition, we find the letters of keys (κλειδας) etched into the background three times:

> Ὅτε οὖν ἠρίστησαν λέγει τῷ Σίμωνι Πέτρῳ ὁ Ἰησοῦς· Σίμων Ἰωάννου, ἀγαπᾷς με πλέον τούτων; λέγει αὐτῷ· Ναί, κύριε, σὺ οἶδας ὅτι φιλῶ σε. λέγει αὐτῷ· Βόσκε τὰ ἀρνία μου. ¹⁶ λέγει αὐτῷ πάλιν δεύτερον· Σίμων Ἰωάννου, ἀγαπᾷς; λέγει αὐτῷ· Ναί, κύριε, σὺ οἶδας ὅτι φιλῶ σε. λέγει αὐτῷ· Ποίμαινε τὰ πρόβατά μου. ¹⁷ λέγει αὐτῷ τὸ τρίτον· Σίμων Ἰωάννου, φιλεῖς με; ἐλυπήθη ὁ Πέτρος ὅτι εἶπεν αὐτῷ τὸ τρίτον· Φιλεῖς με; καὶ εἶπεν αὐτῷ· Κύριε, πάντα σὺ οἶδας, σὺ γινώσκεις ὅτι φιλῶ σε. λέγει αὐτῷ ὁ Ἰησοῦς· Βόσκε τὰ πρόβατά μου. ¹⁸ ἀμὴν ἀμὴν λέγω σοι, ὅτε ἦς νεώτερος, ἐζώννυες σεαυτὸν καὶ περιεπάτεις ὅπου ἤθελες· ὅταν δὲ γηράσῃς, ἐκτενεῖς τὰς χεῖράς σου, καὶ ἄλλος σε ζώσει καὶ οἴσει ὅπου οὐ θέλεις. ¹⁹ τοῦτο δὲ εἶπεν σημαίνων ποίῳ θανάτῳ δοξάσει τὸν θεόν. καὶ τοῦτο εἰπὼν λέγει αὐτῷ· Ἀκολούθει μοι.

Note that the exercise of the keys extends even to the circumstances surrounding Peter's death.

VARIOUS OTHER REIGN-OF-GOD SAYINGS AND THEIR INFLUENCE ON JOHN

The Markan Reign of God and the Johannine Son of Man

The inaugural announcement of God's reign in Mark 1:15 and the anticipation of God's reign in Mark 14:25 place their stamp on the Johannine Evangelist's vision of the Son of Man/Child of Humanity at John 6:53–54:

> So Jesus said to them, "Very truly, I tell you, unless you eat the flesh of the Son of Man and drink his blood, you have no life in you. ⁵⁴ Those who eat my flesh and drink my blood have eternal life, and I will raise them up on the last day. (NRSVCE)

Mark 1:15 declares that the reign of God has drawn near: ἤγγικεν. See the interwoven presence of that verb in the following words of John 6:53:

> εἶπεν οὖν αὐτοῖς ὁ Ἰησοῦς· Ἀμὴν ἀμὴν λέγω ὑμῖν, ἐὰν μὴ φάγητε τὴν σάρκα τοῦ υἱοῦ τοῦ ἀνθρώπου καὶ πίητε αὐτοῦ τὸ αἷμα, οὐκ ἔχετε ζωὴν ἐν ἑαυτοῖς.

At the Supper, in Mark 14:25, Jesus says,

> ἀμὴν λέγω ὑμῖν ὅτι οὐκέτι οὐ μὴ πίω ἐκ τοῦ γενήματος τῆς ἀμπέλου ἕως τῆς ἡμέρας ἐκείνης ὅταν αὐτὸ πίνω καινὸν ἐν τῇ βασιλείᾳ τοῦ θεοῦ.

> Truly I tell you: I will never again drink of the fruit of the vine until that day when I drink it new in the kingdom of God.

John has interwoven the word for "new" (καινὸν) into John 6:54:

> ὁ τρώγων μου τὴν σάρκα καὶ πίνων μου τὸ αἷμα ἔχει ζωὴν αἰώνιον, κἀγὼ ἀναστήσω αὐτὸν τῇ ἐσχάτῃ ἡμέρᾳ.

Concomitantly, the diction of John 6:53–54 presents the phrase "that day" (ἡμέρας ἐκείνης) (Mark 14:25) as background to Jesus' promise about raising them up on the last day:

> εἶπεν οὖν αὐτοῖς ὁ Ἰησοῦς· Ἀμὴν ἀμὴν λέγω ὑμῖν, ἐὰν μὴ φάγητε τὴν σάρκα τοῦ υἱοῦ τοῦ ἀνθρώπου καὶ πίητε αὐτοῦ τὸ αἷμα, οὐκ ἔχετε

ζωὴν ἐν ἑαυτοῖς. ⁵⁴ ὁ τρώγων μου τὴν σάρκα καὶ πίνων μου τὸ αἷμα ἔχει ζωὴν αἰώνιον, κἀγὼ ἀναστήσω αὐτὸν τῇ ἐσχάτῃ ἡμέρᾳ.

In the vision of the Fourth Evangelist, reign-of-God statements spanning almost the entirety of Mark are best understood in the focused intensity of John's eucharistic Son of Man/Child of Humanity.

The Reign of God Intercalated in Matthew 7:8–9 Has Been Rendered Afresh in John 10

Immediately after the commands to ask-seek-knock in Matt 7:7 there is a sprinkling of the letters βασιλεια among the discrete words that follow in verses 8–9. These letters are not present in so compressed a space following similar injunctions to ask-seek-knock in Luke 11:9–13.

Ask-seek-knock have as their result "it will be *given* you—you will *find*—it will *be opened* to you." These same results are presented in reverse order in John 10:8:

> πᾶς γὰρ ὁ αἰτῶν λαμβάνει καὶ ὁ ζητῶν εὑρίσκει καὶ τῷ κρούοντι ἀνοιγήσεται. ⁹ ἢ τίς ἐστιν ἐξ ὑμῶν ἄνθρωπος, ὃν αἰτήσει ὁ υἱὸς αὐτοῦ ἄρτον—μὴ λίθον ἐπιδώσει αὐτῷ;

> For everyone asking receives, and the one seeking finds and to the one knocking it will be opened. What person among you when his son asks for bread will give him a stone? (Matt 7:8, 9)

And in John, we read:

- The doorkeeper *opens* to this one, and the sheep hear his voice, and he calls his own sheep by name, and he leads them out. (10:3)
- I am the gate; whoever enters through me will be saved and will go in and come out and *find* pasture. (10:9)
- I *give* them eternal life. (10:28)[13]

---

13. The subsequent saying in John 10:14, "I know my sheep and mine know me," may be a reverse formulation of the parable in Matt 24:11–12: "Lord, open to us" . . . "I do not know you."

John and the Reign of God in Paul

The evangelist pays particular attention to a handful of places in the Pauline letters where the apostle details his expectation about God's reign, often drawing a dichotomy between what is and is not involved in God's reign. "Not in word, but in power [δυναμει]" (1 Cor 4:20) is the first occurrence of reign-of-God language in that letter. The first lengthy dialogue in the Fourth Gospel appears in John 3, the discourse with Nicodemus, in which the very description of the reign of God turns on what is and is not possible (δυναται) in John 3:3, 5: "Unless born from above, such a one is not able to see, is not able to enter, the reign of God."

This next example portrays Jesus' consummation on the cross (John 19:30–35). The pericope includes an intercalated phrase from 1 Cor 15:24 about the risen Jesus handing over the reign.

> εἶτα τὸ τέλος, ὅταν παραδιδῷ τὴν βασιλείαν τῷ θεῷ καὶ πατρί, ὅταν καταργήσῃ πᾶσαν ἀρχὴν καὶ πᾶσαν ἐξουσίαν καὶ δύναμιν.

> Then comes the end. He hands over the reign to God and Father. (1 Cor 15:24)

The Greek roots τελ- and παραδιδ- are also present in John 19:30:

> ὅτε οὖν ἔλαβεν τὸ ὄξος ὁ Ἰησοῦς εἶπεν· Τετέλεσται, καὶ κλίνας τὴν κεφαλὴν παρέδωκεν τὸ πνεῦμα.

What follows includes the intercalated phrase βασιλεία τῷ θεῷ καὶ πατρί:

> Οἱ οὖν Ἰουδαῖοι, ἐπεὶ παρασκευὴ ἦν, ἵνα μὴ μείνῃ ἐπὶ τοῦ σταυροῦ τὰ σώματα ἐν τῷ σαββάτῳ, ἦν γὰρ μεγάλη ἡ ἡμέρα ἐκείνου τοῦ σαββάτου, ἠρώτησαν τὸν Πιλᾶτον ἵνα κατεαγῶσιν αὐτῶν τὰ σκέλη καὶ ἀρθῶσιν. [32] ἦλθον οὖν οἱ στρατιῶται, καὶ τοῦ μὲν πρώτου κατέαξαν τὰ σκέλη καὶ τοῦ ἄλλου τοῦ συσταυρωθέντος αὐτῷ· [33] ἐπὶ δὲ τὸν Ἰησοῦν ἐλθόντες, ὡς εἶδον ἤδη αὐτὸν τεθνηκότα, οὐ κατέαξαν αὐτοῦ τὰ σκέλη, [34] ἀλλ' εἷς τῶν στρατιωτῶν λόγχῃ αὐτοῦ τὴν πλευρὰν ἔνυξεν, καὶ ἐξῆλθεν εὐθὺς αἷμα καὶ ὕδωρ. [35] καὶ ὁ ἑωρακὼς μεμαρτύρηκεν, καὶ ἀληθινὴ αὐτοῦ ἐστιν ἡ μαρτυρία, καὶ ἐκεῖνος οἶδεν ὅτι ἀληθῆ λέγει, ἵνα καὶ ὑμεῖς πιστεύητε. (John 19:31-35)

The beauty of this juxtaposition effected by the evangelist resides in part in the way in which the temporal occasion of the crucifixion, παρασκευη (the Preparation) in John 19:31, now functions to describe the cross as preparation for the handing over of the reign of Jesus to God the Father.

> Flesh and blood is not able to inherit the reign of God.
> (1 Cor 15:50)

For Paul, that is simply a realistic admission of the limitations of mortal flesh and is enfolded in his discussion of the resurrection flesh made available in Jesus crucified and risen from the dead. In John 6, Jesus insists on not only the possibility of, but the necessity of, eating his flesh and drinking his blood (vv. 53–58), which is not cannibalism, since it is the flesh and blood of God's living Word. That is encompassed by double Amen sayings (6:26, 32, 47, 53) as well as the most unambiguous articulation of the divine I AM in 6:20. Note the four loci of the double Amen sayings, somewhat evenly spaced and limning the name in their quaternity.

> The reign of God is not a matter of food and drink, but rather of righteousness, peace, and joy in the Holy Spirit. (Rom 14:17)

The dinner in John 13–17 is remarkable in its display of each of these terms as such (16:8; 14:27; 16:20; 14:26).

John and the Reign of God in Hebrews

Beginning with John 2:15, John is influenced by three places in Hebrews at which βασιλεια occurs.

> The scepter [ραβδος] of uprightness is the scepter of your reign. (Heb 1:8)

> A whip fashioned from leather strands [φραγέλλιον ἐκ σχοινίων]. (John 2:15)

Both are handheld instruments including the letters ρα-ος.

Two later instances of βασιλεια in Hebrews affect later portions of John as well.

> They conquered [κατηγωνίσαντο] kingdoms. (Heb 11:33)

> My reign is not of this world. If it were, my servants would be fighting [ἠγωνίζοντο ἄν] on my behalf. (John 18:36)

This negative formulation—they would be fighting, but they are not doing so—contains the same verbal root as occurs in the verse of Hebrews. The closer approximation to the thought of Hebrews is the blunt affirmation of Jesus in John 16:33, "I have conquered the world."

> Receiving an unshakable kingdom [βασιλείαν ἀσάλευτον παραλαμβάνοντες]. (Heb 12:28)

> Then they received Jesus [Παρέλαβον οὖν τὸν Ἰησοῦν·]. (John 19:16)

Jesus had just countered "Do you not realize that I have the power to crucify you?" with "You would have no power were it not given you from above" (John 19:10–11). Then the silence, which says what words cannot.[14]

THE NAME OF GOD IN EXODUS 3 AND THE KING OF ISRAEL/THE JEWS IN JOHN

The divine self-description in Exod 3:14 LXX is:

> καὶ εἶπεν ὁ θεὸς πρὸς Μωυσῆν Ἐγώ εἰμι ὁ ὤν· καὶ εἶπεν Οὕτως ἐρεῖς τοῖς υἱοῖς Ισραηλ Ὁ ὢν ἀπέσταλκέν με πρὸς ὑμᾶς.

> And God said to Moses, "I AM WHO AM," and he said, "Thus shall you say to the sons of Israel, 'I AM has sent me to you.'"

John 3 displays a proliferation of participles and other parts of speech that contain, usually at their conclusion, the ων that evokes the I AM of Exod 3:14. We may readily surmise that John 3 alludes to the I AM of Exod 3:14 because both Jesus and the baptizer are described here as being "sent" (3:17, 28). That sent-ness is part and parcel of the event described in Exod 3:14. It is in this third chapter of John, exhibiting some twenty-eight occurrences (considered a *perfect* number in antiquity) of the participial reminder, that we find the only explicit references to the reign of God in John.[15]

---

14. This midrashic exercise on the part of the evangelist, encompassing sources from Matthew to Hebrews, may be compared to the detailed plea of Michael O'Connor for recognition that the poetics of Hebrew verse structure is best seen through a wide lens, attending to syntactical relationships among traditions not immediately adjacent to one another (*Hebrew Verse Structure*).

15. John's riff on the I AM of Exod 3 is not the first time that he attends to the Name. Already in the Prologue's emphasis on creative Being, the evangelist presents Jesus as exegeting the name of God, Yhwh. There is some question about the right of the substantive

Jesus and the Reign of God in John

The Name and the King

One of the most interesting agendas of the evangelist, one that spans almost the entire breadth of the text, traces the presence of the self-identification Ἐγώ εἰμι ὁ ὤν (I AM WHO AM) in Exod 3:14 as interwoven with mention of king.

1. Each of the three places cited here in John 1, 12, and 19 contains the consonantal spine gamma, mu, and nu of Exod 3:14 LXX as well as βασιλευς (king).

   καὶ εἶπεν ὁ θεὸς πρὸς Μωυσῆν Ἐγώ εἰμι ὁ ὤν· καὶ εἶπεν Οὕτως ἐρεῖς τοῖς υἱοῖς Ισραηλ Ὁ ὤν ἀπέσταλκέν με πρὸς ὑμᾶς.

   And God said to Moses: "I AM WHO AM." And he said, "Thus shall you say to the sons of Israel, 'The I AM sent me to you.'" (Exod 3:14)

   ἀπεκρίθη αὐτῷ Ναθαναήλ· Ῥαββί, σὺ εἶ ὁ υἱὸς τοῦ θεοῦ, σὺ <u>βασιλεὺς</u> εἶ τοῦ Ἰσραήλ. . . .
   καὶ λέγει αὐτῷ· Ἀ<u>μὴν</u> ἀμὴν λέγω]ὑ<u>μῖν</u> . . .

   And Nathanael answered him, "Rabbi, you are the son of God, you are the king of Israel." . . .
   And he said to him, "Amen, Amen, I say to you . . ." (John 1:49, 51)

   Ὡσαννά, εὐλογη<u>μέν</u>ος ὁ ἐρχόμενος ἐν ὀνόματι κυρίου, καὶ ὁ <u>βασιλεὺς</u> τοῦ Ἰσραήλ.

   Hosanna, blessed the one coming in the name of the Lord, even the king of Israel. (John 12:13b)

   ἔγραψεν δὲ καὶ τίτλον ὁ Πιλᾶτος καὶ ἔθηκεν ἐπὶ τοῦ σταυροῦ· ἦν δὲ <u>γεγραμμένον</u>· Ἰησοῦς ὁ Ναζωραῖος ὁ <u>βασιλεὺς τῶν Ἰουδαίων.</u>

---

participle ο ων to be considered part of the earliest available reading in John 1:18. It is not present in Sinaiticus. See Schnackenburg, *Gospel According to St John*, 1:280–81. However, even if not the earliest available reading, the phrase epitomizes the clear reference to Being (as distinct from becoming) that is present at the opening of the Prologue (1:1–4). Attention to the name continues throughout John. I agree with those who see in the I AM of John 8:58 an echo of the usage in Exod 3:6, 14. For example, Delebecque, "Autour de verbe *eimi*." See Schnackenburg, *Gospel According to St John*, 2:84, 224.

Sayings

And Pilate also inscribed the sign [τίτλος] and placed it on the cross; and it was inscribed, "Jesus the *Nazōraios*, the king of the Jews." (John 19:19)

These same three places act in concert to replicate the replete self-identification in Exod 3:14: Ἐγώ εἰμι ὁ ὤν (I AM WHO AM).

λέγει αὐτῷ (John 1:51)
ἐν ὀνόματι κυρίου (John 12:13)
ὁ ... Ἰουδαίων (John 19:19)

A close doubling of the γ-μ-ν consonantal components, perhaps intended to reflect the two occurrences of I AM in Exod 3:14, occurs in the following four places in chapters 1–12, culminating at the sign of the crucified king in chapter 19:

ἐμνήσθησαν οἱ μαθηταὶ αὐτοῦ ὅτι γεγραμμένον ἐστίν· Ὁ ζῆλος τοῦ οἴκου σου καταφάγεταί με.

His disciples remembered that it was written, "Zeal for your house consumes me." (John 2:17)

οἱ πατέρες ἡμῶν τὸ μάννα ἔφαγον ἐν τῇ ἐρήμῳ, καθώς ἐστιν γεγραμμένον· Ἄρτον ἐκ τοῦ οὐρανοῦ ἔδωκεν αὐτοῖς φαγεῖν.

Our fathers ate manna in the desert, just as it is written, "He gave them bread from heaven to eat." (John 6:31)

ἀπεκρίθη αὐτοῖς ὁ Ἰησοῦς· Οὐκ ἔστιν γεγραμμένον ἐν τῷ νόμῳ ὑμῶν ὅτι Ἐγὼ εἶπα· Θεοί ἐστε;

Jesus answered them, "Is it not written in your law that I said, 'You are gods'?" (John 10:34)

εὑρὼν δὲ ὁ Ἰησοῦς ὀνάριον ἐκάθισεν ἐπ' αὐτό, καθώς ἐστιν γεγραμμένον· 15 Μὴ φοβοῦ, θυγάτηρ Σιών· ἰδοὺ ὁ βασιλεύς σου ἔρχεται, καθήμενος ἐπὶ πῶλον ὄνου.

And Jesus finding a small donkey sat on it, just as it is written, "Fear not, daughter Zion. Behold, your king comes, seated on the foal of an ass." (John 12:14–15)

These echoes of the name find their completion in the reference to Jesus as king of the Jews in John 19:19:

ἔγραψεν δὲ καὶ τίτλον ὁ Πιλᾶτος καὶ ἔθηκεν ἐπὶ τοῦ σταυροῦ· ἦν δὲ γεγραμμένον· Ἰησοῦς ὁ Ναζωραῖος ὁ βασιλεὺς τῶν Ἰουδαίων.

Note also that here in Ναζωραῖος (*Nazōraios*), we have the vocalic dimensions of the circumlocution for the tetragrammaton, Adōnāy. What we observe here are the four scattered allusions to the name prior to the hour coming to a telescopic concentration of name and king in 19:19.[16]

2. Finally, the following three loci explicitly attend in succession to their Hebrew, Greek, and Roman audiences:

John 1:51's Αμην is translation Greek, rendering Hebrew aleph-mem-nun, following other translations earlier in John 1 from Hebrew to Greek.

Greek Ελληνιστι is limned in John 12:13:

ἔλαβον τὰ βαΐα τῶν φοινίκων καὶ ἐξῆλθον εἰς ὑπάντησιν αὐτῷ, καὶ ἐκραύγαζον· Ὡσαννά, εὐλογημένος ὁ ἐρχόμενος ἐν ὀνόματι κυρίου, καὶ ὁ βασιλεὺς τοῦ Ἰσραήλ.

The Greeks then appear in John 12:20.

Pilate the Roman prefect authors the *titulus* for the cross at John 19:19. Greek τιτλος is a transliteration of Latin *titulus* (sign/placard).

Beginning with a consonantal spine, then proceeding to a replete Greek rendering of the name, and finally sketching an audience of Hebrew, Greek, and Latin speakers, the evangelist has crafted a statement reflecting the name of God the Sovereign. The name is heard first sotto voce, then more clearly in one language pool, and finally in three major audiences of the Hellenistic world, in the person of Jesus. The explicit reference to the name of the *kyrios* in conjunction with the king occupies the central position in this triptych.

Most immediately pertinent to this study's focus is the combination of reign-of-God language in John 3:3, 5 and the γ-μ-ν limning of the name in four places in John 3. We read:

ἀπεκρίθη Ἰησοῦς καὶ εἶπεν αὐτῷ· Ἀμὴν ἀμὴν λέγω σοι, ἐὰν μή τις γεννηθῇ ἄνωθεν, οὐ δύναται ἰδεῖν τὴν βασιλείαν τοῦ θεοῦ.

---

16. During the hour, chs. 13 and following, the sequence γγ-μμ-νν has its sole occurrence in 19:19. A near approximation in 15:25 ends in a sigma: γεγραμμένος. See the more replete discussion in Culpepper, "Jesus' Sayings."

Sayings

Jesus answered and said to him, "Amen, Amen, I say to you, unless someone is born from above, s/he is unable to see the reign of God." (John 3:3)

ἀπεκρίθη Ἰησοῦς· Ἀμὴν ἀμὴν λέγω σοι, ἐὰν μή τις γεννηθῇ ἐξ ὕδατος καὶ πνεύματος, οὐ δύναται εἰσελθεῖν εἰς τὴν βασιλείαν τοῦ θεοῦ.

Jesus answered and said, "Amen, Amen, I say to you, unless someone is born from water and the Spirit, s/he is unable to enter the reign of God." (John 3:5)

ἀμὴν ἀμὴν λέγω σοι ὅτι ὃ οἴδαμεν λαλοῦμεν καὶ ὃ ἑωράκαμεν μαρτυροῦμεν, καὶ τὴν μαρτυρίαν ἡμῶν οὐ λαμβάνετε.

Amen, Amen, I say to you that what we know we speak, and to what we have seen we give witness, and our witness you do not receive. (John 3:11)

ὁ πιστεύων εἰς αὐτὸν οὐ κρίνεται· ὁ δὲ μὴ πιστεύων ἤδη κέκριται, ὅτι μὴ πεπίστευκεν εἰς τὸ ὄνομα τοῦ μονογενοῦς υἱοῦ τοῦ θεοῦ.

The one believing in him is not judged. But the one not believing in him has already been judged, because s/he has not believed in the name of the only begotten Son of God. (John 3:18)

In the first three of these cases, Jesus is the speaker. In the fourth case, the focus is on the name of the Son. I suggest that the reference to the name of the Son refers to the name of Jesus as such, containing a reminder of Yhwh who saves. The sequence of the letters γ-μ-ν runs right to left, as in the Hebrew. The Greek consonantal spine of the I AM declaration is so articulated by the evangelist that it reaches back to the earliest self-declaration of the name in the canonical tradition. Note what else has happened here. The double amen has been pressed into service (perhaps created) precisely to elicit recall of the name in Exod 3:14, in both the Hebrew and Greek. Furthermore, the four occurrences of this special use of γ-μ-ν are, in their very quaternity, a reminder of the tetragrammaton.[17]

---

17. John may be drawing inspiration from Mark here. Jesus speculates on his identity in Mark 8:27–30 ("Who do people say that I am?"), followed by a reference to the reign of God (Mark 9:1). Other themes shared between Mark 8:22—9:13 and John 3 include John the Baptizer, heaven's speech, and the Father's love for the Son.

Chapter Two

Servant

IN THIS CHAPTER, WE *examine Isa 40:10, which describes the reign of God exercised in the strong arm of Yhwh. That statement introduces the name Yhwh as the structuring principle of the four Servant of Yhwh Poems in Isa 42–53. Each of those four Servant Poems in turn informs successive scenes of Jesus with women in John 2, 4, 11, and 12. Luke 1–2 precedes this Johannine agenda by portraying several of its characters as servants of Yhwh. "Mariam" is prominent among them and will initiate the signs in John during the wedding at Cana. For the Johannine signs, we look to the only two psalms in the psalter that begin "Yhwh is my . . ." Finally, I offer two alternative visions of sovereignty from Greco-Roman culture.*

THE RULING ARM OF YHWH AND THE SERVANT POEMS

"His arm rules for him" (Isa 40:10). That introduces Second Isaiah and is the rubric under which to understand its four poems about the servant of Yhwh. The Hebrew letters of the name Yhwh shape each of those poems in succession.

In what follows, I will present the English of the text and underline the details reflecting aspects of the name. In every poetic piece, we see a fourfold repetition of a trait pertinent to successive letters of the name Yhwh.

Delimitation of the Poems

Commentators of the last generation have often followed the decision of Bernhard W. Anderson concerning the extent of the poems: Isa 42:1-4; 49:1-6; 50:4-9; 52:13—53:12.[1] The development of thought about the poems traces an interesting trajectory. In 1875, Bernhard Duhm (in *Die Theologie der Propheten*) saw the poems functioning as a unit created within a post-exilic context and integral to Isaiah. By 1892 (in *Das Buch Jesaia*, his commentary on Isaiah), he had decided that the poems were inserted by an editor at a time later than the formation of the original Second Isaiah text and presented no consistently clear and unifying theme. For example, his delimitation of the second poem to Isa 49:1-4 noted the distinction between the servant as Israel and the servant as a figure distinct within Israel.[2] This discussion continues. Tryggve Mettinger reported in 1983 and again in 1997 his skepticism about an identifiable profile of said Servant Songs.[3] However, the poems continue to attract scholarly attention. A dissertation published in 2015 expands the range of the first poem by examining Isa 42:1-9.[4] In my judgment, that of Anderson, and those who follow him, remains the preferable paradigm because the material in Isa 42:5-9 shifts the primary focus from "*my* servant" to the explicitly named Yhwh/God as speaker. The divine names used in vv. 5-9, however, do reflect the ones that we encounter in later songs:

I note three things concerning the poems pertinent to their use by John:

1. They exhibit increasing levels of suffering on the part of the servant.

> Ch. 42—No suffering
> Ch. 49—Mental and physical fatigue
> Ch. 50—Forensic challenge and physical attack
> Chs. 52-53—Death, burial, and vindication

---

1. B. Anderson, *Understanding the Old Testament*, 456-57.

2. On Duhm, see the Heidelberg dissertation of Ruprecht, "Auslegungsgeschichte," 169-80.

3. Mettinger: *Farewell to Servant Songs*; "Search of Hidden Structure." In this latter essay, Mettinger points to Yhwh's conquest of the forces of chaos and return to inhabit Mount Zion as characteristic of the kingship motif in Second Isaiah.

4. Beaulieu, *Behold My Servant*.

So too in John, the men of the text come into increasing levels of danger because of their association with Jesus.[5]

2. The Isaian poet is attentive to beginnings and endings. Lexical neighbors beginning with Hebrew peh (פשת [linen/wick] and פשע [sin]) bookend the first and fourth poems, which also emphasize the servant's lack of shouted speech on the street as well as silence (Isa 42:3; 53:12). See the domestic dialogue of John 2:1–12 and 19:9. Peh is the seventeenth letter of the Hebrew alphabet, which will be helpful to remember when we explore John's numerical dynamics in the next chapter of this study.

   Furthermore, the letter aleph initiates words in Isa 49–50 pertinent to the Johannine servant narratives in John 11–12. אור (light) in Isa 49:6 corresponds to the life that is light in John 11. אזר (help) in Isa 50:7 prepares for the mention of Lazarus (El-azar) in John 11. The promise of that light in Isa 49 culminates in "salvation reaching to the ends of the earth" as explicated in explicit discussions of Rome and the Greeks in John 11–12.

   Hebrew words beginning with beth, the second letter of the alphabet, inform the Johannine servant narratives in John 2 and 4. ברר (purify) shapes John 2:1–12, and בנה (eat) is a topic of discussion in John 4.

   Together, these aleph-beth words are factors contributing to the preponderant focus on אב (Father) throughout the text. In John 11:41, the lexical neighbors אב (Father) and אבן (stone) are also juxtaposed.

   I mention these foci near the termination and beginning of the Hebrew alphabet because they are like the opening phrase of Genesis, whose first word uses בראשׁת. This phrase includes the first and last letters of the alphabet. In Gen 1:1a, this linguistic feature may be read connotatively as saying that "in the Finality, the Beginning, [God]," which undergirds the denotative statement "In the beginning God created." The Johannine equivalent is the focus on a new creation resulting from God's reign in Jesus.

3. I see the unity of the poems residing in their successive utilization of the letters *y-h-w-h* as organizing principle, to be more fully discussed below as we examine each of the poems in detail. However, now I mention only the thesis itself and some ancillary stylistic observations that support it:

---

5. Van Tilborg, *Imaginative Love in John*, 252.

- Ch. 42—Yod
- Ch. 49—Heh
- Ch. 50—Vav
- Chs. 52-53—Heh

That may be seen as plausible in part because the poetics of these chapters reflect characteristics that track the variety among the letters Yhwh. In their 1998 magnum opus, Korpel and De Moor characterized the cantos' (poems') structural patterns (cola, strophes, canticle/stanzas) with the following phrases:

- Ch. 42—completely regular
- Ch. 49—Symmetric
- Ch. 50—Fairly regular
- Chs. 52-53—Symmetric[6]

That profile is congruent with both the shared and distinctive characteristics of the individual letters of the tetragrammaton:

- 42:1-4—Yod (completely regular and brief; the briefest of the poems)
- 49:1-6—Heh (see also 52-53 as symmetric)
- 50:4-9—Vav (fairly regular, in this case; longer than ch. 42)
- 52:13—53:12—Heh (see also ch. 49 as symmetric)

Before entering a more detailed analysis of the intertextual dialogue between the Servant Poems of Second Isaiah and John, I list here what I judge to be major points of similarity between them as suggested by a theological study of Isaiah's vision of God's reign.[7]

Poem 1: The servant goes about his work in a quiet way. Jesus is working behind the scenes at the wedding at Cana. We see him in dialogue with his mother and the servants. We never see or hear from the couple who are celebrating their marriage.

Poem 2: The servant is Israel bringing Israel back to covenant but is also a light to the nations, guiding them to the salvation of Yhwh. At the well of Jacob (Israel), Jesus relativizes the importance of both Gerizim and

---

6. Korpel and DeMoor, *Classical Hebrew Poetry*, 656–57.
7. Williams, *Kingdom of Our God*, 116, 138–39, 142, 152.

Jerusalem as places of the nation's worship. Through the woman of Samaria, and in a scene that begins at high noon, Jesus draws an entire Samaritan town to himself.

Poem 3: The servant who listens to God also teaches and speaks to humans subject to decay. Jesus is called "the teacher" and is warned by Martha and Mary about the smell of corruption at the tomb of Lazarus.

Poem 4: The servant is destined for a grave with the rich. Expensive ointment is lavished on Jesus' feet by Mary, an action that Jesus interprets as preparation for his burial.

THE SERVANT, A LIGHT TO THE NATIONS (ISA 42:1–4)

> Here is *my* servant, whom I uphold,
> *my* chosen, in whom *my* soul delights;
> I have put *my* spirit upon him;
> he will bring forth justice to the nations.
> ² He will not cry or lift up his voice,
> or make it heard in the street;
> ³ a bruised reed he will not break,
> and a dimly burning wick he will not quench;
> he will faithfully bring forth justice.
> ⁴ He will not grow faint or be crushed
> until he has established justice in the earth;
> and the coastlands wait for his teaching. (NRSVue)

The adjective "my" is represented by the Hebrew letter yod. In this adjectival function, yod occurs four times as the poem opens. The yod is the first letter in Yhwh.

POEM 1: CANA (JOHN 2; ISA 42)

The Wedding at Cana

> On the third day there was a wedding in Cana of Galilee, and the mother of Jesus was there. ² Jesus and his disciples had also been invited to the wedding. ³ When the wine gave out, the mother of Jesus said to him, "They have no wine." ⁴ And Jesus said to her, "Woman, what concern is that to you and to me? My hour has not yet come." ⁵ His mother said to the servants, "Do whatever he tells

you." ⁶ Now standing there were six stone water jars for the Jewish rites of purification, each holding twenty or thirty gallons. ⁷ Jesus said to them, "Fill the jars with water." And they filled them up to the brim. ⁸ He said to them, "Now draw some out, and take it to the chief steward." So, they took it. ⁹ When the steward tasted the water that had become wine, and did not know where it came from (though the servants who had drawn the water knew), the steward called the bridegroom ¹⁰ and said to him, "Everyone serves the good wine first, and then the inferior wine after the guests have become drunk. But you have kept the good wine until now." ¹¹ Jesus did this, the first of his signs, in Cana of Galilee, and revealed his glory; and his disciples believed in him.

¹² After this he went down to Capernaum with his mother, his brothers, and his disciples; and they remained there a few days. (NRSVue)

Here Hebrew *qanah* (reed) is helpful in interpreting the text. Not only is it a homonym of the site Cana, but the term *qanah* refers to a unit of measure. John 2:6 enumerates the number of jars available and the amount of liquid that each could hold. In addition, what happens at this site is congruent with the action of the servant who will not snap a bent reed. The wine has run out, but that is not the end of the story. Moreover, the evangelist could easily have discerned the phrase ὥρα μου (my hour) in Isa 42:1: Ιακωβ ὁ παῖς μου, ἀντιλήμψομαι αὐτοῦ· Ισραηλ ὁ ἐκλεκτός μου.

~

The Servant's Mission (Isa 49:1–6)

Listen to me, O coastlands,
pay attention, you peoples from far away!
Yhwh called me before I was born,
while I was in my mother's womb he named me.
² He made my mouth like a sharp sword,
in the shadow of his hand he hid me;
he made me a polished arrow,
in his quiver he hid me away.
³ And he said to me, "You are my servant,
Israel, in whom I will be glorified."
⁴ But I said, "I have labored in vain,

I have spent my strength for nothing and vanity;
yet surely my cause is with Yhwh,
and my reward with my God."
⁵ And now Yhwh says,
who formed me in the womb to be his servant,
to bring Jacob back to him,
and that Israel might be gathered to him,
for I am honored in the sight of Yhwh,
and my God has become my strength—
⁶ he says,
"It is too light a thing that you should be my servant
to raise up the tribes of Jacob
and to restore the survivors of Israel;
I will give you as a light to the nations,
that my salvation may reach to the end of the earth." (NRSVue)

The name Yhwh occurs four times in this poem.

POEM 2: THE SAMARITAN WOMAN (JOHN 4; ISA 49)

Jesus and the Woman of Samaria

Now when Jesus learned that the Pharisees had heard "Jesus is making and baptizing more disciples than John" ²—although it was not Jesus himself but his disciples who baptized—³ he left Judea and started back to Galilee. ⁴ But he had to go through Samaria. ⁵ So he came to a Samaritan city called Sychar, near the plot of ground that Jacob had given to his son Joseph. ⁶ Jacob's well was there, and Jesus, tired out by his journey, was sitting by the well. It was about noon.

⁷ A Samaritan woman came to draw water, and Jesus said to her, "Give me a drink." ⁸ (His disciples had gone to the city to buy food.) ⁹ The Samaritan woman said to him, "How is it that you, a Jew, ask a drink of me, a woman of Samaria?" (Jews do not share things in common with Samaritans.) ¹⁰ Jesus answered her, "If you knew the gift of God, and who it is that is saying to you, 'Give me a drink,' you would have asked him, and he would have given you living water." ¹¹ The woman said to him, "Sir, you have no bucket, and the well is deep. Where do you get that living water? ¹² Are you greater than our ancestor Jacob, who gave us the well, and with his sons and his flocks drank from it?" ¹³ Jesus said to her, "Everyone who drinks of this water will be thirsty again, ¹⁴ but those who

drink of the water that I will give them will never be thirsty. The water that I will give will become in them a spring of water gushing up to eternal life." [15] The woman said to him, "Sir, give me this water, so that I may never be thirsty or have to keep coming here to draw water."

[16] Jesus said to her, "Go, call your husband, and come back." [17] The woman answered him, "I have no husband." Jesus said to her, "You are right in saying, 'I have no husband'; [18] for you have had five husbands, and the one you have now is not your husband. What you have said is true!" [19] The woman said to him, "Sir, I see that you are a prophet. [20] Our ancestors worshiped on this mountain, but you say that the place where people must worship is in Jerusalem." [21] Jesus said to her, "Woman, believe me, the hour is coming when you will worship the Father neither on this mountain nor in Jerusalem. [22] You worship what you do not know; we worship what we know, for salvation is from the Jews. [23] But the hour is coming, and is now here, when the true worshipers will worship the Father in spirit and truth, for the Father seeks such as these to worship him. [24] God is spirit, and those who worship him must worship in spirit and truth." [25] The woman said to him, "I know that Messiah is coming" (who is called Christ). "When he comes, he will proclaim all things to us." [26] Jesus said to her, "I am he, the one who is speaking to you."

[27] Just then his disciples came. They were astonished that he was speaking with a woman, but no one said, "What do you want?" or "Why are you speaking with her?" [28] Then the woman left her water jar and went back to the city. She said to the people, [29] "Come and see a man who told me everything I have ever done! He cannot be the Messiah, can he?" [30] They left the city and were on their way to him.

[31] Meanwhile the disciples were urging him, "Rabbi, eat something." [32] But he said to them, "I have food to eat that you do not know about." [33] So the disciples said to one another, "Surely no one has brought him something to eat?" [34] Jesus said to them, "My food is to do the will of him who sent me and to complete his work. [35] Do you not say, 'Four months more, then comes the harvest'? But I tell you, look around you, and see how the fields are ripe for harvesting. [36] The reaper is already receiving wages and is gathering fruit for eternal life, so that sower and reaper may rejoice together. [37] For here the saying holds true, 'One sows and another reaps.' [38] I sent you to reap that for which you did not labor. Others have labored, and you have entered into their labor."

⁓³⁹ Many Samaritans from that city believed in him because of the woman's testimony, "He told me everything I have ever done." ⁴⁰ So when the Samaritans came to him, they asked him to stay with them; and he stayed there two days. ⁴¹ And many more believed because of his word. ⁴² They said to the woman, "It is no longer because of what you said that we believe, for we have heard for ourselves, and we know that this is truly the Savior of the world." (NRSVue)

The introduction to the story describes Jesus as fatigued (v. 4). Compare the self-description of the servant:

> I said, "I have labored in vain. I have spent my strength for nothing and vanity." (Isa 49:4)

The Fourth Gospel makes early mention of Jacob (4:12) as Jesus encounters the descendants of those who had returned from exile. The ensuing story of the family of a royal (read, Roman) official indicates even more clearly the trajectory to the nations.

⸺

The Servant's Humiliation and Vindication (Isa 50:4–9)

> Adōnāy Yhwh has given me
> the tongue of a teacher of those who are taught
> that I may know how to sustain
> the weary with a word.
> Morning by morning he wakens—
> wakens my ear
> to listen as those who are taught.
> ⁵ Adōnāy Elohim has opened my ear,
> and I was not rebellious,
> I did not turn backward.
> ⁶ I gave my back to those who struck me,
> and my cheeks to those who pulled out the beard;
> I did not hide my face
> from insult and spitting.
> ⁷ And Adōnāy Yhwh helps me;
> therefore I have not been disgraced;
> therefore I have set my face like flint,
> and I know that I shall not be put to shame;

> ⁸ he who vindicates me is near.
> Who will contend with me?
> Let us stand up together.
> Who are my adversaries?
> Let them confront me.
> ⁹ It is Adōnāy Yhwh who helps me;
> who will declare me guilty?
> All of them will wear out like a garment;
> the moth will eat them up. (NRSVA, modified)

In the Great Isaiah Scroll from Qumran, this poem displays four occurrences of the double indicator of divinity. Usually the phrase is Adōnāy Yhwh (three times) and one time, in v. 5, Adōnāy Elohim. The Masoretes smooth that out and render Adōnāy Yhwh four times. Note also that this item is particularly trenchant in establishing the poetic skill of the Isaian Evangelist. Its pleonastic character, Adōnāy Yhwh rather than simply Yhwh, is congruent with the function of vav, the third letter in Yhwh, which often means "and." I note this without prejudice to the question of whether the scribe wrote Adōnāy so that it, rather than the name Yhwh, as such, might be pronounced.[8] Note also that in v. 7 of the Great Isaiah Scroll at Qumran, it is preceded by the letter vav.[9] That is not the case in any of the other verses of 50:4–9 containing Adōnāy Yhwh. The poet is directing our attention to the letter vav in this third poem and concomitantly to the third position of vav in Yhwh.

POEM 3: MARTHA, MARY, LAZARUS (JOHN 11; ISA 50)

The Death of Lazarus

> Now a certain man was ill, Lazarus of Bethany, the village of Mary and her sister Martha. ² Mary was the one who anointed the Lord

---

8. For a thorough study of reverence for the name Yhwh whereby speakers refrained from pronouncing it outright, see Wilkinson, *Tetragrammaton*.

9. This double asseveration Adōnāy Yhwh is relatively scarce in the Tanak, some strands of Ezekiel also employing the phrase. That makes its presence here in the Great Isaiah Scroll at Qumran even more likely to have been chosen deliberately by the Isaian Evangelist. The Hebrew scroll, in the searchable online format at Digital Dead Sea Scrolls, clearly reveals the vav preceding Adōnāy in Isa 50:7. The verse is accurately rendered as "*But* the Lord God will help me" (Berlin and Brettler, *Jewish Study Bible*). The Isaiah commentary of Paul renders the beginning of the verse similarly (*Isaiah 40–66*, 352).

with perfume and wiped his feet with her hair; her brother Lazarus was ill. ³ So the sisters sent a message to Jesus, "Lord, he whom you love is ill." ⁴ But when Jesus heard it, he said, "This illness does not lead to death; rather it is for God's glory, so that the Son of God may be glorified through it." ⁵ Accordingly, though Jesus loved Martha and her sister and Lazarus, ⁶ after having heard that Lazarus was ill, he stayed two days longer in the place where he was.

⁷ Then after this he said to the disciples, "Let us go to Judea again." ⁸ The disciples said to him, "Rabbi, the Jews were just now trying to stone you, and are you going there again?" ⁹ Jesus answered, "Are there not twelve hours of daylight? Those who walk during the day do not stumble, because they see the light of this world. ¹⁰ But those who walk at night stumble, because the light is not in them." ¹¹ After saying this, he told them, "Our friend Lazarus has fallen asleep, but I am going there to awaken him." ¹² The disciples said to him, "Lord, if he has fallen asleep, he will be all right." ¹³ Jesus, however, had been speaking about his death, but they thought that he was referring merely to sleep. ¹⁴ Then Jesus told them plainly, "Lazarus is dead. ¹⁵ For your sake I am glad I was not there, so that you may believe. But let us go to him." ¹⁶ Thomas, who was called the Twin, said to his fellow disciples, "Let us also go, that we may die with him." (NRSVA)

Jesus, the Resurrection and the Life

When Jesus arrived, he found that Lazarus had already been in the tomb four days. ¹⁸ Now Bethany was near Jerusalem, some two miles away, ¹⁹ and many of the Jews had come to Martha and Mary to console them about their brother. ²⁰ When Martha heard that Jesus was coming, she went and met him, while Mary stayed at home. ²¹ Martha said to Jesus, "Lord, if you had been here, my brother would not have died. ²² But even now I know that God will give you whatever you ask of him." ²³ Jesus said to her, "Your brother will rise again." ²⁴ Martha said to him, "I know that he will rise again in the resurrection on the last day." ²⁵ Jesus said to her, "I am the resurrection and the life. Those who believe in me, even though they die, will live, ²⁶ and everyone who lives and believes in me will never die. Do you believe this?" ²⁷ She said to him, "Yes, Lord, I believe that you are the Messiah, the Son of God, the one coming into the world."

Jesus Weeps

When she had said this, she went back and called her sister Mary, and told her privately, "The Teacher is here and is calling for you." [29] And when she heard it, she got up quickly and went to him. [30] Now Jesus had not yet come to the village but was still at the place where Martha had met him. [31] The Jews who were with her in the house, consoling her, saw Mary get up quickly and go out. They followed her because they thought that she was going to the tomb to weep there. [32] When Mary came where Jesus was and saw him, she knelt at his feet and said to him, "Lord, if you had been here, my brother would not have died." [33] When Jesus saw her weeping, and the Jews who came with her also weeping, he was greatly disturbed in spirit and deeply moved. [34] He said, "Where have you laid him?" They said to him, "Lord, come and see." [35] Jesus began to weep. [36] So the Jews said, "See how he loved him!" [37] But some of them said, "Could not he who opened the eyes of the blind man have kept this man from dying?"

Jesus Raises Lazarus to Life

Then Jesus, again greatly disturbed, came to the tomb. It was a cave, and a stone was lying against it. [39] Jesus said, "Take away the stone." Martha, the sister of the dead man, said to him, "Lord, already there is a stench because he has been dead four days." [40] Jesus said to her, "Did I not tell you that if you believed, you would see the glory of God?" [41] So they took away the stone. And Jesus looked upward and said, "Father, I thank you for having heard me. [42] I knew that you always hear me, but I have said this for the sake of the crowd standing here, so that they may believe that you sent me." [43] When he had said this, he cried with a loud voice, "Lazarus, come out!" [44] The dead man came out, his hands and feet bound with strips of cloth, and his face wrapped in a cloth. Jesus said to them, "Unbind him, and let him go."

Central to understanding the text of Isa 50 in John is the etymology of the name Lazarus. It means God helps, reflecting the twice-repeated assertion of the Isaian servant "God helps" (Isa 50:6, 9). Four of those occurrences of the name Lazarus in John happen within the introduction to the story (John 11:1–6). In the ensuing dialogue with the disciples and entry into the village, the evangelist intones Lazarus three more times. This leads one to expect that there will be a fourth occurrence of Lazarus to complement the previous three. In fact, that is exactly what we have in that "Lazarus" occurs for the next and last time in the mouth of Jesus at the tomb: "Lazarus, come out." There is then a discernible symmetry between the eight occurrences of the name Lazarus and the four double denominators of divinity (Adōnāy Yhwh or Adōnāy Elohim) in the Isaian poem.

Rabbi/teacher: One of the claims made by the servant in Isa 50 is that he has been given the tongue of the learned. That could be understood as "a teacher," and such seems to be the reading made by the evangelist in having Jesus addressed as rabbi (11:8) and referred to as teacher (11:28). (Note, however, that "rabbi" also occurs in John 4:31.)

Finally, a note about the perseverance of the servant. Isaiah 50:7 has him assert:

> The Lord God helps me; therefore, I have set my face like flint.

The analogue in John resides in the perseverance of Jesus displayed in his decision to go to Judea despite recent opposition there (vv. 8, 15).

The Suffering Servant (Isa 52:13—53:12)

> See, my servant shall prosper;
> he shall be exalted and lifted up,
> and shall be very high.
> [14] Just as there were many who were astonished at him
> —so marred was his appearance, beyond human semblance,
> and his form beyond that of mortals—
> [15] so he shall startle many nations;
> kings shall shut their mouths because of him;
> for that which had not been told them they shall see,
> and that which they had not heard they shall contemplate.
> 53 Who has believed what we have heard?
> And to whom has the arm of Yhwh been revealed?
> [2] For he grew up before him like a young plant,
> and like a root out of dry ground;
> he had no form or majesty that we should look at him,
> nothing in his appearance that we should desire him.
> [3] He was despised and rejected by others;
> a man of suffering and acquainted with infirmity;
> and as one from whom others hide their faces

he was despised, and we held him of no account.
⁴ Surely he has borne our infirmities
and carried our diseases;
yet we accounted him stricken,
struck down by God, and afflicted.
⁵ But he was wounded for our transgressions,
crushed for our iniquities;
upon him was the punishment that made us whole,
and by his bruises we are healed.
⁶ All we like sheep have gone astray;
we have all turned to our own way,
and Yhwh has laid on him
the iniquity of us all.
⁷ He was oppressed, and he was afflicted,
yet he did not open his mouth;
like a lamb that is led to the slaughter,
and like a sheep that before its shearers is silent,
so he did not open his mouth.
⁸ By a perversion of justice he was taken away.
Who could have imagined his future?
For he was cut off from the land of the living,
stricken for the transgression of my people.
⁹ They made his grave with the wicked
and his tomb with the rich,
although he had done no violence,
and there was no deceit in his mouth.
¹⁰ Yet it was the will of Yhwh to crush him with pain.
When you make his life an offering for sin,
he shall see his offspring and shall prolong his days;
through him the will of Yhwh shall prosper.
¹¹ Out of his anguish he shall see light;
he shall find satisfaction through his knowledge.
The righteous one, my servant, shall make many righteous,
and he shall bear their iniquities.
¹² Therefore I will allot him a portion with the great,
and he shall divide the spoil with the strong;
because he poured out himself to death,
and was numbered with the transgressors;
yet he bore the sin of many,
and made intercession for the transgressors. (NRSVA)

The name Yhwh occurs four times in the poem. In that regard, it is like the recurrent Yhwh in the second poem of Isa 49. Together, the two poems mimic the double presence of heh in Yhwh.

In tabular form, the tetragrammaton helps to structure the Servant Poems in the following manner:

Isa	42	49	50	52–53
Yhwh	yod	heh	vav	heh

POEM 4: MARTHA, MARY, LAZARUS (JOHN 12; ISA 52–53)

Mary Anoints Jesus

> Six days before the Passover Jesus came to Bethany, the home of Lazarus, whom he had raised from the dead. ² There they gave a dinner for him. Martha served, and Lazarus was one of those at the table with him. ³ Mary took a pound of costly perfume made of pure nard, anointed Jesus' feet, and wiped them with her hair. The house was filled with the fragrance of the perfume. ⁴ But Judas Iscariot, one of his disciples (the one who was about to betray him), said, ⁵ "Why was this perfume not sold for three hundred denarii and the money given to the poor?" ⁶ (He said this not because he cared about the poor, but because he was a thief; he kept the common purse and used to steal what was put into it.) ⁷ Jesus said, "Leave her alone. She bought it so that she might keep it for the day of my burial. ⁸ You always have the poor with you, but you do not always have me." (NRSVA)

The text depicts a prophetic sign of the future burial of Jesus, congruent with the reference to the grave of the servant in Isa 53:9.

(There is also a reference in John 12:38 to the arm of Yhwh at work in Jesus' signs. This is reminiscent of the arm of Yhwh in Isa 40:10, which undergirds part of the Johannine depiction of the reign of God.)

Note too that there may be a pertinent lexical dynamic to this fourth poem. Of all the canonical Gospel texts that have women attending to the body of Jesus at a dinner, only here do we find the double entendre in דלה, which, depending on the vocalic pointing, can mean either hair or poor. In the first half of the Fourth Gospel, the narratives of these women do the heavy lifting of depicting Jesus as servant of Yhwh.

Servant

The Samaritan woman especially exemplifies the *mebasseret* of Isa 40:9, a female herald, but the women of the other Johannine narratives are also relevant to the *mebasseret*. The Hebrew of the Isaian verse simply places in apposition the words "herald" (f.) and "Jerusalem." That allows us to read "herald, Jerusalem" as preferred, for example, by Joseph Blenkinsopp in his commentary on Isaiah.[10] However, the grammar also allows us to render the sense as "herald to Jerusalem" as preferred by Shalom Paul in his commentary on Isa 40–66.[11] The Fourth Evangelist, I would argue, also reads it as "herald to Jerusalem." The women in these four narratives are not in Jerusalem. However, the evangelist has placed them in increasingly close proximity to Jerusalem. Moreover, the mother of Jesus in chapter 19 is in Jerusalem proper. Within the narrative world of the evangelist, they are heralds to Jerusalem. And what do they announce? What is the message of the *mebasseret*? The b-s-r in that word, again depending on the vowels provided, means both to announce good news and flesh. Collectively these women announce the enfleshed good news of Jesus, servant of Yhwh.

Shem and Implied Mashal in John 20:24–29

I suggest that the delineation of the ruling arm and the name in the texts just examined also affects John 20:24–29. The name is present in this text both implicitly and explicitly and implies consideration of the ruling arm of the Lord.

The implicit presence of the name in this part of John 20 is predicated on a numerical dynamic. Twenty-one is the sum of the numerical equivalents of the discrete letters in the name Yhwh: yod (ten), heh (five), vav (six). As pointed out several decades ago, though to the best of my knowledge not mentioned since regarding John 20, Exod 4:1 presents the reader with twenty-one words prior to Moses pronouncing the name Yhwh for the first time.[12] Arriving at the number twenty-one is achieved by counting the prepositions and their pronominal endings as separate words.

וַיַּעַן מֹשֶׁה וַיֹּאמֶר וְהֵן לֹא־יַאֲמִינוּ לִי וְלֹא יִשְׁמְעוּ בְּקֹלִי כִּי יֹאמְרוּ לֹא־נִרְאָה אֵלֶיךָ יְהוָה׃

---

10. Blenkinsopp, *Isaiah 40–55*, 184–86.
11. Paul, *Isaiah 40–66*, 135–36.
12. Scholem, "Name of God."

Then Moses answered and said, "But suppose they do not believe me or listen to my voice, but say, 'The LORD did not appear to you.'" (Exod 4:1 NRSVA)

How does this affect John? Thomas utters thirty-three words in John 20:25:

Ἐὰν μὴ ἴδω ἐν ταῖς χερσὶν αὐτοῦ τὸν τύπον τῶν ἥλων καὶ βάλω τὸν δάκτυλόν μου εἰς τὸν τύπον τῶν ἥλων καὶ βάλω μου τὴν χεῖρα εἰς τὴν πλευρὰν αὐτοῦ, οὐ μὴ πιστεύσω.

Unless I see in his hands the imprint of the nails and put my finger into the imprint of the nails and put my hand into his side, I will in no way believe.

That may be accounted as twenty-one words plus twelve, a preparation for his confession in 20:28, "My Lord and my God," on behalf of the Twelve in whose number he resides (see v. 24). His refusal to believe reflects the very stance about which Moses fretted in Exod 4:1. The *shem* (name) is certainly present here. So too is the Lord's ruling arm; present in the displayed hands, of course, with the wounds of the hands and side emphasized as the cost of such an exercise in regency.

Servants of Yhwh and the Characters in Luke 1–2

The Fourth Evangelist did not create this tableau of Jesus as Isaian servant of Yhwh out of thin air. Luke 1–2 preceded him in portraying a similar profile drawn from Isaiah's Servant Poems for the narrative that opens the Third Gospel:

	Servants of Yhwh	
Isa		Luke
42:1	Spirit on	1:35
49:5	From the handmaiden's womb	1:38, 48
49:6	Covenant	1:72
49:6	Light/dawn from on high	1:78; 2:36
50:4	Open ear	2:26
50:6–8	Opposition	2:34
52:15	Astonishment	2:47
53:5	Discipline	2:51

Noteworthy for our present purpose is the preponderant presence of Mary throughout the Lukan sketch. As mother of Jesus, she will be prominently placed at the beginning of the signs in John, at the wedding at Cana. Those signs may therefore be read as an expression of the reign of God being established in and through Jesus and his fellow servants of Yhwh.[13]

The Name Yhwh as Organizing the Johannine Signs

The letters of the name Yhwh organize a large swath of material in the Servant Poems of Second Isaiah and in the summary notices of Jesus' ministry in Matt 4, 8, 9, and 12.[14] The same process is discernible in John's presentation of the signs of Jesus, where the name functions as an organizing principle, though in a somewhat different way.

"Rabbi, you are the Son of God, you are the king of Israel" (John 1:49). One may readily hear in the latter phrase an echo of Israel's acclamation of Yhwh as king, though perhaps at a level not intended to be part of the speaker's consciousness. What follows in John 2 is the first of Jesus' signs that are collectively shaped by the name Yhwh.

Only Pss 23 and 27 among all the psalms begin "Yhwh is my . . ."—in Ps 23, "Yhwh is my shepherd"; in Ps 27, "Yhwh is my light and salvation." These two psalms are a narrative exposition of the name Yhwh. In the table below, I present the essential data that suggest that the evangelist had these two psalms in mind when choosing which of Jesus' miracles to relate as well as the details of some of them.

Signs in John 1–11	Pss 23 and 27
Lack of wine at Cana is reversed (John 2:3). Large amount of liquid is turned into excellent wine (John 2:6, 10).	Nothing is lacking for me (Ps 23:1). My cup is the best/overflows (Ps 23:5c).[15]
Healing of the child in the Jordan River Valley who was "about to die" (John 4:47, 49, 51)	Even though I walk through the valley of the shadow of death (Ps 23:4a)

13. These Lukan observations were shaped in part by an Advent homily given by Rev. Ben Hawley, SJ, in 2024 at the church of St. Francis Xavier, Manhattan.

14. Kiley, "Yhwh in Servant Poems."

15. All of the letters in καὶ τὸ ποτήριόν σου μεθύσκον ὡς κράτιστον (your drinking cup

Signs in John 1–11	Pss 23 and 27
Healing of the paralytic at the still pool (John 5:7, 9)	He leads me beside still waters (Ps 23:2b).
Feeding the crowd in the grass (John 6:10–11)	He makes me lie down in green pastures . . . you spread a table before me (Ps 23:2a, 5a).
Appearance in the sea storm and words of assurance to the fearful disciples, "It is I; do not be afraid" (John 6:20)	I fear no evil, for you are with me (Ps 23:4b).
Giving sight to the blind man and seeking him out following his brave responses under questioning and desertion by his parents (John 9)	The Lord is my light and salvation; whom should I fear? (Ps 27:1). Even though my father and mother have forsaken me, the Lord will take me up (Ps 27:10).
Return of Lazarus to life (John 11)	He restores my life (Ps 23:3a).

These signs conclude with a reminder that servant sovereignty is at work. John 12:38 quotes from the Fourth Servant poem at Isa 53:1:

> *Kyrie*, who has believed our report and to whom has the arm of *kyrie* been revealed?

This is said in the shadow of Jesus' entry into Jerusalem, where the evangelist has added the phrase "king of Israel" to his traditional quote from Ps 118:

> Hosanna, blessed be the one coming in the name of *kyrie*, [even] the king of Israel. (John 12:13)

These data suggest that the evangelist has chosen to relay only particular signs in a particular way in order to underscore their function as acts of Yhwh, the I AM.[16] Indeed, the first word in the Hebrew Ps 23 is יהוה, to which corresponds the Johannine Prologue's attention to being (John 1:1) and becoming (John 1:12). The tetragrammaton of Pss 23 and 27 order the minor signs. They are bookended by an acclamation of Jesus as king of Israel and servant of Yhwh. This designation has "school exercise" written all over it.

---

is the best) are interspersed, in the correct order, in John 2:1–11. The reproduction of this part of the psalm begins at και (John 2:1) and concludes at εν in John 2:11.

16. Kiley, "Exegesis of God."

Of course, what we have just examined is a mere skeletal structure for the minor signs. Another text, Pss. Sol. 17, gives us more of the muscle and sinew of these signs:

The text is variously dated from the middle of the first century BCE to the period immediately following 70 CE and includes a complaint about gentile oppressors of Israel.[17] It begins and ends with an acclamation of the *kyrios* as king (vv. 1, 46). Its forty-second verse extols the king of Israel as such. The following three citations give some insight into the ways in which it is used in John 9:

- Pss. Sol. 17:16 depicts forced separation from the assemblies of the devout. Compare the threat of expulsion from the synagogue in John 9.
- Pss. Sol. 17:25 says that the Davidic king will condemn sinners for the thoughts of their heart. See the give-and-take between Jesus and the Pharisees in John 9.
- Pss. Sol. 17:32 uses the title "Lord Messiah." That is reflected in John 9's use of Ps 27, "The Lord is my . . . ," as well as in the portrayed tensions about confessing Jesus as the Christ. It is worth noting that there is no hint in John 9 that gentiles are the oppressors. Instead, the tension portrayed is Jewish and wholly intramural.

In addition, Pss. Sol. 17:40 affects John 6 in that the psalm celebrates the king as shepherd of the Lord's flock and focuses on the surpassing value of his words as such. Remember that Jesus refuses to be acclaimed king by the crowd in John 6. One of the longest discourses in the text, John 6 concludes by asserting, "You have the words of eternal life" (John 6:68).

Another resource lies close at hand for understanding the attention to Jesus as king in the Fourth Gospel. Consider the prophetic roots of "guileless" and "fig" at the end of John 1. These two distinctive phrases in John 1:47–51 are best understood as initiating a dialogue with two prophetic texts, Isa 53 and Jer 23–24, both of which concern the theme of a burden.

"No deceit" in his mouth (Isa 53:9)	
Amnos (lamb) (Isa 53; John 1)	
	"Fig" (Jer 24:1–8)

17. See G. Buchanan Gray, "Psalms of Solomon," *APOT* 2:625–52, esp. 2:625–30, 647–51; R. B. Wright, "Psalms of Solomon," *OTP* 2:639–70. See also the discussion of "Son of God" (Pss. Sol. 17:27) in Richey, *Roman Imperial Ideology*, 92.

	Massā', meaning both oracle and burden (Jer 23:33–40)
	"What says the oracle?" (Jer 23:33)[18]
"It was our sins he bore, our burden he carried." (Isa 53:4)	"*You* are the burden." (Jer 23:33 LXX)
	King of Israel (Jer 23:1–8)
	Massā' < *nasā'* (lift up) (Jer 23:39)

With the cues "guileless" and "fig," Jesus prompts Nathanael to reflect on these two prophetic texts (all happening rather quickly, in narrative time; a reflection of the school context of the Gospel?). From their shared theme of bearing a burden, Nathanael is able in John 1:49 to identify Jesus as king of Israel who, in the tradition of Ps 2, is also Son of God.[19]

In Jer 24:1–10, the vision of the two baskets of figs, like the vision of fruit in Amos 8:1–3, is followed by a question asked by Yhwh and then the meaning of the vision. So too in John 1:47–51, the fig tree saying is followed by a question, "Because I said I saw you . . . do you believe?" and finally a promised seeing.[20]

Now, how does the vision of Jesus as servant-king stack up to extracanonical visions concerned with sovereignty? I limit the potentially gargantuan list to citation of a few pertinent examples from Greco-Roman culture.

Some Greek and Roman Parallels to Isaiah's Vision of Servant Kingship

Bread—Fish—Lambs (John 21; Odyssey 19)

One of the enduring puzzles of chapter 21 resides in the combination of both fish and lamb imagery. Appealing to one or the other theme earlier in the emerging church's tradition as source for John 21 has not yielded

---

18. An emendation in v. 33. See Couturier, "Jeremiah," 284–85.

19. The Johannine audience will also recognize that the same combination of Son-king is present at Mark's cross. It might have helped them to do so by remembering that *massā'* also means test, trial, something Jesus undergoes in the crowd's taunts at Mark's cross.

20. Does Jer 23 forbid the use of the term מַשָּׂא (oracle, burden), because of the insistence of Moses in Deut 30:11 (Jeremiah's favorite book) that "the command I enjoin on you today is not υπερογκος/נִפְלֵאת—of excessive bulk"? Rad suggests "too hard" (*Deuteronomy*, 184).

widely recognized results. However, in one of the speeches of Odysseus to Penelope, Odysseus celebrates Penelope's fame as akin to that of a

> king without blemish, master of many men; the black earth bears wheat and barley . . . sheep bear young continuously, and the sea provides fish, because of his good leadership, and people attain excellence under him. (*Od.* 19.107–14)

I would suggest that, at one level, this Johannine use of Homeric scenery alludes to Jesus as blameless king.

The evangelist also employs this same section of *Od.* 19 in John 19 in which Pilate questions Jesus. Upon his return to Ithaca, Odysseus in disguise as a poor beggar is invited by Penelope to tell her about himself. She wants to ask him some questions. Penelope has a servant draw up a chair, on which Odysseus sits (*Od.* 19.100–104). Commentators have long noted that the grammar of John 19:13 allows us to read that it is Jesus who sits down on the seat of Pilate's platform. Jesus sits there clothed in the purple cloak in which he has recently been dressed, even as Odysseus in disguise recounts a tale told of a purple cloak given to him upon his embarking to war in Troy. As Penelope asks where the stranger has come from (*Od.* 19.105), so Pilate asks Jesus the same (John 19:9). John's Jesus has already said in the presence of his disciples that he is returning to the Father whence he came (John 17). The evangelist fills out that portrait with details of the homecoming at the heart of the Greeks' Bible, *The Odyssey*. It is no accident that the more recent Greek author draws on the theme of kingship present in his antique model.

John's version of Second Isaiah's servant kingship is and is not like *The Odyssey*. It is also similar to and perceptibly different from the Roman experiment in representative self-governance. To that topic we now turn.

Conjugation of Jesus and the Roman Senate

The *Romanitá* in the Tiberias reference in John 21:1 is echoed earlier in John as well. Jesus acts in various ways to image the Roman Republic amid the Roman Empire.[21]

> 21. Carter: *John*, 170–74; and the entirety of *John and Empire* are concerned with John as he engages imperial Rome. The latter study is especially riveted on Ephesus.

In his first encounter with the disciples, Jesus enacts the role of *quaestor*, asking, "What do you seek?" (1:38).

In the initial confrontation with the temple proceedings in 2:13–22, he performs the role of *aedile*, whose concern included the public buildings of the republic.

When discussing the shared authority that he enjoys with the Father in John 5, he enacts the role of *consul*.

When defending his sheep whom no one will snatch out of his hand in John 10, he performs the function of *tribune*, especially concerned during the republic with the protection of plebeians.

As foot washer/cleanser in chapter 13, he enacts the role of *censor*, a role whose duties also included the identification and exclusion of names on the membership rolls of the citizenry.

And in the praetorium, very possibly sitting on the judgment seat in 19:13, he adjudicates at his own trial, turning the questioning process on Pilate and thereby performing the role of *praetor*.

All of these roles had been subsumed into the person of the emperor by the first century CE. But John's Jesus embodies a republican profile in an imperial time.

Senate Issues

Cursus honorum. The six republican offices just described do not follow the normal order in which candidates would progress. The last office in the Senate was often that of *consul*, whereas John presents the consular analogue in John 5. The evangelist seems to address this disparity from the *cursus honorum* at the very point at which the Roman hearer might be expected to notice the political dimension of the portrait, at the temple cleansing in John 2. It is here that John's Jesus explicitly discusses his fixed concern for his Father's house and implicitly *his Father's* honor. It becomes even more pronounced and explicit in chapter 5 where he castigates his audience for seeking more their own than God's glory. His official public course will not mimic the secular Roman concern for personal honor but seek the glory of God.

INRI/SPQR. The *titulus* on the cross also participates in the republican thrust of the evangelist's work. The four-word inscription, unique among

---

The present study complements Carter's focus by delineating some of the ways in which John's elevation of the republican Roman profile provides a counter ballast to empire.

the canonical Gospels, is in its quaternity and character as signpost analogous to the insignia placed on the lead banner of every Roman army detachment sent to battle: *SPQR*. It is the abbreviation for *Senatus Populusque Romanorum*, the Senate and People of the Romans. It harks back to the republican era in which the Senate, at least in theory, represented the interests of the people. Its adumbration by Jesus lifted up offers an alternative to the reality of first-century CE Rome in which these relationships existed in rhetoric alone due to the actions of the emperor.[22]

Last, we turn to the *victory breakfast*, held at the shore of the Sea of Tiberias (hear the echo of the emperor Tiberius here). A passage in Josephus describing the conquest of Jerusalem by Vespasian's army provides an admirable parallel to the breakfast ($\alpha\rho\iota\sigma\tau\eta\sigma\alpha\tau\epsilon$) of John 21:

> After the prayers, Vespasian made a short speech to the whole gathering, dismissed the soldiers to the breakfast [$\alpha\rho\iota\sigma\tau\text{o}\nu$] which it was customary for victorious generals to provide.[23]

---

22. For the representational aspects of office as such during the republic, see Ando, *Law, Language, and Empire*.

23. Josephus, *J.W.* 7.129 (Williamson, 371). Compare to John 21:12–14.

Chapter Three

Sophia

IN THIS CHAPTER, WE *explore some of the ways in which divine sovereignty in wisdom literature affects the Fourth Gospel.*[1] *We will make excursions into Sir 1, 1 Kgs 3, and the Wisdom of Solomon (esp. chs. 6–10), with special attention to the phrase "reign of God" in Wis 10:10. Other aspects of God's reign in Wisdom and John follow, including the use of numbers. On the way, we inspect some of the parallels from philosophy in antiquity that the evangelist has reshaped into a statement about some aspects of divine sovereignty. This is intended as a subsidiary exercise in appreciating Jesus' saying in John 14:23 concerning what it is to love Sophia (philo-sophize) in Jesus.*

The following is an itinerary for this, the lengthiest chapter of the present study:

1 Kgs 3: The wise king unites mother and son
Sir 1: The Enthroned One in creative command
Wis 10: Reign—Yhwh—signs, wonders, labors
Wis 8: Sophia and Jesus' female disciples, again
Wis 6: Ladder progression and the Farewell Discourse in John
Wisdom of Solomon, Number and Text
Philo-sophia and love of Jesus

---

1. These observations about the presence of Sophia/Wisdom in John are intended as a complement to those made by Coloe (*John 1–10, 11–21*).

Sophia

1 KINGS 3 AND THE GOSPEL OF JOHN

In the explicit text, John's Jesus joins mother to son at the cross. In the subtext, a more replete accounting of Jesus' identity is taking place. The text of 19:26–27 reads, "Then Jesus, seeing the mother and the disciple standing there whom he loved, says to the mother, 'Woman, behold your son.' Then he says to the disciple, 'Behold your mother.' From that hour the disciple took her to his own." The text is particular to this Gospel. Therefore, one might well suspect that it has something to say bearing its own integrity.

Consider in this regard the role of Solomon in 1 Kgs 3. Being confronted by two women, each claiming that she is the rightful mother of the child they bring to the king, presents an opportunity for Solomon to display the wisdom for which he prays. Because of the king's offer to cut the child in two and give half to each woman, the real mother verifies her identity when calling for the child to be allowed to live with her competitor.

The Greek of John 19:26–27 contains, sprinkled, each of the correctly ordered letters of the name Σ-α-λ-ω-μ-ω-ν (Solomon):

Ἰησοῦς οὖν ἰδὼν τὴν μητέρα καὶ τὸν μαθητὴν παρεστῶτα ὃν ἠγάπα λέγει τῇ μητρί· Γύναι, ἴδε ὁ υἱός σου· ²⁷ εἶτα λέγει τῷ μαθητῇ· Ἴδε ἡ μήτηρ σου. καὶ ἀπ' ἐκείνης τῆς ὥρας ἔλαβεν ὁ μαθητὴς αὐτὴν εἰς τὰ ἴδια.

As in 1 Kgs 3:1, where Solomon's effort in building "his own house" is explicitly mentioned in the Hebrew בֵּיתוֹ, so too the Beloved Disciple will bring the mother of Jesus εις τα ιδια (to his own [house, implied]).

The Greek describing the bystanders at the cross sprinkles the letters spelling σοφια (Sophia):

Εἱστήκεισαν δὲ παρὰ τῷ σταυρῷ τοῦ Ἰησοῦ ἡ μήτηρ αὐτοῦ καὶ ἡ ἀδελφὴ τῆς μητρὸς αὐτοῦ, Μαρία ἡ τοῦ Κλωπᾶ καὶ Μαρία ἡ Μαγδαληνή.

There stood at the cross of Jesus his mother, and the sister of his mother, Mary the wife of Klopas and Mary the Magdalene. (John 19:25)

At one level, the narrative asserts that Jesus is a Solomonic figure filled with God's wisdom, active here at the cross that acclaims him king.[2]

---

2. Congruent with this Solomonic emphasis in John 19, see also the letters of the alternative spelling Σολομων sprinkled throughout John 2:19, where Jesus describes his resurrection as the raising of a temple.

SIRACH 1 AND THE FOURTH GOSPEL

> One there is who is wise exceedingly awesome, seated on his throne. (Sir 1:8)

This is the God of Israel, as indicated in the Prologue to Sir v. 1. Its analogue in the Fourth Gospel is John 1:49b, "You are the king of Israel."

> The Sovereign himself created her and saw and apportioned [εξηριθμησεν] her.
> He poured her out upon all his works. (Sir 1:9)

The analogue in John is the crafting of the opening days of Jesus' appearance, which may be counted as six. The phrase "on the next day" (ἐπαύριον) occurs at John 1:29, 35, 43. Then at 2:1 we hear καὶ τῇ ἡμέρᾳ τῇ τρίτῃ (and on the third day). Note that the acclamation of Jesus as king of Israel occurs amid these counted days, at 1:49. Sovereignty is at the heart of this Johannine exercise, yet it is a sovereignty exercised through Sophia. The wedding at Cana in John 2:1–12 instantiates the vision of Sir 1:16, "She intoxicates [people] with her fruits."

John's Transformation of Sirach 1:1–30

Of all the canonical books, and here I advert to inclusion in the Catholic canon, the Wisdom of Jesus ben Sirach is the one that most thoroughly explores the fear of the Sovereign. Alexander A. DiLella estimated that the phrase or its equivalents occurs some fifty-five to sixty times in the book.[3] In the more circumscribed focus adopted here, I will point out some features of this theme in the text's opening gambit before suggesting how John uses it.

My thesis here is basically simple, though not simplistic. *Greek phobos (fear/awe) is a Greek amalgam containing the sound of the Hebrew letter beth within the creation account of Gen 1:1 and becomes for the author of Sirach a cipher for God's creative activity.* In addition, the letters of the word σοφος (wise) are contained within Greek φοβος (fear). Sirach 1 reads the Gen 1 creation account through that lens such that φοβος, six times as a noun and four times as verb, becomes emblematic of God's creative activity. How does this work? Hebrew Gen 1:26 names two classes of creatures containing *ph-* and *s-*:

---

3. DiLella, "Fear of the Lord," esp. 188.

[gave dominion]
also over the flying creatures [וּבְעוֹף]
and
over the creeping things [הָרֶמֶשׂ]

When the author of Sirach reads the first phrase of Gen 1:1, יִתְבָּרֵאשׁ, beginning with the letter beth, he has found the linguistic basis for his promotion of the reverential awe that the word φοβος conveys. The author of Greek Sirach combines the beth of Hebrew Gen 1:1 with σ-φ of σοφος (wise) to form φοβος. *Sophos* is, so to speak, hidden in *phobos*. As a member of the highly literate wisdom school, he finds in Gen 1:1 a linguistic hook on which he will display the notion that God's Sophia is integrally responsible for God's act of bringing creation into being. Perhaps, for the wisdom thinker, she is even the primary referent of *us* in "Let us make the human in our image."[4]

The author of Sir 1 is quite open about his interest in creation. The verbal root κτιζ- appears in vv. 4 and 9. And he is something of a poet in making this presentation, choosing words as much for their sound as for their ideological content. Leaving aside for the moment the *f-* and *s-* combination in the phrase φοβος του κυριου, he presents two other words in *f-s*, φρονησεως (v. 5) and ευφροσυνη (vv. 11, 12). He also reverses the lens from *f-s* to *s-f*, offering two words in *s-f*, σφοδρα (v. 8) and στεφανος (vv. 11, 18). These words are framed by four discrete words containing the letter beta: αβυσσον (v. 3), παραβολαι, βδελυγμα, and θεοσεβεια (v. 25). Counted as discrete words, these ten words containing some combination of *s-b-f* are mirrored in the ten occurrences of the *fob kuriou* (fear of the Sovereign) in this chapter.

| φρονησεως (v. 5) |
| ευφροσυνη (v. 11) |
| ευφροσυνη (v. 12) |
| σφοδρα (v. 8) |
| στεφανος (v. 11) |
| στεφανος (v. 18) |
| αβυσσον (v. 3) |
| παραβολαι (v. 25) |
| βδελυγμα (v. 25) |
| Θεοσεβεια (v. 25) |

---

4. Job 28:21 exemplifies such a hidden aspect of wisdom: "It is hidden from the eyes of all the living and concealed from the birds of the air."

Counted as discrete words, these ten are mirrored in the ten occurrences of the phrase *fob κυριου* (fear of the Sovereign) in Sir 1.

Φοβος κυριου (v. 11)
Φοβος κυριου (v. 12)
Φοβουμενῳ τον κυριον (v. 13)
Φοβεῖσθαι τον κυριον (v. 14)
Φοβεῖσθαι τον κυριον (v. 16)
Φοβος κυριου (v. 18)
Φοβεῖσθαι τον κυριον (v. 20)
Φοβος κυριου (v. 27)
Φοβῳ κυριου (v. 28)
Φοβῳ κυριου (v. 30)

That tenfold symmetry may function as a gesture toward the commandments of v. 26. In short, Sir 1 is a poetic rendition of the fear of the Sovereign resulting from a reading of Gen 1 through the lens of God's hidden wisdom.

And what of John in this regard? The categories of "flying creatures" and "those that crawl" in the creation account of Gen 1 appear in John 1:32 and 3:14, dove and serpent. Fear in the sense of awe or reverence is to the fore here, and it bespeaks the unfolding of a new creation. That the Spirit descends, and the serpent is lifted up suggests that the new creation finds its center in Jesus as Son of Man/Child of Humanity on whom those verbal activities are visited (John 1:51).

Since *Φοβος κυριου* occurs ten times in Sir 1 and is integrally related to keeping the commandments, those who desire to be *σοφος* (wise) are to keep the commandments (Sir 1:26). That initiates a program in John whereby the Ten Words are embodied in Jesus.

The evangelist introduces the exploration of Jesus and the Decalogue in John 5 by recognizing a connection to the Prologue of Sirach, where he finds the letters of *ὑγιης* (healthy) amid this statement:

> ἐν γὰρ τῷ ὀγδόῳ καὶ τριακοστῷ ἔτει ἐπὶ τοῦ Εὐεργέτου βασιλέως παραγενηθεὶς εἰς Αἴγυπτον καὶ συγχρονίσας, εὑρὼν οὐ μικρᾶς παιδείας ἀφόμοιον.
> For in the eight and thirtieth year coming into Egypt, when Euergetes was king, and continuing there some time, I found a copy [of a book] of no small learning. (vv. 27–29)

The word ὑγιης (healthy) is part of John 5:14 and the preceding healing narrative (John 5:6, 8):

μετὰ ταῦτα εὑρίσκει αὐτὸν ὁ Ἰησοῦς ἐν τῷ ἱερῷ καὶ εἶπεν αὐτῷ· Ἴδε ὑγιὴς γέγονας· μηκέτι ἁμάρτανε, ἵνα μὴ χεῖρόν σοί τι γένηται.

After this, Jesus found him in the temple and said to him, "Look; you have become healthy; do not sin, so that nothing worse befall you." (John 5:14)

In turn, the evangelist has incorporated the letters of Σειραχ into the same John 5:14.

μετὰ ταῦτα εὑρίσκει αὐτὸν ὁ Ἰησοῦς ἐν τῷ ἱερῷ καὶ εἶπεν αὐτῷ· Ἴδε ὑγιὴς γέγονας· μηκέτι ἁμάρτανε, ἵνα μὴ χεῖρόν σοί τι γένηται.

Lest there be any doubt about this interplay between Sirach and John, note that the thirty-eight years that Sirach spent in Egypt are mirrored in the thirty-eight-year duration of the paralytic's illness (John 5:5).

Then commences the narrative rendering of Jesus as Decalogue embodied.

DECALOGUE

- John 5

    Only God (v. 44)
    Come in Father's name; you do not receive (v. 43)
    Sabbath; life's works (v. 18)

- John 8

    I honor my Father (v. 49)
    You try to kill me (v. 40)
    True witness (v. 17)
    No *adultery* but fornication (v. 41)
    Your father's desires (v. 44)

- John 10

    Steal and kill (vv. 8–10)

Love of God is exercised by keeping the commandments (Deut 6:1–3, 17). I think that this has direct relevance for the presentation of the Johannine Jesus. For ease of reference, I supply here a chart that correlates each word of the Decalogue with the pertinent chapter of the Fourth Gospel.

Chapter in John → Word ↓	5	6	7	8	9	10
1	44					
2	19					
3	43					
4	16, 17		(22–24)			
5				49		
6	18		19	40		
7				41		
8						8–10
9				13–14		
10				44, 35		

Variant forms of the Decalogue occur in Exod 20 and Deut 5. Note that the evangelist's hypothetical narrativization occurs in the block of chapters from John 5 through 10, excepting chapters 6 and 9. And the order of the transformed commandments is approximately the same in John as one would expect from their presentation in Exodus and Deuteronomy. It is broadly true that the first three words concerning love of God per se find their analogues in John 5, whereas the social commandments are primarily presented in chapters 7, 8, and 10.[5]

Furthermore, we may hear the larger background to the Decalogue in John both in the evangelist's dialogue with the Hebrew language and in the treatment of the Decalogue in Matthew.

First, the dialogue with the Hebrew lexicon. It is of more than passing interest to me that the water Jesus promises in John 7, widely seen as reflecting the water from the rock in the wilderness (Exod 17), also incorporates the lexical neighbors for two different words for rock. Hebrew סֶלַע (rock) is near סָלַק (ascend) in the lexicon. See the extended discussion of going up to Jerusalem that opens John 7. Another word for rock (צוּר) is near צוּף (overflow). See the description of waters flowing from the middle

---

5. That John's Jesus is the perfection of the gift of Torah is one of the emphases present in Keener, *Gospel of John*, 1:360–63.

of the believer in John 7:38. This exercise in John 7 demarcates the discussion of the theologically focused commandments in John 5 from the social commandments in John 8–10.

Similar observations about lexical neighbors may be made regarding the delight (חֵפֶץ) one takes in Torah (e.g., in Ps 1:2) and the freedom (חָפְשָׁה) that is discussed in John 8:31–38. Or consider the delight (שָׁעַע) one takes in the Lord's commands (e.g., Ps 119:47) and the Hebrew for door or gate (שַׁעַר) that forms part of the discussion of command in John 10:18 (itself the first of ten instances of εντολη [command] in John).

JOHN'S DECALOGUE AND MATTHEW'S

If one considers the yoke of Jesus in Matt 11:29–30 a reference to his interpretation of law, then it behooves us to inspect the sweep of Matt 11 (oral or written is a secondary question) as possible conversation partner with the Decalogue in John:

Matt 11		John 5–8
Verses		Chapters
2	John the Bapist	
5	Lame healed	5
4	Hear and see	6
12	Violence	
16–19	Schism	7
22	Judgment	
25–27	Revelation of Father and Son	8
29–30	Yoke of Jesus	5, 8
28	Wisdom	6–7

WISDOM OF SOLOMON AND THE GOSPEL OF JOHN

At the center of this Wisdom text is the explicit use of the phrase "reign of God" (10:10). I suggest that Wisdom offers material on both the macro- and micro-level for the Fourth Evangelist, who is also sparing in his use of the phrase.

Similar Thematic Profiles of Wisdom and FG, in Differing Scales

Macro

Wisdom of Solomon		Fourth Gospel
1–4 Immortality		1–12 Signs of eternal life
5–9 Characteristics of, and relationship with, God's Sophia		13–19 I AM … in …
9	Guard … glory	17
10–19 Creation's benefits for God's chosen		18–21 Jesus lifted up to the Father and giving Spirit
13, 15 Critique of idolatry	Four questions	16 Exploration of the disciples' limited understanding of Jesus' words

Micro

Wisdom of Solomon		Fourth Gospel
7:13	Without guile	1:46–48
11:1–14	Thirst, water	2, 4
16:1–4	Hunger	4
16:5–14	Dying, healing	4–5
16:15–29	Hail, manna	6
17:1—18:4	Darkness, light	8–9
18:5–25	Death, salvation	10–11
19:1–17, 22	Drowning, crossing, doxology	21

A Note About Analogy and the Reign of God

Again, the explicit phrase "reign of God" occurs only at Wis 10:10, the approximate center of the book. In that regard, it resembles the sparse usage in the Fourth Gospel, which cites the phrase only at John 3:3, 5. That is not to say that Wisdom deals with the theme only here. When the author discusses analogical thought in 13:5, "And so the architect is known through analogy from the majesty and beauty of created things," we have a hint of how he thinks about his topics. I see the themes treated below as indicative of the author's wide range of analogical thinking about God's reign.

WISDOM OF SOLOMON 10:10 AND JOHN

A key text in our consideration of the reign of God in Wisdom and John is Wis 10:10:

> ὡδήγησεν ἐν τρίβοις εὐθείαις ἔδειξεν αὐτῷ βασιλείαν θεοῦ καὶ ἔδωκεν αὐτῷ γνῶσιν ἁγίων εὐπόρησεν αὐτὸν ἐν μόχθοις καὶ ἐπλήθυνεν τοὺς πόνους αὐτοῦ

> She guided him on right paths and showed him God's reign and gave him knowledge of holy things. She prospered him in his labors and increased the fruit of his toil.

The *she* is Sophia. What she shows is God's reign. Note that there is no definite article present; not *the* reign of God. What does John do with this?

Showed (δεικνυμι) is what Jesus does in John 20:20, displaying his wounds to the disciples.

In the underlined letters of John 20:27–28 below, in which Jesus speaks and displays his wounds, please find σοφια (Sophia, Wisdom) and βασιλεία του θεοῦ (God's reign):

> εἶτα λέγει τῷ Θωμᾷ· Φέρε τὸν δάκτυλόν <u>σου</u> ὧδε καὶ ἴδε τὰς χεῖράς μου, καὶ <u>φέρε</u> τὴν χεῖρά σου καὶ <u>βάλε</u> εἰς τὴν πλευράν μου, καὶ <u>μὴ</u> γίνου ἄπιστος ἀ<u>λλὰ</u> πιστός. ²⁸ <u>ἀπεκρίθη</u> Θωμᾶ<u>ς</u> καὶ εἶπεν αὐτῷ· Ὁ κύριός μου καὶ ὁ <u>θεός</u> <u>μου</u>.

Critical commentaries frequently note the oddity of the verbal diction; Βάλε (throw) in v. 27 describing what Thomas is invited by Jesus to do with his hand. A simple τίθημι (put, place) would have satisfied a punctilious grammarian. But John is not playing to the cranky pedagogues in the back row. Βάλε (throw) is integral to his shimmering presentation of God's βασιλεια (reign).

We are dealing here with Wisdom's explicit use of the phrase "reign of God." As many have said, Wis 10:10 exegetes the ladder vision of Jacob (referred to here as "him") in Gen 28. This verse may be seen as influencing two groups of Johannine verses. The more concentrated appear in the beginning of the Farewell Discourse.

Wis 10:10	Johannine Farewell Discourse
She [ὡδήγησεν] guided him on straight paths	I am the [ὁδὸς] Way (John 14:6)
She showed [δεικνυμι] him the reign of God	Show [δεικνυμι] us the Father (John 14:8)
She gave him knowledge of holy things	The Holy Spirit (John 14:26)
She prospered him in his labors	You will do greater works than these (John 14:12)
And increased the fruit of his toil	That you should bear more fruit (John 15:2)

WISDOM OF SOLOMON 10 AND THE NAME YHWH

Αὕτη πρωτόπλαστον πατέρα κόσμου μόνον κτισθέντα διεφύλαξεν καὶ ἐξείλατο αὐτὸν ἐκ παραπτώματος ἰδίου
2 ἔδωκέν τε αὐτῷ ἰσχὺν κρατῆσαι ἁπάντων.
3 ἀποστὰς δὲ ἀπ' αὐτῆς ἄδικος ἐν ὀργῇ αὐτοῦ ἀδελφοκτόνοις συναπώλετο θυμοῖς.
4 δι' ὃν κατακλυζομένην γῆν πάλιν ἔσωσεν σοφία δι' εὐτελοῦς ξύλου τὸν δίκαιον κυβερνήσασα.
5 αὕτη καὶ ἐν ὁμονοίᾳ πονηρίας ἐθνῶν συγχυθέντων ἔγνω τὸν δίκαιον καὶ ἐτήρησεν αὐτὸν ἄμεμπτον θεῷ καὶ ἐπὶ τέκνου σπλάγχνοις ἰσχυρὸν ἐφύλαξεν.
6 αὕτη δίκαιον ἐξαπολλυμένων ἀσεβῶν ἐρρύσατο φυγόντα καταβάσιον πῦρ Πενταπόλεως,
7 ἧς ἔτι μαρτύριον τῆς πονηρίας καπνιζομένη καθέστηκε χέρσος, καὶ ἀτελέσιν ὥραις καρποφοροῦντα φυτά, ἀπιστούσης ψυχῆς μνημεῖον ἑστηκυῖα στήλη ἁλός.
8 σοφίαν γὰρ παροδεύσαντες οὐ μόνον ἐβλάβησαν τοῦ μὴ γνῶναι τὰ καλά, ἀλλὰ καὶ τῆς ἀφροσύνης ἀπέλιπον τῷ βίῳ μνημόσυνον, ἵνα ἐν οἷς ἐσφάλησαν μηδὲ λαθεῖν δυνηθῶσιν.
9 σοφία δὲ τοὺς θεραπεύοντας αὐτὴν ἐκ πόνων ἐρρύσατο.
10 αὕτη φυγάδα ὀργῆς ἀδελφοῦ δίκαιον ὡδήγησεν ἐν τρίβοις εὐθείαις· ἔδειξεν αὐτῷ βασιλείαν θεοῦ καὶ ἔδωκεν αὐτῷ γνῶσιν ἁγίων· εὐπόρησεν αὐτὸν ἐν μόχθοις καὶ ἐπλήθυνεν τοὺς πόνους αὐτοῦ·
11 ἐν πλεονεξίᾳ κατισχυόντων αὐτὸν παρέστη καὶ ἐπλούτισεν αὐτόν·
12 διεφύλαξεν αὐτὸν ἀπὸ ἐχθρῶν καὶ ἀπὸ ἐνεδρευόντων ἠσφαλίσατο· καὶ ἀγῶνα ἰσχυρὸν ἐβράβευσεν αὐτῷ, ἵνα γνῷ ὅτι παντὸς δυνατωτέρα ἐστὶν εὐσέβεια.
13 αὕτη πραθέντα δίκαιον οὐκ ἐγκατέλιπεν, ἀλλὰ ἐξ ἁμαρτίας ἐρρύσατο αὐτόν·

14 συγκατέβη αὐτῷ εἰς λάκκον καὶ ἐν δεσμοῖς οὐκ ἀφῆκεν αὐτόν, ἕως ἤνεγκεν αὐτῷ σκῆπτρα βασιλείας καὶ ἐξουσίαν τυραννούντων αὐτοῦ· ψευδεῖς τε ἔδειξεν τοὺς μωμησαμένους αὐτὸν καὶ ἔδωκεν αὐτῷ δόξαν αἰώνιον.
15 Αὕτη λαὸν ὅσιον καὶ σπέρμα ἄμεμπτον ἐρρύσατο ἐξ ἔθνους θλιβόντων·
16 εἰσῆλθεν εἰς ψυχὴν θεράποντος κυρίου καὶ ἀντέστη βασιλεῦσιν φοβεροῖς ἐν τέρασι καὶ σημείοις.
17 ἀπέδωκεν ὁσίοις μισθὸν κόπων αὐτῶν, ὡδήγησεν αὐτοὺς ἐν ὁδῷ θαυμαστῇ καὶ ἐγένετο αὐτοῖς εἰς σκέπην ἡμέρας καὶ εἰς φλόγα ἄστρων τὴν νύκτα.
18 διεβίβασεν αὐτοὺς θάλασσαν ἐρυθρὰν καὶ διήγαγεν αὐτοὺς δι᾽ ὕδατος πολλοῦ·
19 τοὺς δὲ ἐχθροὺς αὐτῶν κατέκλυσεν καὶ ἐκ βάθους ἀβύσσου ἀνέβρασεν αὐτούς.
20 διὰ τοῦτο δίκαιοι ἐσκύλευσαν ἀσεβεῖς καὶ ὕμνησαν, κύριε, τὸ ὄνομα τὸ ἅγιόν σου τήν τε ὑπέρμαχόν σου χεῖρα ᾔνεσαν ὁμοθυμαδόν·
21 ὅτι ἡ σοφία ἤνοιξεν στόμα κωφῶν καὶ γλώσσας νηπίων ἔθηκεν τρανάς.

Wisdom protected the first-formed father of the world, when he alone had been created;
she delivered him from his transgression,
2 and gave him strength to rule all things.
3 But when an unrighteous man departed from her in his anger,
he perished because in rage he killed his brother.
4 When the earth was flooded because of him, Wisdom again saved it,
steering the righteous man by a paltry piece of wood.
5 Wisdom also, when the nations in wicked agreement had been put to confusion,
recognized the righteous man and preserved him blameless before God,
and kept him strong in the face of his compassion for his child.
6 Wisdom rescued a righteous man when the ungodly were perishing;
he escaped the fire that descended on the Five Cities.
7 Evidence of their wickedness still remains:
a continually smoking wasteland,
plants bearing fruit that does not ripen,
and a pillar of salt standing as a monument to an unbelieving soul.
8 For because they passed Wisdom by,
they not only were hindered from recognizing the good,

but also left for humankind a reminder of their folly,
so that their failures could never go unnoticed.
9 Wisdom rescued from troubles those who served her.
10 When a righteous man fled from his brother's wrath,
she guided him on straight paths;
she showed him the kingdom of God,
and gave him knowledge of holy things;
she prospered him in his labors,
and increased the fruit of his toil.
11 When his oppressors were covetous,
she stood by him and made him rich.
12 She protected him from his enemies,
and kept him safe from those who lay in wait for him;
in his arduous contest she gave him the victory,
so that he might learn that godliness is more powerful than anything else.
13 When a righteous man was sold, Wisdom did not desert him,
but delivered him from sin.
She descended with him into the dungeon,
14 and when he was in prison she did not leave him,
until she brought him the scepter of a kingdom
and authority over his masters.
Those who accused him she showed to be false,
and she gave him everlasting honor.
15 A holy people and blameless race
Wisdom delivered from a nation of oppressors.
16 She entered the soul of a servant of the Sovereign,
and withstood dread kings with wonders and signs.
17 She gave to holy people the reward of their labors;
she guided them along a marvelous way,
and became a shelter to them by day,
and a starry flame through the night.
18 She brought them over the Red Sea,
and led them through deep waters;
19 but she drowned their enemies,
and cast them up from the depth of the sea.
20 Therefore the righteous plundered the ungodly;
they sang hymns, O Sovereign, to your holy name,
and praised with one accord your defending hand;
21 for Wisdom opened the mouths of those who were mute,
and made the tongues of infants speak clearly. (RSV)

I find it a signal of the studious pleasure that grounds this text that Hebrew Yhwh informs the Greek of Wis 10, something perhaps to be expected since Wis 10:20 explicitly mentions the name of the *kyrios*. Furthermore, Βασιλεια is intercalated in John 2:13-14, intertwined with σοφια in vv. 14-15 and concluding with reference to the name in v. 23. These characteristics are derived from some contact with Wis 10.

Καὶ ἐγγὺς ἦν τὸ πάσχα τῶν Ἰουδαίων, καὶ ἀνέβη εἰς Ἱεροσόλυμα ὁ Ἰησοῦς. ¹⁴ καὶ εὗρεν ἐν τῷ ἱερῷ τοὺς πωλοῦντας βόας καὶ πρόβατα καὶ περιστερὰς (John 2:13-14)

and

καὶ εὗρεν ἐν τῷ ἱερῷ τοὺς πωλοῦντας βόας καὶ πρόβατα καὶ περιστερὰς καὶ τοὺς κερματιστὰς καθημένους, ¹⁵ καὶ ποιήσας φραγέλλιον ἐκ σχοινίων πάντας ἐξέβαλεν ἐκ τοῦ ἱεροῦ τά τε πρόβατα καὶ τοὺς βόας, καὶ τῶν κολλυβιστῶν ἐξέχεεν τὰ κέρματα καὶ τὰς τραπέζας ἀνέστρεψεν, (John 2:14-15)

The Johannine pericope concludes with explicit attention at John 2:23 to the name.[6] This twin emphasis on kingdom and name is also present in Wis 10:10 in which Sophia shows Jacob the reign of God in a chapter that concludes with explicit attention to the holy name in Wis 10:20. And the same verb δεικνυμι (show/display) at John 2:18 occurs in Wis 10:10.[7]

The Way in Which the Name Yhwh Shapes Wisdom 10 Also Affects John 17

There are four occurrences of the name Σοφια in Wis 10, at vv. 4, 8, 9, and in its last verse, 21. Close attention to the following features suggests that Yhwh is the unspoken partner in this profile.

The first occurrence in v. 4a places Sophia at the end of the bicolon about her action during the flood. That is, Sophia occurs where the yod in יהוה is placed, to the far right of the name.

The occurrence of Sophia in v. 8 is preceded by ἅλας. The rough breathing in the beginning of this word for "salt" mimics the sound of the letter heh.

---

6. Those interested will also find the divine self-predication Ἐγώ εἰμι ὁ ὤν (Exod 3:14) intercalated into John 2:23-25.

7. "That one knows all" (Wis 9:11) leaves its footprint in the memory of the Johannine author at John 2:21, 24.

The nearby σοφια δε in v. 9 functions, together with that in v. 8, as meme for the additive function of the letter vav in Yhwh.

Finally, the fourth occurrence of Sophia in v. 21 is preceded by the definite article ἡ, whose rough breathing functions as it does in v. 8, to limn the sound of heh, the fourth letter in Yhwh.

Subsidiary dynamics in the chapter also gesture toward Yhwh. There is a set of references in vv. 1, 2, and 6 to what she does, expressed with the pronoun αυτη. A complementary set of occurrences of αυτη appears in vv. 10, 13, and 15. In the approximate center of these two sets of aute are three occurrences of Sophia in vv. 4, 8, 9. We could read this arrangement as a reminder that in the tetragrammaton, we are dealing, after all, with three discrete letters.

This reading bears fruit when hearing the text of John 17. Mirroring the fourfold occurrence of Sophia in Wis 10, there are four and only four occurrences of the word ονομα (name) in John 17 (vv. 6, 11, 12, and in the last verse of the chapter, v. 26). Just as importantly, their relative distribution precisely mirrors that of Sophia in Wis 10.

Wis 10—Sophia	Wis 10—Sophia	Wis 10—Sophia
vv. 4	8, 9	21
John 17—*Onoma*	John 17—*Onoma*	John 17—*Onoma*
vv. 6	11, 12	26

The evangelist even uses αυτη, though without the rough breathing, in John 17:3, a whisper of an echo of its frequent occurrence in Wis 10.

At the literary level, John 17 takes one of its cues concerning Yhwh from the structure of Wis 10.

Signs, Wonders, Labors (Wis 10:16–17; John 4)

As we have just seen, Wis 10 displays four occurrences of the name Sophia (vv. 4, 8, 9, 21), intimating that we are in the presence of Yhwh exercising the sovereignty of Wis 10:10. I find it entirely plausible that Jesus' response, "I AM," in John 4:26, while capable of being read as answer to the question about the Messiah, is also sufficiently ambiguous as to connote the divine name. In addition, John 4 presents us with other themes reflective of Wis 10. When alluding to Moses, Pseudo-Solomon says:

She entered the soul of a servant of the Sovereign,
and he withstood frightening kings [βασιλεις] with signs and wonders. She repaid the labors [μισθον κοπων] of holy ones.
(Wis 10:16–17a)

This complex is reflected in the comments of Jesus in John 4:36–38 concerning the payment of labor (μισθον κοπον αυτων) of the harvesters and his complaint to a royal official (βασιλικος) that "unless you see signs and wonders you will not believe" (John 4:48).

SOPHIA, THE REIGN OF GOD, AND JESUS' FEMALE DISCIPLES (WIS 8:5–8)

The text of Wis 8:5–8 renders a Greek portrait of Sophia that is demonstrably incorporated into the very servant narratives we examined in chapter 2 of this study (Cana wedding—Samaritan woman—siblings Mary, Martha, Lazarus—and dinner with the siblings). A stylistic feature binds together these verses in Wis 8:5–8 in that each one begins with some variant of the phrase *ei de kai*. Furthermore, the letters of the phrase βασιλεια του θεου (reign of God), here underlined, are present and extend throughout each verse of the passage:

> εἰ δὲ πλοῦτός ἐστιν ἐπιθυμητὸν κτῆμα ἐν βίῳ, τί σοφίας πλουσιώτερον τῆς τὰ πάντα ἐργαζομένης; ⁶ εἰ δὲ φρόνησις ἐργάζεται, τίς αὐτῆς τῶν ὄντων μᾶλλόν ἐστι τεχνῖτις; ⁷ καὶ εἰ δικαιοσύνην ἀγαπᾷ τις, οἱ πόνοι ταύτης εἰσὶν ἀρεταί· σωφροσύνην γὰρ καὶ φρόνησιν ἐκδιδάσκει, δικαιοσύνην καὶ ἀνδρείαν, ὧν χρησιμώτερον οὐδέν ἐστιν ἐν βίῳ ἀνθρώποις. ⁸ εἰ δὲ καὶ πολυπειρίαν ποθεῖ τις, οἶδε τὰ ἀρχαῖα καὶ τὰ μέλλοντα εἰκάζειν, ἐπίσταται στροφὰς λόγων καὶ λύσεις αἰνιγμάτων, σημεῖα καὶ τέρατα προγινώσκει καὶ ἐκβάσεις καιρῶν καὶ χρόνων.

> If riches be a possession to be desired in this life; what is richer than wisdom, who works all things? ⁶ And if prudence work; who of all that are is a more cunning laborer than she? ⁷ And if a man love righteousness, her labors are virtues: for she teaches temperance and prudence, justice and fortitude which are such things, as people can have nothing more profitable in their life. ⁸ If a man desire much experience, she knows things of old, and conjectures aright what is to come: she knows the subtleties of speeches, and can expound dark sentences: she foresees signs and wonders, and the outcomes of seasons and times.

The Fourth Evangelist has noted that female evangelists bring good news to Jerusalem in Isa 40:9–10. (The form used for "herald" is feminine.) He incorporates traits of God's female Sophia into four successive scenes in the Fourth Gospel that include women. The following chart collects much of the diction that will be incorporated into the chapters with women disciples and is followed by a more extensive discussion of those passages.

Citation in Wisdom	Sophia Language	Citation in John
8:5	τι (what, in a question)	What to me and you? (2:4)
8:6	Τις (who, in a question)	Who brought him food? (4:33)
8:7	Αγαπ (love)	Jesus loved Martha and Mary and Lazarus. (11:5)
	Ανδρεια (courage)	Resolve to enter dangerous territory (11:6–7)
	Δικαιοσυνη (just[ice])	These letters are here intercalated. (11:42–43)
8:8	Πολυπειρια (wide experience)	These letters are here intercalated. (12:3)
	Αρχαια (antiquities)	The feet of Gen 3:15 (12:3)
	Στροφος λογων και λυσεις αινιγματων (turns of phrase and solutions of puzzles)	The letters in the saying about αναστασις (resurrection) in 11:25 are here intercalated. (12:3)
	Σημεια (signs)	These letters are here intercalated. (12:3)

The Wedding at Cana and Wisdom of Solomon 8:5

εἰ δὲ πλοῦτός ἐστιν ἐπιθυμητὸν κτῆμα ἐν βίῳ, τί σοφίας πλουσιώτερον τῆς τὰ πάντα ἐργαζομένης;

And if wealth is to be desired as a possession in life, who is wealthier than Sophia, who effects everything? (Wis 8:5)

The abundant quantity of excellent wine in John 2:1–11 is generally congruent with the theme of riches in v. 5 above. At a linguistic level, moreover, the very word *ploutos* (wealth) is present in reverse order in the letters of the words spoken in John 2:5, which I here underline:

καὶ λέγει αὐτῇ ὁ Ἰησοῦς· Τί ἐμοὶ καὶ σοί, γύναι; οὔπω ἥκει ἡ ὥρα μου. λέγει ἡ μήτηρ αὐτοῦ τοῖς διακόνοις Ὅ τι ἂν λέγῃ ὑμῖν ποιήσατε.

And Jesus said to her, "What is your concern to me, woman? My hour has not yet come." His mother said to the servants, "Do whatever he tells you."

Subsequently read left to right, those same letters appear once Jesus has acted on his mother's request:

ὡς δὲ ἐγεύσατο ὁ ἀρχιτρίκλινος τὸ ὕδωρ οἶνον γεγενημένον, καὶ οὐκ ᾔδει πόθεν ἐστίν, οἱ δὲ διάκονοι ᾔδεισαν οἱ ἠντληκότες τὸ ὕδωρ, φωνεῖ τὸν νυμφίον ὁ ἀρχιτρίκλινος.

When the chief steward tasted the water become wine, indeed he did not know whence it came (though the servants who had drawn the water knew), the chief steward called the bridegroom. (John 2:9)

And again in John 2:10:

καὶ λέγει αὐτῷ· Πᾶς ἄνθρωπος πρῶτον τὸν καλὸν οἶνον τίθησιν, καὶ ὅταν μεθυσθῶσιν τὸν ἐλάσσω· σὺ τετήρηκας τὸν καλὸν οἶνον ἕως ἄρτι.

And he said to him, "Every person serves the good wine first, and when they have drunk their fill, the lesser; you, however, have kept the good wine until now.

Even the reader who is open to the possibility of such intercalated construction will perhaps wonder about the order in which the requisite letters occur. I would suggest that Wis 8:1, just a handful of verses prior, offers a rationale for what occurs in this text:

Διατείνει δὲ ἀπὸ πέρατος εἰς πέρας εὐρώστως καὶ διοικεῖ τὰ πάντα χρηστῶς.

She reaches from end to end powerfully and orders all things well.

The verb διοικεῖ can mean order or administer but also provide or furnish. One of the things that the Johannine author has Sophia order is the very order of the letters in the word πλοῦτός.[8] And as Sophia orders all things well (in the sense of provide), so the chief steward orders all things

---

8. In regard to John 2:1–12, note the fact that the word *oinos/oinon* (wine) occurs within the letters of Wis 8:5, εἰ δὲ πλοῦτός ἐστιν ἐπιθυμητὸν.

at a banquet. Indeed, I see the attention given by the narrator to the chief steward as a deliberate reflection at one level of Sophia. However, when the banquet's wine falls short, Sophia's wealth, active in Jesus and his mother, makes up the deficit, and then some.

A metaphorical referent of this wealth resides in the adjacent chapter 7 of Wisdom in which Wisdom's instruction is depicted as itself a superior kind of wealth (Wis 7:8, 11, 13–14). And this is only one aspect of the symmetry between this portrait of Wisdom and the mother of Jesus in the Fourth Gospel.[9] Finally, the change from water to wine and its particular brand of wealth is perhaps best understood as a manifestation of the change in key mentioned in Wis 19:18a whereby various elements of creation are reconfigured at the behest of Wisdom.[10]

The Woman of Samaria and Wisdom of Solomon 8:6

εἰ δὲ φρόνησις ἐργάζεται, τίς αὐτῆς τῶν ὄντων μᾶλλόν ἐστι τεχνῖτις;

And if foresight effects [things], who more than she is a craftsperson of all that is? (Wis 8:6)

Regarding John 4:1–42, Jesus and the woman of Samaria, note that the particle *tis* (who) occurs in John 4:10, 33 and only there in the story. That reflects the double occurrence of *tis* that brackets the concluding phrase in Wis 8:6:

τίς αὐτῆς τῶν ὄντων μᾶλλόν ἐστι τεχνῖτις;

Note also that *edei* (it was necessary) in John 4:4 is a variant of the letters that open Wis 8:6, *ei de*. And the *ergon* (work) to which Jesus refers in John 4:34 is the nominal aspect of the verb *ergazetai* in Wis 8:6.

Remember also that the reign of God in Wis 10:10 is related to Jacob specifically.

---

9. Wisdom 8:9, "I took her [Sophia] to live with me," might have been one influence on John 19:27 in which the Beloved Disciple takes the mother of Jesus to live with him. The voice of Solomon makes this choice because he perceives that she would be "good counsel in care and grief." Compare the mother of Jesus addressing the lack of wine in John 2 and the image of the woman whose grief yields to joy at birth in John 16.

10. Note also that the Mary of the Magnificat gives attention to the πλουτοῦντας rich (Luke 1:53).

When the righteous fled from his brother's wrath she guided him in right paths, shewed him *the kingdom of God*, and gave him knowledge of holy things, made him rich in his travels, and multiplied the fruit of his labors.

This is particularly pertinent to John 4:5-6, 12 where Jacob is mentioned. These are the only mentions of Jacob in John.

Moreover, the letters βασιλεια (reign) are intercalated in John 4:1-3:

Ὡς οὖν ἔγνω ὁ Ἰησοῦς ὅτι ἤκουσαν οἱ Φαρισαῖοι ὅτι Ἰησοῦς πλείονας μαθητὰς ποιεῖ καὶ <u>βα</u>πτίζει ἢ Ἰωάννης—² καίτοιγε Ἰησοῦς αὐτὸς οὐκ ἐβάπτιζεν ἀλλ' οἱ μαθηταὶ αὐτοῦ—³ ἀφῆκεν τὴν Ἰουδα<u>ία</u>ν καὶ ἀπῆλθεν πάλιν εἰς τὴν Γαλιλαία.

So when Jesus knew that the Pharisees heard that Jesus was making more disciples than John and was baptizing—though Jesus himself did not baptize; his disciples did—he left Judea and came again into Galilee.

The Raising of Lazarus and Wis 8:7

καὶ εἰ δικαιοσύνην ἀγαπᾷ τις, οἱ πόνοι ταύτης εἰσὶν ἀρεταί· σωφροσύνην γὰρ καὶ φρόνησιν ἐκδιδάσκει, δικαιοσύνην καὶ ἀνδρείαν, ὧν χρησιμώτερον οὐδέν ἐστιν ἐν βίῳ ἀνθρώποις. (Wis 8:7)

Regarding John 11:1-44, two clear linguistic parallels to Wis 8:7 are present: *agap-* (love) (John 11:3, 5), and *didask-* (teacher) (John 11:28). Furthermore, four of Wisdom's virtues are named in Wis 8:7. One of them, αρετη, is present in descriptions of both sisters:

ἡ οὖν Μά<u>ρ</u>θα ὡς ἤκουσεν ὅτι Ἰησοῦς ἔρχεται ὑπήντησεν αὐτῷ· Μαρία δὲ ἐν τῷ οἴκῳ ἐκαθέζετο. (John 11:20)

οἱ οὖν Ἰουδαῖοι οἱ ὄντες μετ' αὐτῆς ἐν τῇ οἰκίᾳ καὶ παραμυθούμενοι αὐτήν, ἰδόντες τὴν Μα<u>ρ</u>ιάμ ὅτι ταχέως ἀνέσ<u>τη</u> καὶ ἐξῆλθεν, ἠκολούθησαν αὐτῇ δόξαντες ὅτι ὑπάγει εἰς τὸ μνημεῖον ἵνα κλαύσῃ ἐκεῖ. (John 11:31)

This virtue of excellence is equated with *ponos* in Wis 8:7. *Ponos*, meaning labor, is implicit in the introduction to John 11, that is, John 10:40, when Jesus goes to the

Jesus and the Reign of God in John

το<u>πον</u> <u>ο</u>που η Ιωαννης

place where John was [baptizing at first].

The other meaning of *ponos* is grief, apparent in the friends and family of Lazarus, who has died. The combined sense of both labor and grief is present in Exod 2:11, "Moses went out and looked on his people and considered their burden [πονον]," and may therefore be seen as one of the best structuring principles of John 11 in that Jesus' command "unbind him and let him go" (11:44) is readily understood as an echo of exodus liberation.

One of the virtues named in Wis 8:7 is φρονησις (providence), the ability to foresee the link between present action and the future, and is arguably present in Jesus' assertion about the link between Lazarus and the revelation of the glory of God (11:40). Another of Sophia's virtues, bravery, named in Wis 8:7 (ανδρεια), is seen in Jesus' decision to return to Judea in John 11:7–8. Just as interesting, perhaps, is the open vocalic formation that opens Wis 8:7, *kai ei*. The *aiei* vowels contain within them the adverb *aei* (forever). Compare the phrase εις τον αιωνα in John 11:26.

Also noteworthy is the fact that διδασκαλος (teacher) (John 11:28) contains within it all the letters of δικαιος (just), since δικαιοσυνη (justice) is emphasized twice in Wis 8:7.

The Dinner at Bethany and Wisdom of Solomon 8:8

εἰ δὲ καὶ πολυπειρίαν ποθεῖ τις,
οἶδε τὰ ἀρχαῖα <u>καὶ</u> τὰ μέλλοντα εἰκάζειν,
ἐπίσταται στροφὰς λόγων <u>καὶ</u> λύσεις αἰνιγμάτων,
σημεῖα <u>καὶ</u> τέρατα προγινώσκει καὶ
ἐκβάσεις καιρῶν <u>καὶ</u> χρόνων. (Wis 8:8)

Formally a doublet, the names Martha and Mary are in that regard reflected in the sequence of four doublets in Wis 8:8. There is also a symmetry between their names and the four doublets in that their shared Μαρ- component, when added to the letters that follow in each name, ιαμ and θα, yields a total of eight letters.

Because of her purity, Sophia pervades and permeates all things (Wis 7:24d), a reality surely intended in the myrrh that, uniquely in this account, permeates the house where they eat (John 12:3). In Wis 8:8, Sophia is said to know realities past and also intuit the future. That is also relevant to

John 12:18. At the most basic level, noted by many commentators, the action of Mary in anointing Jesus for his upcoming burial is congruent with Wisdom's presence in her.

Moreover, the concluding phrase εκβασεις καιρων (outcome of times) contains within it the letters ισ-κᾱ-ρῑ. The Fourth Evangelist uses this to draw Ἰσκαριωτης (*Iskariot*) into the mix, which is missing from the other canonical accounts of the anointing. John's attention to names is complemented by including ten instances of ων in John 12:1–8. The four pairs of doublets joined by καὶ plus two other instances of καὶ in Wis 8 serve as background to this Johannine pericope. The replete presence of ων in this account of the anointing is also part of the divine self-predication of Exod 3:14, I AM.

λέγει δὲ Ἰούδας ὁ Ἰσκαριώτης εἷς τ<u>ῶν</u> μαθητ<u>ῶν</u> αὐτοῦ, ὁ μέλλ<u>ων</u> αὐτὸν παραδιδόναι·⁵ Διὰ τί τοῦτο τὸ μύρον οὐκ ἐπράθη τριακοσί<u>ων</u> δηναρί<u>ων</u> καὶ ἐδόθη πτωχοῖς; ⁶ εἶπεν δὲ τοῦτο οὐχ ὅτι περὶ τ<u>ῶν</u> πτωχ<u>ῶν</u> ἔμελεν αὐτῷ, ἀλλ' ὅτι κλέπτης ἦν καὶ τὸ γλωσσόκομον ἔχ<u>ων</u> τὰ βαλλόμενα ἐβάσταζεν. ⁷ εἶπεν οὖν ὁ Ἰησοῦς · Ἄφες αὐτήν, ἵνα εἰς τὴν ἡμέραν τοῦ ἐνταφιασμοῦ μου τηρήσῃ αὐτό ·⁸ τοὺς πτωχοὺς γὰρ πάντοτε ἔχετε μεθ' ἑαυτ<u>ῶν</u>, ἐμὲ δὲ οὐ πάντοτε ἔχετε. (John 12:4–8)

The other portion of the divine name ἐγώ εἰμι (I AM) is present in the longer self-description "I am the resurrection and the life" in John 11:25:

<u>Ἐγώ εἰμι</u> ἡ ἀνάστασις καὶ ἡ ζωή.

That is, the two narratives in John 11–12, each portraying the characters of Martha and Mary, also work together to convey the twice-told divine self-predication of Exod 3:14. The Fourth Evangelist presents the God of Israel and the Sophia of the same as active in the stories of these women in John 2, 4, 11, and 12.

ΠΙΠΙ (WIS 8:5–8)

There is another feature that holds together the four verses in Wis 8:5–8. The successive verses limn the occasional Septuagintal rendering of the divine name as PIPI (letters chosen for their rather rough approximation to the shape of the Hebrew letters in the name):

v. 5 Πloutos

v. 6 εI de

v. 7 Ποnoi

v. 8 εI de

THE REIGN OF GOD AS A LADDER (WIS 6)

As already noted, John 3:3, 5 are the only two occurrences of the phrase "reign of God" in John. I suggest that this spare accounting corresponds deliberately to an aspect of Wisdom of Solomon in which the reign of God is to a certain extent twice depicted in the image of a ladder.

Commentators frequently note that Wis 10:10, in which Sophia reveals the kingdom of God to Jacob, is grounded in the narrative of the staircase/ladder of Gen 28. It is common to observe also that the vision of the Son of Man/Child of Humanity in John 1:51 is based on the ladder vision of Gen 28. What has not been explored, to the best of my knowledge, is that the interlocking steps of Sophia's *paideia* in Wis 6:17–20, also crafted as analogous to a ladder, help to shape the Farewell Discourse in John:

> [17] For the very true beginning of wisdom is the desire for learning; and the concern for learning is love (of her);
> [18] And love is the keeping of her laws; and giving heed to her laws is the assurance of incorruption;
> [19] And incorruption makes (one) near to God:
> [20] Therefore the desire for wisdom leads to sovereignty.
> (Wis 6:17–20)

Consider the following sketch of similarities between Wis 6:17–20 and the Farewell Discourse in John. To reinforce the visual image of a ladder, the texts may be read from bottom to top of the columns:

Wis 6:17–20		John 13–17	
Verse		Chapter and Verse	
20	βασιλεια	17:2	εξουσια (authority over all flesh)
		17:3	θεον
19	θεω (to God) *aphtharsia* (incorruption)	16:2 16:33	θεῳ (to God) *alla tharseite* (be brave)

Wis 6:17–20	John 13–17
Verse	Chapter and Verse
18 αγαπ- (love) (2x) τηρησις (keep her laws)	15:12 αγαπ- (love) 15:12, 14, 17 τηρειν (keep commands, words) 14:21 αγαπ- (love)
17 παιδεια (instruction)	13:33 τεκνια (children)

The answer to the question "Where are you going?" in John 14:5 is modeled in part on Jacob's ladder depicting God's reign and receives a plausible answer in that context: Jesus is going to the Father/God. It is exhilarating to recognize that the "rise [εγειρεσθε], let us go from here" in John 14:31b is, on this reading, an invitation to a literally presented ascent analogous to Jacob's arising (εξηγερθη) in Gen 28:16. That backstory of Jacob's ladder acts as the peg on which the Johannine ladder's themes are mounted and addresses the universally recognized conundrum that Jesus continues to talk for three more chapters following this invitation to rise and go.[11]

WISDOM OF SOLOMON, NUMBER AND TEXT

I suggest that attention to numerical dynamics in the construction of Wisdom of Solomon was inspired in part at least by the vision of Sir 1:2, 9, 19 wherein the one on the throne creates wisdom, who is then apportioned among the elements of the world. The word for apportioned is εξαριθμειν, in whose αριθμ- component one may see the attention to number. As we begin these observations, I emphasize that their referents are an exercise of the Sovereign, who creates with a kind of mathematical precision. In what follows, we will pursue mathematical aspects per se of the Wisdom of Solomon in relation to the Gospel of John:

- Ps 62:5 LXX
- The arm of the Sovereign/Son of the Magnificat's Mary
- 153 fish of the new creation

---

11. Perhaps Luke 22:15 that speaks of Jesus' desire (επιθυμ-) to eat this meal with the disciples is inspired by the true desire (επιθυμια) of Wis 8:5. And nothing that has been argued about the importance of this ladder of wisdom cancels the fact that Song 2:13 also contains language shared by John 14–15, i.e., vineyard, arise, friend.

Most major sections of the Wisdom of Solomon are structured according to a discernible numerical sequence.[12] Here we attend to structuring mathematical procedures in Wisdom that inspired the author of John in at least three ways.

Wisdom of Solomon and Psalm 62:5 LXX

Counting either mono-cola-, bi-cola-, or tri-cola-exhibiting literary devices such as *inclusio* as well as thematic development, Addison Wright reports the following number of verses in the listed sections of Wisdom.[13]

A	1:1—6:21	138 verses
B	6:22—9:18	84 verses
C	11:2-16; 12:23-27; 15:18—16:29	54 verses
D	17:1—19:22	84 verses

Note that the verse totals in B and D are identical. Note also that the sum of verse totals in B and C (i.e., 138 verses) matches the sum of verse totals in C and D. Adding the sum of A and B (222 verses) and then adding to 222 either of the other couplets BC or CD (each 138 verses) produces a total of 360 verses. Wright also holds that groupings of the verse divisions exhibit relationships arising out of the following numerical sequence—1, 4, 5, 9, 14, 23, 37, 60—times 6 (yielding 6, 24, 30, 54, 84, 138, 222, 360) in which each number is the sum of the two preceding numbers. He suggests that the ratio of a smaller to a larger unit equals the proportion of the larger unit to the sum of the larger and smaller unit.[14]

Formulaically expressed:
$m/M = M/M + m$

Using the ABCD groupings of verses cited previously:
$222/360 = .618$

and

---

12. The procedure was also known to Virgil, Aratus, Lucretius, and others. See the pioneering study of Duckworth, *Patterns and Proportions*.

13. Wright: "Structure of Wisdom"; "Wisdom."

14. See a summary report of Wright's work in Glicksman, *Wisdom of Solomon 10*, 48–49.

222 + 360= 582
360/582= .618

The graded relationships, in part numerically determined, among verse clusters in Wisdom may be intended in part as a stylistic ladder or staircase image of the reign of God that is alluded to in Wis 10:10, and, as already mentioned, perhaps the sequential educational steps of 6:17–21 as well.

I suggest that the ratio .618 indeed led the author of John to Ps 62:5 LXX, which says: "In your name I will lift up my hands."

In our upcoming chapter 5, I will provide a sketch of Jesus glorified and lifting the arms as a structuring principle of John.

The Arm of the Sovereign/Son of the Magnificat's Mary

Within Virgil, the proportions of smaller to larger units approximating .618 also open a window to another Johannine statement about Jesus. John 12:38's βραχιων (arm) is word 9611 in the text as critically received in recent times. The length of the entire text, without John 5:4 and John 8:1–11 (the angel at the water and the near stoning of the adulteress) is 15,315.

The golden mean employed by Virgil states that the smaller segment is to the larger as the larger is to the sum of the smaller and larger. In formulaic language, as just mentioned:

$m/M = M/m + M$
or
m is to M as M is to m + M

In Virgil, that often works out to be around .618 on both sides of the equal sign.

Does this apply to the Johannine numbers? *Remember, however, that we are counting not verses as in Virgil but John's individual words.*

Does 9611/15,315 = 15,315/24,926?

Not exactly: We have .627 on the left and .614 on the right.

Now consider the fact that βραχιων (arm) is the sixty-third word in Isaiah's Fourth Servant Poem and that βραχιων (arm) is the sixty-first word in the Magnificat in Luke 1. The percentages on both sides of the equal sign closely approximate the placement of βραχιων (arm) in both Isa 53 and Luke 1. Now, this is presented here in Arabic computation, not yet available to the Greco-Roman world. Nevertheless, the Greeks and Romans knew fractions/ratios sufficiently to be able to construct buildings composed of circle and line.

What can we say about βραχιων in John 12:38? The location of the word in John 12:38 suggests that the arm of the Sovereign mentioned in John is that of the servant of the Sovereign in Isaiah. By itself, this would be unremarkable, because John is quoting Isa 53 at this juncture. However, the location of βραχιων in John 12:38 also suggests that the Isaianic servant is the son of Mary. John gestures to both Isaiah's servant and the announced child of Luke 1 by placing βραχιων where he does.

A salutary footnote: The total word count in John (15,315 words) is achieved by eliminating from the received text the story of the near stoning of a woman. This section (John 8:1–11) imagines what the arms of the men might have done had they not been reminded by Jesus of their own stash of sins. The voluntary withdrawal of their arms in the narrative makes way for the revelation of the Lord's arm in Jesus throughout the text. The excision of the story from the Gospel at large, on the best of text-critical principles, enables us to see the location of *brachiōn* in John 12 as a gesture toward the arm of the Lord active in Jesus, servant of Yhwh and son of Mary.

153 Fish

When John 21 asserts that the disciples caught 153 fish at Jesus' direction, a reader may note with Augustine that the numbers from one through seventeen add up to 153. Attention to eight and nine in that sequence provides another means of arriving at 153. They are the only contiguous numbers adding up to seventeen, and these numbers play a role in the narratives of the glorification of the crucified in John 20–21. Jesus encounters the disciples as a group for the second time after eight days (20:26). And if one takes seriously the fact that the Beloved Disciple is not named as such among the original group who set out to go fishing, we find a total of nine persons in John 21. In deference to this attention to eight and nine in the glorification narratives, we may add that eight plus nine equals seventeen and multiply the result by nine to arrive at 153. This procedure of increase and multiply may very well render an innovative presentation of the increase-and-multiply commands in Gen 1. In my judgment, it is entirely conceivable that the integration of salvation history and numerical considerations in Wisdom inspired in John a similar, yet distinctive, exercise of the same.

Sophia

PHILO-SOPHIA (LOVE OF WISDOM) AND LOVE OF JESUS

Perhaps as influential in shaping the Johannine agenda is the linguistic meaning of the word "philosophy," which is "love of Sophia." In Wisdom, that discussion is conducted in terms of personal intimacy with the addressees, perhaps young male inhabitants of Alexandria in the first century BCE. I suggest that the Fourth Gospel is aware of a variety of philosophical trends and teachers in antiquity, and that we have not yet mined the full array of parallels between the Johannine text and those philosophers.[15]

The scene at the cross with Jesus, his mother, and the Beloved Disciple (BD) is an etiology of Christian love of wisdom, philo-sophy. That is, Jesus' talk of "loving him" (14:23–24) is consistent with his mediation of Sophia: *philo-sophia*. Sophia is loved in loving Jesus. By paronomasia within the Johannine vocabulary, e.g, ἰδε-ἰδια (see his own) (John 19:26–27), we are led to consider John's *idea*/form(s), which he employs to articulate the Word as made flesh in the mother of Jesus. The evangelist understands Jesus the incarnate Word as the measuring rod against which he tests the viability of various forms for expressing the mystery at work in Jesus.

Where is *philosophia* transformed in the Gospel of John? In many places. Here we focus on philosophical tracts having some bearing on sovereignty, broadly defined, but with some relation to political theory and practice in antiquity. We examine aspects of Socrates, Plato, Diogenes of Sinope, and Aristotle in relation to sovereignty in John.

SOCRATES

Socrates the questioner is present in Jesus and his approximately forty-five questions (half the number of the entirety of his questions in the canonical Gospels). In John the Baptist's directing his disciples to Jesus, can we not hear an echo of the story of Zeno (ca. 280–207 BCE), founder of the Stoa, who, when seeking someone like Socrates, was directed by a bookseller to the Cynic Crates who happened by, saying, "Follow that man."[16] And regarding the fact that neither Socrates nor Jesus wrote anything, it is worth considering whether the following comparison applies:

Socrates: Plato :: Jesus : BD

15. See Adamson, *Hellenistic and Roman Worlds*.

16. See discussion in Greene, *Moira*, 337. See also 280 for a discussion of the inseparability of the presentations of Socrates and Plato.

Particularly notable is the way in which both Socrates and Jesus are personally present to/aware of the actions related to their dying.[17] The reader is prepared for Jesus' death in part by the discussion of kingship with Pilate.

PLATO

The Hour of Jesus and the Dialogues of Plato

A broad schematic inspection of some Platonic dialogues in relation to John 13–21 yields a list of similarities that give insight into part of the evangelist's intentions.[18]

John	Theme	Plato
13	Promulgating the new	*Laws*
14	Teaching	*Meno*
15	Love and death, friendship	*Phaedo, Phaedrus, Lysis*
16	Courage	*Laches*
17	(The) One	*Parmenides*
19	Justice for its own sake	*Republic*

The Republic and the Conversation with Nicodemus (John 3)

In examining the first part of this interaction, we are at a formal advantage because we are comparing two examples of *discourse*.

> Ἐὰν μή, ἦν δ' ἐγώ, ἢ οἱ φιλόσοφοι βασιλεύσωσιν ἐν ταῖς πόλεσιν ἢ οἱ βασιλῆς τε νῦν λεγόμενοι καὶ δυνάσται φιλοσοφήσωσι γνησίως τε καὶ ἱκανῶς, καὶ τοῦτο εἰς ταὐτὸν συμπέσῃ, δύναμίς τε πολιτικὴ καὶ φιλοσοφία, τῶν δὲ νῦν πορευομένων χωρὶς ἐφ' ἑκάτερον αἱ πολλαὶ φύσεις ἐξ ἀνάγκης | ἀποκλεισθῶσιν, οὐκ ἔστι κακῶν παῦλα, ὦ φίλε Γλαύκων, ταῖς πόλεσι, δοκῶ δ' οὐδὲ τῷ ἀνθρωπίνῳ γένει, οὐδὲ αὕτη ἡ

---

17. Gooch, *Jesus and Socrates*, ch. 6, "Love and Death," 230–305, esp. 247. Gooch, a philosopher, offers extensive observations on the imbrications of love, death, and glory.

18. See Howatson, "Plato."

πολιτεία μή ποτε πρότερον φυῇ τε εἰς τὸ δυνατὸν καὶ φῶς ἡλίου ἴδῃ, ἥν νῦν λόγῳ διεληλύθαμεν.

Until philosophers rule or kings are capable of philosophizing genuinely and adequately, and this comes together in the same person, a power both political and philosophical, and the many natures of those pursuing only the one or the other are by necessity shut out, there will be no halt in evils, Glaucon my friend, in the city nor even in the human race. Neither this polity nor any prior one may grow to its potential and this polity we have been discussing will never see the light of the sun. (*Resp.* 5.473D)

This offers several points of comparison with Jesus' conversation happening "at night":

Republic	John 3:3, 5
Δύναμίς (capability)	Δυναται (capability)
Πολιτικη (political power)	Nicodemus an αρχων (leader)
Φιλοσοφια (love of wisdom)	(Jesus as Sophia) and God's love
Ιδε ... πολιτεια (see such a polity)	Ιδειν ... βασιλεια του θεου (see God's reign)

This section of the discourse also has Plato asserting that [even] some of those who are "not mean in social status" (nevertheless) attack the lover of wisdom, who loves the truth (*Resp.* 5.473E, 475E). The word used for "of no mean status" (φαυλοι) occurs also in John 3:20–21:

> Those doing common, mean, substandard things [φαυλα] hate the light; not so, those doing the truth.

Plato seems to protest the tendency to settle for a perception that is merely mundane. Those who rejoice in mere spectacle only, says Plato, are not those who love the whole truth (*Resp.* 5.475D). True love of learning, in the Platonic vein, tends toward holism (*Resp.* 5.475C).

This may profitably be compared to the discussion about cleansing that erupts among the learners/disciples of the baptizer in John 3:25. The baptizer avers that his joy is complete when, as friend of the Bridegroom, he hears his voice, that of the one from heaven: "It is necessary that that one increase and I decrease" (John 3:29–30).

Both Plato and the evangelist are riding a wave of variegated reality from sensible to supersensible, coaxing those who would learn to attend to the words and deeds of the higher level of reality. Their definitions of what constitute higher and lower differ, of course, because of the evangelist's dedication to the incarnation.[19]

The Republic offers yet another strong parallel to the Fourth Gospel. At one level, the discussion of truth by Pilate and Jesus is a rendition of Plato's cave (*Resp.* 7). But it reverses the roles as described by Plato: In Plato, prisoners are chained in a cave so that they can see only the back of the cave, perceiving moving shadows on a wall, shadows cast by a light from the outside, above and behind them. John depicts Jesus as that light of truth, even as he is bound and his back flayed after the narrative moves beyond the firelight of the courtyard. As Pilate exits, he is, unlike the case of Plato's cave, moving away from the light, who is Jesus inside. It is Pilate who in ignorance of the truth and in fear of Caesar is the functional prisoner. (Mark anticipated some of this scenario, but John crosses the *t* of the tradition by introducing a discussion of truth.)

John began working with this Platonic lens even earlier than chapter 19. Working backwards:

- Lazarus emerges from a cave, in a chapter that begins with Jesus' saying, "If anyone walks in the day, he does not stumble, because he sees the light of the world" (ch. 11).

- In the healing of the man born blind (ch. 9). It is important that he has never seen; there's the link to Plato's cave.

- Nicodemus speaks up for Jesus in chapter 7, a movement beyond his earlier curiosity exercised in private (ch. 3) and itself a movement toward the light that Jesus will declare himself to be as chapter 8 opens. Plato is explicit that the vision of those emerging from their confinement in the dark cave is a gradual process.

Of course, there are other themes at work in the Gospel text, some having parallels in the *Republic*: e.g., authority and truth. In seeing Jesus, one enters an awareness of ideal law, whose authority is derived from the vision of the true.[20]

---

19. For Plato, earthly persons and things are shadows of ideas, persons, and things in heaven. For John, they are reflections of Jesus, the Word of God become flesh, who is rejected, who has gone to the cross to be exalted there to God (paraphrase of Schweizer "Johannine 'Parables,'" 216).

20. See authority in John 5 and 10, truth in John 14. For a twentieth-century reflection on their relationship to one another, see Arendt, "What Is Authority?"

Meno

Interestingly also, Plato's *Meno* serves as a helpful background for understanding John's agenda. They are not saying the same thing, but John is using some of the same apparatus. The Platonic dialogue concerns learning (μαθησις) as a recollection (αναμνησις) of knowledge obtained in the previous lives of a soul. *Meno* 81B concerns souls that undergo death and are born again, asserting that those whom Persephone requites from ancient wrong are raised again in the ninth year to the upper sun. John 21:23 conveys Jesus' nine words, one of them *menein*, about the Beloved Disciple:

Ἐὰν αὐτὸν θέλω μένειν ἕως ἔρχομαι, τί πρὸς σέ;

Socrates spends the latter half of the *Meno* in discussion with a boy (παις) eliciting from him the correct measurements, eight and nine, of extended permutations of a square (82E, 83E). John's exploration of eight and nine in chapters 19–21 culminates in his address to the disciples as *paidia*. While the vision of being born again (παλιν) in *Meno* differs from John's being born (ανωθεν), John's frequent use of *menein* (forty-two times) deliberately invites us to understand that the current instantiation of Logos in Jesus is not unrelated to the previous exploration of Platonic wisdom.[21]

Hippias Maior

Our understanding of John is furthered by another dialogue in the Platonic tradition, *Hippias Maior* (*Greater Hippias*). Its authorship is contested, but it is ancient. The rationale for John's using it? In 281D, we hear Socrates say,

> Why do the wise refrain from politics? Because they are unable to compass with their wisdom both public and private matters.

I suggest that the themes drawn from *Hippias Maior* collect in the middle portion of the Gospel, at the juncture of public and private. In John 12, we have just heard from the chief priests about provincial and imperial Realpolitik, and we are about to enter the meal discourse between Jesus and disciples alone. In the Farewell Discourse (John 13–17), we will hear of decidedly nonpolitical *realia*, indirectly drawn from Paul: manifestation to disciples, not to the world (Gal 1); an asking and receiving crafted to reflect

---

21. For another assemblage of Platonic tradition in John, see P. Anderson, *Riddles*, 188–90.

the Lukan (Pauline) infancy narratives, which offer only an incipient counter witness to the world. Moreover, this shift in John mirrors that in Mark, from the love theme with Hebrew Bible materials to the same theme of love as seen in Paul; should we say that this is a shift from the public wisdom of the covenant people to the hidden wisdom of the cross?[22] Is the qualification of the role of public charity in chapter 12 presented in dialectical tension with the lifting up, so that public charity does not assume primary or independent significance? So that *the gift* remains in central focus:

Hippias Maior 301C is a *proverb*: "Human affairs . . . are not what a man *wishes* but what he *can* [Παροιμιαζομενοι . . . βουλεται . . . δυναται]." Compare the vocabulary in John 10–12:

- παροιμια (John 10:6)
- εδυνατ (John 11:37)
- εβουλευσαντο (John 12:10)

In *Hippias Maior* 302B, ostensibly reflecting the single Greek word *kalos*, meaning both beautiful and good, we encounter "What both are, each is and what each is, both are." Compare to:

> I and Father are One. (John 10:30)

> What shall I say? . . . I have glorified [the name]. (John 12:27–28)

This interchange in John 12:27–28, where a voice speaks to be heard by the crowd, exemplifies John's christological take on *Hippias Maior*'s two-in-one theme: Plato asserted that even when the wise man leaves the marketplace and goes home, he is not alone. In Plato, that means he acts as a thinking, judging agent in conversation with himself. "When Socrates goes home, he is not alone; he is *by* himself,"[23] unlike the unwise who, when alone, are truly alone. John's Jesus is also not alone. The Father is always with him (explicitly stated in John 16:32).

It is, I believe, in great high spirits that John modifies the following section of *Hippias Maior* 304D:

> It happens that the man who is continually refuting me is a very close relative of mine and lives in the same house. Whenever I go home to my own house and he hears me saying these things, he asks . . .

22. Kiley, "Marcan Love." Chennattu can discuss Johannine covenant without reference to public/private distinctions (*Johannine Discipleship*).

23. Arendt, *Portable Hannah Arendt*, 410; emphasis in original.

Compare to:

- The Father's speech (John 12:27–28)
- In my Father's house (John 14:2)

In addition to public/private and two-in-one themes, John is in dialogue with *Hippias Maior* 304B:

> You are blessed because you know the things a person ought to practice and have practiced them sufficiently well.

Compare to:

> If you know these things, blessed are you if you do them. (John 13:17)

But *Hippias Maior*'s influence is not restricted to the fulcrum at John 12–13. *Hippias Maior* 283E discusses persuading fathers to entrust children to Hippias as teacher. See the references to Jesus as teacher that span the text (in John 1, 13, 20).

Even Socrates's commendation of Hippias for having a technical memory, enabling him to present the past to his hearers (285E), has an analogue in John 14:26: "The Advocate will teach you and remind you of all I have told you."

Also, see *Hippias Maior* 291E:

> For everyone everywhere it is most beautiful to be beautifully and splendidly buried by his own offspring.

See the royal burial of John 19:38–42.

Transcendentals

Now an interesting ancillary question occurs because of John's use of this dialogue about beauty. Consider the following anthropology of the ancients:

- The emotions find their bearings regarding the beautiful.
- Intellect is oriented toward the true.
- The will is directed toward the good.[24]

---

24. See Viladeseau, *Theological Aesthetics*, 124–34, esp. 126.

Are we correct in thinking that the final lifting-up saying in John 12:32 is appropriately preceded by a discussion of the *kalos* (good/beautiful) shepherd in John 10 and the statement of the Greeks arriving at the feast, "We want to see Jesus" (will)?

The second lifting-up saying in John 8:13 is accompanied by the statement "Your witness is not true/cannot be verified" (intellect).

The first lifting-up saying in John 3:14 is adjacent to a polemic against one whose deeds are evil and who therefore hates the light and does not come to the light (emotion).

Plato and a Canon

Before leaving Plato, we turn our attention to Thrasyllus (d. 36 CE), a court astrologer to Tiberius. Thrasyllus is credited with organizing the Platonic dialogues, which constituted a sort of Scripture for Platonists in that world, into four sets of nine (including some of the spurious works). This arrangement has been taken as programmatic for subsequent students of Plato.[25] Is it likely that the Fourth Evangelist was one of those so affected? The evangelist attends to the number nine (if one counts the Beloved Disciple in John 21:7 as a character separate from the other eight in the chapter) as well as to the tetragrammaton. The latter might have functioned as part of a dialogue with the Synoptic Gospels, a dialogue in which the evangelist is implicitly making a case for *four* Gospels almost a century before Irenaeus.

Judas a Sophist?

John 12:1–8 offers another opportunity to gauge the extent to which the Fourth Gospel is articulating a sophiological vision. It is the story of a dinner at which Jesus receives extravagant attention from Mary, who anoints him. Judas objects, ostensibly because the money spent on the ointment could have been better used to assist the poor. The narrator insists that this is spoken out of greed because Judas was a thief (a note unique to this Gospel). Jesus' responds in 12:8:

> The poor you always have with you, but me you do not always have.

---

25. See Poster, "Idea(s) of Order," esp. 288–92.

Jesus in John is among friends, and the house in which they dine is filled with the aroma of the anointing oil. Listen again to these lines in praise of Sophia:

> Because of her purity, she *pervades and penetrates all things*. . . .
> In every generation she passes into holy souls and makes them friends of God and prophets. (Wis 7:24b, 27c–d)

The setting is indeed sophiological. What happens therefore with Judas occurs at the edges of sophism. Insofar as the *Gorgias* of Plato is explicit in saying that Sophists often use language solely for its utility in helping them accrue wealth, we might well consider this version the one most riveted on the sophism of Judas.[26]

DIOGENES OF SINOPE, CYNIC PHILOSOPHER

This early fourth-century BCE son of a banker hailed from the south-central shore of the Black Sea.[27] He is often thought to be one of the initial sources of Cynic philosophy that lasted intermittently throughout the first century CE and beyond. My immediate reason for discussing him resides in the frequently used word for worship (προσκυν-) in John 4:20–27. The κυν therein, similar to the Greek word for dog (κυων), is the basis for the appellation κυνικος (Cynic). However, these observations are related to an expression of Roman civic life under the republic, which constitutes a parallel to this chapter's concern with the nature of sovereignty.

There is a broad similarity between the concerns of Jesus in John 4 and the Cynics. The Cynics were dedicated to a critique of what they considered those inadequate societal props chosen by weak humans in the search for happiness. In a similar vein, John's Jesus advocates worship in spirit and truth and seems indifferent to any ultimate claims of either Gerizim or Jerusalem temples. Cynics praised a strong will exercised in a choice for poverty and self-abnegation, as a buffer against the eventual vicissitudes of time. When urged by his disciples to eat something, Jesus says that his food is to do the will of the One who sent him. The Cynics are credited with developing the *chreia*, useful sayings and actions that they believed promoted their universally relevant thought. Similarly, Jesus quotes two sayings as illustrations of his missionary concerns (John 4:35, 37).

---

26. Cassin, "Sophists," esp. 958–66.
27. See the discussion in Diogenes Laertius, *Lives of Eminent Philosophers*.

At this level, the parallels are rather broad and do not overpower the other particularly Jewish concerns in the chapter, such as the identity of the Christ. But when one adds related Latinate considerations, the picture changes to some degree. Cognate to Greek κυων is Latin *canis* (dog). And nearby *canis* in the Latin dictionary is the word for white (*caneo*). The fields are described as white in John 4:35. More importantly, the chapter's diction implicitly gestures toward ideas associated with the *can-* root, even as it explicitly discusses marital themes. The *Lex Canuleia* provides ample material for parallel consideration. This law was enacted in the Roman republican period (445 BCE) at the behest of the tribune Gaius Canuleius, against stiff opposition from the patricians. It allowed for marriage between plebeians and patricians, i.e., commoners and aristocrats, replacing the prohibition thereof in the Twelve Tables. Here we have one plausible background for understanding this frequently espoused woman as representative of her people and the one who talks of worshipping and doing the will of his *pater* (Father). Important to note is that two out of the three references to Jesus' Father in the chapter are in an oblique case, *patri*. In addition, Jesus' travel into Galilee becomes the occasion for saying that "A prophet has no honor in his own fatherland [*patridi*]" (4:44), which is followed by the narrative of the royal official, a father. In a chapter that discusses strained relations between her Samaritans and his Jews, these linguistic similarities to the word "patrician" hint at the Roman republican marital arrangements undergirding the chapter and give added resonance to the acclamation of Jesus as Savior of the world in 4:42. That title had been widely used by propagandists on behalf of Caesar Augustus.

Perhaps most significantly, the word for worship (προσκυν-) occurs ten times throughout John 4:20–27. I see that as a literary cue preparing us for the fact that Jesus will instantiate the Decalogue in the following chapters (5–10). The parallel with the Twelve Tables is completed with the articulation of the command to love one another in *two* subsequent places, at 13:34a–b and 15:12, 17. Note also that there is a twoness to the presence of the command in both places. Might we read with fresh eyes the invitation of the woman to the townspeople to come and see Jesus (4:29), as well as their enthusiastic response and endorsement of what they hear in Jesus (4:39–42); might we best understand this as reflecting this description by Livy of the unveiling of the tables?

> This prompt justice, of an almost superhuman purity and enjoyed alike by the highest and lowest of the country was one aspect of the

decemvirs' work; at the same time they were busy with framing a code, until a day came when, amid tremendous public excitement, they published Ten Tables of Law, and with a solemn prayer for heaven's blessing on themselves, their country, and their children, invited the whole population of Rome to come and read the statutes that were there offered for approval.[28]

So we have progressed from an appreciation of Greek *kyn-* as dog and philosopher to Latin *can-* as marital legislation. A site of betrothal opens the chapter at the well of Jacob (4:5).[29] The narrative is then adorned stylistically by a plebeian-patrician cast derived from the *Lex Canuleia*, lending a unity to the chapter.[30] Lest this dog-and-bride thematic seem far fetched, remember that Hebrew כֶּלֶב (dog) is proximate to the Hebrew word for bride (כַּלָּה). Indeed, I would think that these lexical neighbors in the Hebrew form the generating nucleus of the evangelist's agenda in John 4. The chapter is laying a building block in an overarching program wherein Jesus is proleptically fashioning a bride for himself, later to be known as the church.

ARISTOTLE

Aristotle's ten categories that describe Being may best explain much of the diction in chapter 18. John 18:29 has Pilate ask, "What κατηγορια do you bring against this man?" That is rightly translated in its forensic sense of "accusation, charge." However, things are rarely so simple in John's world. Remembering that Jesus is the Word of God in whom all things come to be, we can also hear this as "What category do you apply to this man?" At one point in his writings, Aristotle posited ten such categories, including "How many? How great? What stance?" Yet here is the fascinating point: After Aristotle, the Stoa followed his lead in reducing the number of these somewhat; they reduced his categories to four.[31] Within this frame of reference, we note that John's eighteenth chapter includes ten instances of the

28. Livy, *History of Rome*, 3.34. These ten, completed in 450 BCE, were complemented the following year by two others.

29. For a discussion of Jacob and Jesus' identity, see Neyrey, "Greater Than Father Jacob?"

30. Some scholars who inspected Jesus' parables in comparison with Cynic tradition frequently decided that the Jewish element was vastly more important than Cynicism for appreciating Jesus' teaching in the Synoptic Gospels. But John 4 moves the teaching of Jesus into the philosophical arena where it basks in a subtle but distinct Cynic aura.

31. Copleston, *History of Philosophy*, 1:386.

word αρχιερευς (high priest) in the singular, whose first syllable mimics the αρχη (First Principle) of the Prologue (18:10, 13, 15, 16, 19, 22, 24, 26; 18:3, 35 are in the plural). And the chapter opens with Jesus' self-declaration I AM, the tetragrammaton. I think that, at one level of the theology of this chapter, we are witnessing nothing less than an investigation of Being.

Second, Aristotle's vision of friendship is both immanent (shared activity) and transcendent (shared virtue/character). John, unlike many Hellenistic authors, preserves these twin emphases, in the fishing and love of John 21.[32]

Finally, Aristotle perceived the difficulty with Plato's Forms, *ideas*. They are immutable and therefore do not explain how things fall apart. Moreover, their generative activity is intermittent.[33] Compare that with the scenario in John 11:

- See [Ιδε] how he loved him.
- It is now the fourth day; he will smell.
- I know that you always hear me.

Yet one other link to Aristotle may be discerned. Upon the death of Aristotle, his student Theophrastus founded a school to carry on Aristotle's tradition of investigating and cataloguing empirical phenomena. It was situated in a garden in Athens that included a walkway (περιπατος), where its exercitants demonstrated a concern to preserve books of the master and hand them down to successors. It is when Jesus is walking by (περιπατ) that the baptizer points him out to some of his disciples (John 1:36). The other features mentioned have their analogues in John, including this: Theophrastus refused to let the school bear his own name, since it was dedicated to furtherance of the legacy of the master, Aristotle.[34]

---

32. See Schroeder, "Friendship in Aristotle."
33. Greene, *Moira*, 286.
34. Natali, "Schools."

Chapter Four

Stories

OVERVIEW

This chapter further explores some of the ways in which the reign-of-God theme affects the formation of John, including but not limited to two dozen synoptic parables of God's reign that have been transformed in John. We also examine the puzzle knot of God's reign present in Dan 5 as it appears in the narrative of Jesus lifted up in John 19 and 20.

PERIPHERAL INFLUENCE OF REIGN-OF-GOD NARRATIVES ON THE FOURTH GOSPEL

We can identify a few antecedent ways in which the reign of God has shaped the Fourth Gospel: the debates in 1 Sam 8–12, the first letters of the announcement of the reign in Mark 1:15, and the possible transmutation of reign-of-God language into that of eternal life.

1. The long-recognized debate in 1 Samuel about whether to recognize a human regent may be seen as informing the Gospel of Mark:

Jesus and the Reign of God in John

1 Samuel		Mark	
8	Evil	8	Satan
9	High place of sacrifice Father and son	9	Mountain Son of a father
10	New heart How will this one rescue us?	10	Hard heart Who can be saved?
11	Oxen butchered as threat	11	Fig tree cursed
12	Show good and right way Fraud	12	Good teacher Defraud

Of these, only the women who draw water and point out the prophet in 1 Sam 9:11 resemble John, i.e., the Samaritan woman of John 4, though it is interesting that John also juxtaposes to the Samaritan account the narrative of the royal official and his son.

2. I think that Jesus' inaugural announcement of God's reign in Mark 1:15 presents elements that have a distinct effect on the diction of John, even though the Johannine Jesus makes no announcement that closely resembles Mark 1:15. I underline letters pertinent to my argument:

Πεπλήρωται ὁ καιρὸς	The opportune time is fulfilled
καὶ ἤγγικεν ἡ βασιλεία τοῦ θεοῦ·	And the reign of God has drawn near
μετανοεῖτε καὶ πιστεύετε	Repent and believe
ἐν τῷ εὐαγγελίῳ	in the gospel

The letters π-ε-μ-π in those Markan clauses form the root of the verb πεμπ- (send). Πεμπ- occurs thirty-three times in John, far more times than in any other New Testament text. I offer this as clear evidence that John is aware of the Gospel tradition of the reign of God but is presenting it in his own key.

3. Commentators continue to reflect on the presence of reign-of-God material in the Synoptic Gospels and in John. Chrys C. Caragounis notes that the image of *entering* the reign of God in John 3:3, 5 is also present in Matt 5:20; 7:21; 18:13; and Mark 10:23–25. He joins many others before and after him who note the language of Jesus as king in all four of the canonical Gospels. He suggests that the phrase "eternal life," repeated seventeen times in John, is the equivalent to

reign-of-God language in the Synoptics, and judges that the use of the phrase "reign of God" in the Gospels indeed has a future orientation but in such a way that shapes the present by Jesus' call to decision.[1]

However, the relative impact of these dynamics on John is rather scant when compared to what I judge to be the much more extensive influence of the parables of God's reign on the Fourth Gospel.

JESUS AND THE PARABOLIC REIGN OF GOD IN JOHN

By far the most usual means of presenting the reign of God in the Synoptic Gospels is the parable, and it is to the Johannine riff on that parabolic speech that I devote most of this chapter. We turn first to examine specific parables of the reign of God and their transformation in John. However, because the form of the parable is not unique to the Gospel tradition, I also offer an example of a puzzle from Daniel that the Fourth Gospel presents in its own way.

The parade example of a parable in the triple tradition of the Synoptic Gospels is the seed parable of Mark 4:

> And he said to them, "Do you not understand this parable? Then how will you understand all the parables? 14 The sower sows the word. [15] These are the ones on the path where the word is sown: when they hear, Satan immediately comes and takes away the word that is sown in them. [16] And these are the ones sown on rocky ground: when they hear the word, they immediately receive it with joy. [17] But they have no root, and endure only for a while; then, when trouble or persecution arises on account of the word, immediately they fall away. [18] And others are those sown among the thorns: these are the ones who hear the word, [19] but the cares of the world, and the lure of wealth, and the desire for other things come in and choke the word, and it yields nothing. [20] And these are the ones sown on the good soil: they hear the word and accept it and bear fruit, thirty and sixty and a hundredfold. (Mark 4:13–20 RSV)

Here are some of the schematized aspects of that parable as they are rendered by narratives in the Fourth Gospel:

---

1. Caragounis, "Kingdom of God."

Threats to Seed	John
Lack of comprehension	They knew not whence (John 2)
	You have no bucket. How . . . (John 4)
Cares of the world	Grief; concern that Romans will take this place (John 11)
Persecution	Lure of wealth and plot to kill (John 12)
Received by good and generous heart	Expensive oil (John 12)

Like the seed parable, the story of the mustard seed is present in the triple tradition as a depiction of God's reign. The plant is foreseen as the greatest of herbs, putting forth great branches such that the birds of heaven can shelter under its shadow (Mark 4:32). Herbs (λαχανων) find their linguistic echo at Jesus' cross when the soldiers decide to cast lots (λαχωμεν) for his tunic (John 19:24). Do we find a clumsy misstep when the text continues, "Then the soldiers did these things"? Has the evangelist suddenly become lead footed in his report? I doubt it. The Greek of those few words contains each letter in πετεινα (birds):

Οἱ μὲν οὖν στρατιῶται ταῦτα ἐποίησαν.

The greatness of the shrub forecast in the parable is delineated by what happens under the shadow of Jesus' cross. Might this have something to do with the word for tunic (χιτων), whose ending, ων, proffers the garment as a pledge of eternal Being?[2] Perhaps. In any case, the letters σκια/shadow are present within the pluperfect verb ειστηκεισαν, took their stand (John 19:25).

Moreover, there is a Semitic logic to this scene under the cross of the king of the Jews, arising from the Hebrew Psalter and extending into the sayings tradition Q. Ps 84:4 reads:

גַּם־צִפּוֹר ׀ מָצְאָה בַיִת וּדְרוֹר ׀ קֵן לָהּ אֲשֶׁר־שָׁתָה אֶפְרֹחֶיהָ אֶת־מִזְבְּחוֹתֶיךָ
יְהוָה צְבָאוֹת מַלְכִּי וֵאלֹהָי׃

> Even the sparrow finds a home,
> and the swallow a nest for herself,
> where she may lay her young,
> at your altars, O LORD of hosts,
> my King and my God. (NRSV)

---

2. "All things are One, and this One is Being" (Aristotle, *Metaphysics*, 3.4.1001 a 29). This teaching of Aristotle is already present in the pre-Socratic Parmenides.

This psalm is a reflection on life at the Jerusalem temple. It displays a lovely soft rhyme between צִפּוֹר (*tsifōr*) and דְּרוֹר (*d rōr*), partly replicated in the English rendering "sparrow" and "swallow." I suggest that early study of the avian tradition now represented in Luke 17:37 and Matt 24:18 ("Where the corpse is, there will the eagles gather") drew attention to another soft rhyme, that between נֵזֶר (*nezer*, consecrated) and נֶשֶׁר (*nesher*, eagle). The word נֵזֶר was then also read as an allusion to the Nazarene. Such fancy footwork betrays the smell of the lamp and is productive for understanding the inner workings of this scene at the foot of the crucified Johannine king. The Holy One, who has already forecast the destruction and raising of the temple of his body, arranges for the ongoing mutual relationship of mother and son, evincing the spirit of Deut 22:6 that allows for the capture of a bird in the nest but insists on setting free the mother bird. Jesus' activity on behalf of his mother and the Beloved Disciple also reflects the context of the Lukan version of the avian saying. He does not save himself and, in so doing, saves lives.[3]

Furthermore, there are affinities of this scene at the cross with the reign of God as depicted in Jacob Neusner's understanding of evolving Mishnaic traditions.[4] Neusner asserts that the reign of God is constituted by attention to several appointed times (in the second division of Mishnah), framed by attending to blessings (division 1—Mishnah-Berakhoth) and the slaughter of animals for domestic use (division 5—Hullin). These considerations of God's reign are preceded by attention to overcoming death, involving the purifying effect of water, especially when exercised with maximal human agency. The reflections of the Mishnaic tradition, approximating a systematic distillation of the halakic commands of Torah, also happen to resemble aspects of the Johannine effort.

Several appointed times/festivals are cited in John 1–12, framed by foot washing in anticipation, at the least, of the disciples' contact with Jesus' corpse, as well as by analogues to Hullin, whose twelfth section concerns Deut 22:6–7. Again, the Deuteronomic text treats bird nests encountered on one's way or in a tree. The Israelite may take the young but is enjoined to send away the mother bird who has been incubating eggs or nurturing

---

3. The Jesus Seminar gave the Q saying a grey rating, indicating their judgment that it *might* proceed from the historical Jesus (Funk, *Five Gospels*, 248–49, 366–68). Their dubiety is justified. It is more likely that if the historical Jesus crafted the saying, it was along the Hebraic lines just outlined. See also the discussion of alternative understandings in Greek language traditions in Davies and Allison, *Gospel According to Saint Matthew*, 3:355–56.

4. Neusner, *Rabbinic Literature*, 133–34; *Mishnah*.

fledglings, so that the death of the young is not exacerbated by hers as well. Thus, it will go well with you, and long lived will you be (v. 7). John's Jesus, from the tree infiltrated by birds/soldiers, that is, the cross, sends mother and son to their home, as Jesus crucified enters the glory of God.

BEYOND THE UR-SEED: FURTHER PARABOLIC DYNAMICS IN JOHN

Note that many of the following traditions occur only in their respective Synoptic Gospels.[5]

MARKAN AND MATTHEAN PARABLES IN JOHANNINE INTEGRATION

In John, the burial of Jesus includes at least three thematic echoes of material in special synoptic parabolic material concerning God's reign:

- Hiddenness
- Night-first motifs in the growth of a plant
- Extravagant outlay for a priceless treasure

1. Joseph of Arimathea, who asks Pilate for Jesus' body and buries it, is described as a "hidden disciple" (John 19:38–42). Consider this saying concerning the parabolic presence of the kingdom of God/heaven:

   > The kingdom of heaven is like a treasure *hidden* in a field, which a man found and hid, and in his joy went and sold everything he had and bought that field. (Matt 13:44)

   However, this Matthean saying also generates a narrative development of the reign of God in John 6 and 13. In Matt 13:44, we read in the Greek:

---

[5]. My intention here is not primarily to explore the rich tapestry of the synoptic parabolic interweaving in and of themselves. That is admirably represented in the work of Donahue (*Gospel in Parable*). The massive study of Snodgrass is also valuable for its breadth and depth (*Stories with Intent*). For a lucid and cogent discussion of some of the synoptic parables, see Levine, *Short Stories by Jesus*; see also Zimmermann, *Puzzling the Parables*. For the parables at the historical Jesus layer of tradition, see Meier, *Authenticity of the Parables*.

Ὁμοία ἐστὶν ἡ βασιλεία τῶν οὐρανῶν θησαυρῷ κεκρυμμένῳ ἐν τῷ ἀγρῷ, ὃν εὑρὼν ἄνθρωπος ἔκρυψεν, καὶ ἀπὸ τῆς χαρᾶς αὐτοῦ ὑπάγει καὶ πωλεῖ πάντα ὅσα ἔχει καὶ ἀγοράζει τὸν ἀγρὸν ἐκεῖνον.

The reign of heaven is like a treasure hidden in a field, which someone found and hid and out of his joy went away and sold all that he had and bought that field.

The letters of treasure (θησαυρος) are present in the correct order in John 6:68, beginning at ἀπεκρίθη and ending at ἔχεις:

ἀπεκρίθη αὐτῷ Σίμων Πέτρος· Κύριε, πρὸς τίνα ἀπελευσόμεθα; ῥήματα ζωῆς αἰωνίου ἔχεις.

Simon Peter answered, "Lord, to whom shall we go? You have the words of everlasting life."

Jesus and his words of eternal life constitute the hidden treasure, and the reader shares in the joy of that discovery as s/he traces out the hidden letters of the word θησαυρος (treasure).

Moreover, the commercial terms of the Matthean parable reappear in the presentation of the Beloved Disciple in John 13.[6] Πωλεῖ (sell) is present in the words of the Beloved Disciple at John 13:25 as he asks (disingenuously) about the identity of the betrayer. The letters of πωλεῖ are present, beginning with ἀναπεσὼν and ending with λέγει:

ἀναπεσὼν ἐκεῖνος οὕτως ἐπὶ τὸ στῆθος τοῦ Ἰησοῦ λέγει αὐτῷ· Κύριε, τίς ἐστιν;

That one reclining on the breast of Jesus says to him, "Lord, who is it?"

The verb ἀγοράζει (buy) of Matt 13:44 is present in the disciples' musing about the meaning of Jesus' words to Judas:

τινὲς γὰρ ἐδόκουν, ἐπεὶ τὸ γλωσσόκομον εἶχεν Ἰούδας, ὅτι λέγει αὐτῷ ὁ Ἰησοῦς· Ἀγόρασον ὧν χρείαν ἔχομεν εἰς τὴν ἑορτήν, ἢ τοῖς πτωχοῖς ἵνα τι δῷ.

Some thought, since Judas had the common purse, that Jesus said to him, "Buy what we need for the feast or in order to give something to the poor." (John 13:29)

6. I have argued elsewhere that the narrative identity of the Beloved Disciple is Judas Iscariot. See Kiley, "Beloved Disciple, Judas Iscariot."

The Johannine imperative form Ἀγόρασον is a variant of Matthew's indicative verb ἀγοράζει.

The Beloved Disciple, who has already fallen under Satanic influence (13:1), decided to betray Jesus and sold his soul but will be enabled at his exorcism at the arrest of Jesus to buy into the full mystery of Jesus crucified and glorified.

2. Joseph's partner in burying Jesus, Nicodemus, is described in language evocative of another parable of the kingdom. Of Nicodemus, the evangelist says that he is "the one who came to him [Jesus] at night [νυκτος] at the first [πρωτον]" (John 19:39). Listen to this uniquely Markan parable of the reign of God concerning the seed that grows of itself:

> And he said, "The kingdom of God is like a man who casts seed in the ground. And he sleeps and rises night [νυκτα] and day, and the seed sprouts and grows, he knows not how.[7] The earth automatically [αυτοματη] yields fruit, first [πρωτον] the blade, then the ear, then the full grain in the ear. And when it produces fruit, straightway he sends in the sickle because the harvest has come." (Mark 4:26–29)

The letters of αυτοματη are present in John 19:39–40. The designation αυτοματη is also used of a gate that spontaneously opens in Acts 12:10, which might have inspired the image of Jesus as door in John 10. May not the automatic nature of the seed's growth in this passage of Mark also be profitably compared to the following saying of Jesus in John 10:14–15, 17–18 especially regarding what (here, *who*) is known during the process of laying down and taking up of his own accord?

> I am the good shepherd, and I know my own and mine know me. Just as the Father knows me and I know the Father, and I lay down my life for the sheep. . . . Because of this, the Father loves me, because I lay down my life, in order that I may take it up again. No one takes it from me, but I lay it down of my own accord [εξ εμαυτου]. I have authority to lay it down, and I have authority to

---

7. At the parabolic level, Mary's "we don't know" in John 20:13 is her attestation of the unknown quotient of the mystery of the kingdom available in Jesus. Jesus as the seed growing of itself (αυτοματη), one knows not how, is also attested in the frequent occurrence of intensive αυτος in John, seven times, more than in the other canonical Gospels.

take it up again. This command I have received from my Father. (NRSV)[8]

Note too that

3. Virtually all commentators note the *extravagance* of the hundred-liter outlay of myrrh and aloe with which the body of Jesus is dressed in John 19:39. And this has often been seen as appropriate for a royal burial, no surprise in a text in which the question of the kingship of Jesus has been elaborated at some length in the dialogue with Pilate. However, this extravagance may also be seen in concert with other details that work together in a complementary direction.

Consider this saying, one that occurs in Matthew and Luke as well but that is placed only by Mark in a parables context:

> And he said to them, "Listen up. In the measure with which you give [lit. *measure*] it will be measured out to you, and even more will be given to you." (Mark 4:24)

The extravagant outlay at the burial mimics the lavish expenditure for the pearl of great price in Matt 13:46.

THE PRODIGAL SON AND JOHN

Luke 15:11–32		John
		Prologue (1:1–18)
After not many days, he gathered everything		
	Journey of ουσια (that which exists, property/belongings) into a far country παντα (everything) (3x)	
I never broke your command		His command is life (12)
Your brother lives		The one sending me gave me command.

8. Theobald argues that the seed growing automatically receives further interpretation in the forces of resistance to the seed in Matt 13:24–30 ("Johannine Dominical Sayings"). I would add that John 10:14–15, 17–18 is a further stage of response to the same Markan parable.

MATTHEW 13:35 AND THE JOHANNINE PROLOGUE

> I will open my mouth in parables. I will utter what has lain hidden *since the foundation of the world.* (Matt 13:35)

Is this an impetus to the portrait of creation in the Prologue?

THE BARREN FIG TREE (LUKE 13:6–9) AND JOHANNINE CHRONOLOGY

Visits for three years, expecting fruit from the fig. Cut it down. Leave it this year also; perhaps it will bear in the future (Luke 13:6–9). In John, this becomes:

- A three-year ministry (John 2, 6, 13)
- Bearing fruit, pruning (John 15)

THE COMING OF THE MASTER (LUKE 12:35–38; JOHN 13:4–5)

The center of what Luke explicitly calls a parable (Luke 12:41) depicts a master whose coming is awaited. It is not unique to Luke, having a proximate parallel in Matt 24:45–51. However, the Matthean parallel lacks precisely the motif on which I want to focus our attention. Uniquely in Luke, when the master arrives to find his servants alert, and so considered blessed, he girds a towel around himself and serves them at table. This is a plausible parabolic background for the depiction of Jesus in John 13:4–5, not only in the toweling service at a meal but in the elaboration of what it is to be blessed (John 13:17).

In addition, the structure of this Lukan parable also lends us some assistance in understanding the scope of John. The parable begins with an exhortation to servants to keep their lamps burning brightly as they await the return of their master from a wedding banquet. Bridegroom and lamp imagery is part of the structure of John 3 and 5. The Lukan parable concludes with renewed attention to the details of a coming, this time of the Son of Man/Child of Humanity. The servants are exhorted to be alert for his coming in whichever watch that occurs and thereby be considered blessed. The conclusion of John is similarly shaped by attention to blessedness in

John 20:29. The Fourth Evangelist also integrates this third manifestation of Jesus in John 21:14 at dawn with the two earlier ones at night in chapter 20. Jesus feeds them breakfast (21:12), and the evangelist transfers the girding to Simon Peter (21:7, 18) who is commissioned to carry on this act of feeding. The Lukan parable that occurs near the middle of Luke inspires the portrait in John 13 near the middle of John, and the frame of the Lukan parable informs part of the frame of John.

In the next section, we shall see that the good Samaritan has been utilized similarly in structuring the Johannine text.

INTRODUCTION TO AND PARABLE OF THE GOOD SAMARITAN (LUKE 10)

> [25] Just then a lawyer stood up to test Jesus. "Teacher," he said, "what must I do to inherit eternal life?" [26] He said to him, "What is written in the law? What do you read there?" [27] He answered, "You shall love the Lord your God with all your heart, and with all your soul, and with all your strength, and with all your mind; and your neighbor as yourself." [28] And he said to him, "You have given the right answer; do this, and you will live."
>
> [29] But wanting to justify himself, he asked Jesus, "And who is my neighbor?" [30] Jesus replied, "A man was going down from Jerusalem to Jericho, and fell into the hands of robbers, who stripped him, beat him, and went away, leaving him half dead. [31] Now by chance a priest was going down that road; and when he saw him, he passed by on the other side. [32] So likewise a Levite, when he came to the place and saw him, passed by on the other side. [33] But a Samaritan while traveling came near him; and when he saw him, he was moved with pity. [34] He went to him and bandaged his wounds, having poured oil and wine on them. Then he put him on his own animal, brought him to an inn, and took care of him. [35] The next day he took out two denarii, gave them to the innkeeper, and said, 'Take care of him; and when I come back, I will repay you whatever more you spend.' [36] Which of these three, do you think, was a neighbor to the man who fell into the hands of the robbers?" [37] He said, "The one who showed him mercy." Jesus said to him, "Go and do likewise." (NRSV)

The question "How do you read?" and the parable of the Samaritan itself, are L material and so exemplify those traditions occurring uniquely in only one of the Synoptic Gospels. John is intensely interested in these stray bits of special tradition and acts to preserve them by transforming them.

Behind the single Greek verb αναγινωσκειν (read) resides the Latin verb *lego*, bearing more than one sense. One aspect of the Latin verb *lego* refers to choosing. For a related reason, that of the eyes picking out which letters and sounds to combine in the act of reading, often done aloud in antiquity, *lego* also came to refer to reading.

It is appropriate that the discussion beginning with Jesus' question "How do you read?" proceeds through a parable in which various levels of chosenness are exemplified. *Lego*'s sense of being chosen is embodied in priest and Levite, particular vocations. The least-chosen character of the parable from their point of view is the Samaritan who acts as neighbor to the robbed and beaten man. The narrative sweep of the parable resists the supposition inherent in the legal scholar's question, "Who is my neighbor?" (paraphrase, "How might I identify/choose those who are worthy of the designation *neighbor*?"). And it presents Jesus' counter challenge, "Who was neighbor to the man?" (paraphrase, "Can you read yourself as fitting this category of *neighbor*?").

The following characteristics of the Fourth Gospel exemplify multiple contours of this parable. Of all the synoptic parables examined here, this is one of the most thoroughly integrated into the overall structure of John:

Theme	John
Going down from Jerusalem, priest, Levite	1:19
Someone a victim of robbers	10:8
Came and saw	11:34
Gave wine (for trauma)	2:1–11
Put him on *his own* mule (ιδιον)	19:26–27 (BD and mother of Jesus)
Left wounded in care of another	19:26–27 (BD and mother of Jesus)
Do likewise	13:15
When I come (again)	21:23

Note that the Samaritan places the one mugged on his own mule and *leads* him to an inn, that is, walks beside the mule and the injured one, having yielded his place to the one attacked. So too, Jesus yields his own place as Son of the mother to the Beloved Disciple. Most importantly, perhaps, is the question asked of Jesus in John 8:48—"Are you not a Samaritan?" This is not a confused misplacement of Jesus in the wrong tribal phylum. Rather, it is an ironically precise identification of the parabolic Jesus.

This parable is important to John insofar as it is a one-shot piece of tradition in its synoptic setting, as are so many of the other parables we inspect in this chapter. But in this case, I think it worth considering whether its location near the center of the Lukan text, like the parable of the master's coming, was equally influential in attracting the attention of the Fourth Evangelist. In imitation of Luke, John placed aspects of these Lukan parables near the center of his text as well. And from that shared central position the author sent out tendrils that give shape to the entire Johannine endeavor.

PARABLE OF THE WIDOW AND JUDGE (LUKE 18:1-8)

Here resides an especially svelte instance of Johannine transformation of a Lukan parable.

Ἔλεγεν δὲ παραβολὴν αὐτοῖς πρὸς τὸ δεῖν πάντοτε προσεύχεσθαι αὐτοὺς καὶ μὴ ἐγκακεῖν, ² λέγων· Κριτής τις ἦν ἔν τινι πόλει τὸν θεὸν μὴ φοβούμενος καὶ ἄνθρωπον μὴ ἐντρεπόμενος. ³ χήρα δὲ ἦν ἐν τῇ πόλει ἐκείνῃ καὶ ἤρχετο πρὸς αὐτὸν λέγουσα· Ἐκδίκησόν με ἀπὸ τοῦ ἀντιδίκου μου. ⁴ καὶ οὐκ ἤθελεν ἐπὶ χρόνον, μετὰ ταῦτα δὲ εἶπεν ἐν ἑαυτῷ· Εἰ καὶ τὸν θεὸν οὐ φοβοῦμαι οὐδὲ ἄνθρωπον ἐντρέπομαι, ⁵ διά γε τὸ παρέχειν μοι κόπον τὴν χήραν ταύτην ἐκδικήσω αὐτὴν ἵνα μὴ εἰς τέλος ἐρχομένη ὑπωπιάζῃ με. ⁶ εἶπεν δὲ ὁ κύριος· Ἀκούσατε τί ὁ κριτὴς τῆς ἀδικίας λέγει· ⁷ ὁ δὲ θεὸς οὐ μὴ ποιήσῃ τὴν ἐκδίκησιν τῶν ἐκλεκτῶν αὐτοῦ τῶν βοώντων αὐτῷ ἡμέρας καὶ νυκτός, καὶ μακροθυμεῖ ἐπ᾽ αὐτοῖς; ⁸ λέγω ὑμῖν ὅτι ποιήσει τὴν ἐκδίκησιν αὐτῶν ἐν τάχει. πλὴν ὁ υἱὸς τοῦ ἀνθρώπου ἐλθὼν ἆρα εὑρήσει τὴν πίστιν ἐπὶ τῆς γῆς;

Then Jesus told them a parable about their need to pray always and not to lose heart. ² He said, "In a certain city there was a judge who neither feared God nor had respect for people. ³ In that city there was a widow who kept coming to him and saying, 'Grant me justice against my opponent.' ⁴ For a while he refused; but later he said to himself, 'Though I have no fear of God and no respect for anyone, ⁵ yet because this widow keeps bothering me, I will grant her justice, so that she may not wear me out by continually coming.'" ⁶ And the Lord said, "Listen to what the unjust judge says. ⁷ And will not God grant justice to his chosen ones who cry to him day and night? Will he delay long in helping them? ⁸ I tell you, he will quickly grant justice to them. And yet, when the Son of Man comes, will he find faith on earth?" (Luke 18:1–8 NRSV)

The conclusion to Luke's pericope reads, "But at the Son of Man's coming, will he find faith on the earth?" John 9:35 has Jesus seek out the man expelled from the synagogue, asking, "Do you believe in the Son of Man?" After the man's profession of faith, the text has Jesus say, "For judgment have I come into this world" (9:39).[9]

Other less direct verbal resonance of this parable may be found in these aspects of the Farewell Discourse (John 15:18—16:33):

- Petitions
- Elect/chosen
- δικ (just)
- From χηρα (widow) to χαρα (joy)
- ερχ (come)
- πιστ (believe)

THE PHARISEE AND TAX COLLECTOR (LUKE 18) AND BELIEVING (JOHN 14)

> He also told this parable to some who trusted in themselves that they were righteous and regarded others with contempt: [10] "Two men went up to the temple to pray, one a Pharisee and the other a tax collector. [11] The Pharisee, standing by himself, was praying thus, 'God, I thank you that I am not like other people: thieves, rogues, adulterers, or even like this tax collector. [12] I fast twice a week; I give a tenth of all my income.' [13] But the tax collector, standing far off, would not even look up to heaven, but was beating his breast and saying, 'God, be merciful to me, a sinner!' [14] I tell you, this man went down to his home justified rather than the other; for all who exalt themselves will be humbled, but all who humble themselves will be exalted." (Luke 18:9–14 NRSV)

The parable compares those who trusted in themselves with those who trust in God. Compare to "Believe in God, believe also in me" (John 14:1).

---

9. Both narratives share an atmosphere fraught with the threat of violence (Levine, *Short Stories by Jesus*, 221–46).

Stories

THE REIGN OF GOD IS LIKE YEAST THAT A WOMAN HIDES IN FORTY TO SIXTY POUNDS OF FLOUR UNTIL THE WHOLE IS LEAVENED (LUKE 13:21)

ὁμοία ἐστὶν ζύμῃ, ἣν λαβοῦσα γυνὴ ἔκρυψεν εἰς ἀλεύρου <u>σάτα τρία</u> ἕως οὗ ἐζυμώθη ὅλον. (Luke 13:21)

Matthew 13:33 also records this saying, but John better embodies the Lukan language of the reign of God in John 3:3, 5. The parabolic woman's hiding the agent responsible for the massive amount of rising bread is reflected in John's having the mother of Jesus, addressed as "woman," secretly initiate the process whereby Jesus transforms six containers, each holding two or three measures of water, into wine (approx. 120–180 gallons). The letters σατα τρια/three measures are sprinkled throughout John 2:6 that describe the jars and their capacity. By text's end, her Bread of Life will have manifested his glorified life three times and engaged in a triform dialogue with Simon Peter.

THE RICH MAN AND LAZARUS (LUKE 16:19-31) AND THE RAISING OF LAZARUS

"There was a rich man who was dressed in purple and fine linen and who feasted sumptuously every day. [20] And at his gate lay a poor man named Lazarus, covered with sores, [21] who longed to satisfy his hunger with what fell from the rich man's table; even the dogs would come and lick his sores. [22] The poor man died and was carried away by the angels to be with Abraham. The rich man also died and was buried. [23] In Hades, where he was being tormented, he looked up and saw Abraham far away with Lazarus by his side. [24] He called out, 'Father Abraham, have mercy on me, and send Lazarus to dip the tip of his finger in water and cool my tongue; for I am in agony in these flames.' [25] But Abraham said, 'Child, remember that during your lifetime you received your good things, and Lazarus in like manner evil things; but now he is comforted here, and you are in agony. [26] Besides all this, between you and us a great chasm has been fixed, so that those who might want to pass from here to you cannot do so, and no one can cross from there to us.' [27] He said, 'Then, father, I beg you to send him to my father's house—[28] for I have five brothers—that he may warn them, so that they will not also come into this place of torment.' [29] Abraham replied, 'They have Moses and the prophets; they should listen to them.' ³⁰ He said, 'No, father Abraham; but if someone goes to them from the dead, they will repent.'" ³¹ He said to him, "If they do not listen to Moses and the prophets, neither will they be convinced even if someone rises from the dead." (Luke 16:19–31 NRSV)

Many commentators have long been persuaded that at one level what we have in John 11 is a response to the dictum in Luke 16:31, "If they will not listen to Moses and the prophets, neither will they be persuaded if someone should rise from the dead."

MANY ARE CALLED, FEW ARE CHOSEN: THE WEDDING FEAST (MATT 22:2–14)

> The kingdom of heaven may be compared to a king who gave a wedding banquet for his son. ³ He sent his slaves to call those who had been invited to the wedding banquet, but they would not come. ⁴ Again he sent other slaves, saying, "Tell those who have been invited: Look, I have prepared my dinner, my oxen and my fat calves have been slaughtered, and everything is ready; come to the wedding banquet." ⁵ But they made light of it and went away, one to his farm, another to his business, ⁶ while the rest seized his slaves, mistreated them, and killed them. ⁷ The king was enraged. He sent his troops, destroyed those murderers, and burned their city. ⁸ Then he said to his slaves, "The wedding is ready, but those invited were not worthy. ⁹ Go therefore into the main streets, and invite everyone you find to the wedding banquet." ¹⁰ Those slaves went out into the streets and gathered all whom they found, both good and bad; so the wedding hall was filled with guests.
>
> ¹¹ But when the king came in to see the guests, he noticed a man there who was not wearing a wedding robe, ¹² and he said to him, "Friend, how did you get in here without a wedding robe?" And he was speechless. ¹³ Then the king said to the attendants, "Bind him hand and foot, and throw him into the outer darkness, where there will be weeping and gnashing of teeth." ¹⁴ For many are called, but few are chosen. (Matt 22:2–14 NRSV)

The schism in the crowd of disciples, only some of them *chosen*, is explicit in John 6:66–70, as is the statement of Jesus to the remaining disciples at supper, "You did not choose me, I chose you" (John 15:16).

COME TO THE BRIDEGROOM (MATT 25:1–13): JOHN 4 AND BEYOND

> Then the kingdom of heaven will be like this. Ten bridesmaids took their lamps and went to meet the bridegroom. ² Five of them were foolish, and five were wise. ³ When the foolish took their lamps, they took no oil with them; ⁴ but the wise took flasks of oil with their lamps. ⁵ As the bridegroom was delayed, all of them became drowsy and slept. ⁶ But at midnight there was a shout, "Look! Here is the bridegroom! Come out to meet him." ⁷ Then all those bridesmaids got up and trimmed their lamps. ⁸ The foolish said to the wise, "Give us some of your oil, for our lamps are going out." ⁹ But the wise replied, "No! there will not be enough for you and for us; you had better go to the dealers and buy some for yourselves.: ¹⁰ And while they went to buy it, the bridegroom came, and those who were ready went with him into the wedding banquet; and the door was shut. ¹¹ Later the other bridesmaids came also, saying, "Lord, lord, open to us." ¹² But he replied, "Truly I tell you, I do not know you." ¹³ Keep awake therefore, for you know neither the day nor the hour. (Matt 25:1–13 NRSV)

Many commentators hear an echo of Jacob wooing a bride in John 4. Perhaps that is one of the lynchpins in the chain of events that follow Jesus' dialogue with the Samaritan woman. She goes to town to announce Jesus' presence, and they come to see for themselves.

But the parallels are much more extensive than that:

The parable discusses a lamp and a bridegroom. John the Baptist is described as a lamp in John 5:35 and Jesus is explicitly called a bridegroom in John 3:29.

The presence of Martha and Mary with their resuscitated brother who had fallen asleep in John 11 evinces a link to this parable in Matt 25. The parable, after all, explores the theme of those who fall asleep and are awakened at the shouted announcement that the bridegroom is near. They are young women. And the deficient supply of oil noted in the parable was identified by Donfried, rightly in my opinion, with a lack of good deeds.[10] It is thus no surprise that at the dinner in John 12, with many of the same persons present as in John 11, a plea is made for money to be given to the poor. Not the good deed that Jesus is valorizing in the moment, but a good deed, nonetheless.

---

10. Donfried, "Allegory of Ten Virgins."

In Matt 25:6, we hear, "A great cry went up, 'Behold the bridegroom! Let us go out to meet him." Similarly, in John 12:13b, "The crowd went out to meet him and cried out." Much of that phrasing is unique to John and this verse of Matthew.

And the parable concludes by saying, "You know neither the day nor the hour." In John 11:9, Jesus discusses the day and rejoicing in it, echoing Ps 118:24. And in John 11:49, after Jesus has raised Lazarus from the dead, the chief priest says, "You know nothing." And once the hour has been made known in chapter 13, we have a string of statements concerning what the disciples do not know (13:7, 28; 14:5).

The cast of Gospel characters has been differently characterized from the way they performed in the Matthean parable, but some of the narrative underpinnings in John 3, 5, and 11–13 are in dialogue with the parable of the ten virgins (25:1–13).

SHAMELESS GENEROSITY (LUKE 11:5-8; JOHN 20-21)

> Καὶ εἶπεν πρὸς αὐτούς· Τίς ἐξ ὑμῶν ἕξει φίλον καὶ πορεύσεται πρὸς αὐτὸν μεσονυκτίου καὶ εἴπῃ αὐτῷ· Φίλε, χρῆσόν μοι τρεῖς ἄρτους, ⁶ ἐπειδὴ φίλος μου παρεγένετο ἐξ ὁδοῦ πρός με καὶ οὐκ ἔχω ὃ παραθήσω αὐτῷ· ⁷ κἀκεῖνος ἔσωθεν ἀποκριθεὶς εἴπῃ· Μή μοι κόπους πάρεχε· ἤδη ἡ θύρα κέκλεισται, καὶ τὰ παιδία μου μετ' ἐμοῦ εἰς τὴν κοίτην εἰσίν· οὐ δύναμαι ἀναστὰς δοῦναί σοι. ⁸ λέγω ὑμῖν, εἰ καὶ οὐ δώσει αὐτῷ ἀναστὰς διὰ τὸ εἶναι φίλον αὐτοῦ, διά γε τὴν ἀναίδειαν αὐτοῦ ἐγερθεὶς δώσει αὐτῷ ὅσων χρῄζει.

> And he said to them, "Suppose one of you has a friend, and you go to him at midnight and say to him, 'Friend, lend me three loaves of bread; ⁶ for a friend of mine has arrived, and I have nothing to set before him.' ⁷ And he answers from within, 'Do not bother me; the door has already been locked, and my children are with me in bed; I cannot get up and give you anything.' ⁸ I tell you, even though he will not get up and give him anything because he is his friend, at least because of his persistence he will get up and give him whatever he needs. (Luke 11:5–8 NRSV)

"My children [παιδια] and I are in bed. I cannot arise [αναστας] to give you anything," says the friend being solicited for bread by his importunate friend at midnight. Jesus, having arisen (αναστηναι) (John 20:9), does give bread to those he calls "children" (*paidia*) (John 21:5). It is just a bonus that

Luke's Jesus explains this parable with reference to a father whose son asks for a fish (John 21:13). And lest there be any doubt that John has Luke 11 in view here, the acknowledgment of John's Jesus that the Father has sent him and his gift of the Spirit to the disciples in John 20:21-22 embodies the script of the concluding line to Luke's parable:

> If you who are evil know how to give good gifts to your children, how much more will the heavenly Father give Holy Spirit to those who ask him? (Luke 11:13)

Even the locked doors at the start of both accounts (Luke 11:7; John 20:19) witness to their interrelation.

"WHO MADE ME JUDGE OVER YOU?" (LUKE 12:13-21; JOHN 8)

> Someone in the crowd said to him, "Teacher, tell my brother to divide the family inheritance with me." [14] But he said to him, "Friend, who set me to be a judge or arbitrator over you?" [15] And he said to them, "Take care! Be on your guard against all kinds of greed; for one's life does not consist in the abundance of possessions." [16] Then he told them a parable: "The land of a rich man produced abundantly. [17] And he thought to himself, 'What should I do, for I have no place to store my crops?' [18] Then he said, 'I will do this: I will pull down my barns and build larger ones, and there I will store all my grain and my goods. [19] And I will say to my soul, Soul, you have ample goods laid up for many years; relax, eat, drink, be merry.' [20] But God said to him, 'You fool! This very night your life is being demanded of you. And the things you have prepared, whose will they be?' [21] So it is with those who store up treasures for themselves but are not rich toward God." (Luke 12:13-21 NRSV)

Is not John 8:15 ("I judge no one") a reflection of this sentiment, even though it creates some tension with statements elsewhere in the Gospel (such as at 5:27 and 9:39)?

MUSTARD SEED, CAST INTO HIS GARDEN (LUKE 13:18–19; JOHN 20)

John alone places the burial of Jesus and its aftermath in a garden. This is widely recognized as, in part, a return to the garden of Genesis. And I agree. All three Synoptic Gospels contain the parable in which the birds of the air come to nest in the branches of what grows (a shrub in Mark, a tree in Matthew and Luke). However, Luke 13:18–19 has a man casting mustard seed, uniquely among the synoptic mustard seed parables, into his *garden*.[11] Should we not see in the crucified Jesus of glory the parabolic rendering of this mustard seed that grows into a tree in whom dwell disciples who are filled with one like a dove (John 1:32; 20:22)? This seems especially likely because of the way it coheres with the evangelist's earlier description of the disciples as "branches" (John 15:5). The birds of Luke 13 nest in the "branches" of the mustard seed tree. The crucified and glorified Jesus in John 20 breathes Holy Spirit (as a dove) into the disciples (as branches).

THE SONS OF LIGHT (LUKE 16:8; JOHN 12:36)

The phrase also occurs in the Qumran literature, but Luke is a source closer to hand. The use of the phrase in John 12 is particularly apposite, in that Judas's theft from the poor box reflects the parable of the dishonest manager in Luke 16.

THE DEVIL SOWING WEEDS (MATT 13:39; JOHN 13:2)

> Then he left the crowds and went into the house. And his disciples approached him, saying, "Explain to us the parable of the weeds of the field." [37] He answered, "The one who sows the good seed is the Son of Man; [38] the field is the world, and the good seed are the children of the kingdom; the weeds are the children of the evil one, [39] and the enemy who sowed them is the devil; the harvest is the end of the age, and the reapers are angels. [40] Just as the weeds are collected and burned up with fire, so will it be at the end of the age.

---

11. This has parallels in Mark 4:30–32; Matt 13:31–32. Again, it is one of four parables identified by John Meier as emerging from the historical Jesus tradition. The others are the evil tenants of the vineyard (Mark 12:1–11; Matt 21:33–43; Luke 20:9–18); the great supper (Matt 22:1–14; Luke 14:16–24); the talents/pounds (Matt 25:14–30; Luke 19:11–27) (*Authenticity of the Parables*, 230–362).

> ⁴¹ The Son of Man will send his angels, and they will collect out of his kingdom all causes of sin and all evildoers, ⁴² and they will throw them into the furnace of fire, where there will be weeping and gnashing of teeth. ⁴³ Then the righteous will shine like the sun in the kingdom of their Father. Let anyone with ears listen!" (Matt 13:36–43 NRSV)

Matthew's devil adulterates the wheat crop with weeds. Coming soon after Jesus' assertion that the seed must be put in the ground and die to bear fruit (John 12:24), the assertion at the opening of the Johannine supper is in sync with Matthew: "the devil placed the betrayal into Judas's heart" is the personalized negative extension of the agricultural metaphor.

MATTHEW 13:44–50 AND THE FOURTH GOSPEL

> The kingdom of heaven is like treasure hidden in a field, which someone found and hid; then in his joy he goes and sells all that he has and buys that field.
> ⁴⁵ Again, the kingdom of heaven is like a merchant in search of fine pearls; ⁴⁶ on finding one pearl of great value, he went and sold all that he had and bought it.
> ⁴⁷ Again, the kingdom of heaven is like a net that was thrown into the sea and caught fish of every kind; ⁴⁸ when it was full, they drew it ashore, sat down, and put the good into baskets but threw out the bad. ⁴⁹ So it will be at the end of the age. The angels will come out and separate the evil from the righteous ⁵⁰ and throw them into the furnace of fire, where there will be weeping and gnashing of teeth. (Matt 13:44–50 NRSV)

Three Matthean reign-of-God parables unique to Matthew have joy at their center. The unalloyed joy of the Johannine disciples at encountering Jesus glorified is almost wholly distinctive among the canonical resurrection accounts, with the exception of Luke 24:52. The other Gospels in the canon mention just about everything else but this joy (fear in Mark; fear mixed with joy, as well as belief and doubt in Matthew; burning hearts, troubled and doubting hearts in Luke). The joy of the Lukan disciples described in Luke 24:52 constitutes the culmination of their progress through these other reactions within the resurrection narratives, whereas the joy of the Johannine disciples is apparent in their first encounter with Jesus in his glorified state.[12]

---

12. Snodgrass, *Stories with Intent*, 246.

However, much more may be seen in John's transformation of the Matt 13 parables concerning the reign of heaven. Each one of them has a linguistic peg, drawn from Matt 13:44–50, on which John strings a series of developments:

Matt 13:44–50	John
Merchant (13:45)	Marketplace (2:16)
Treasure (13:44)	Treasure (θησαυρος) (6:68)
Seashore (13:48)	Seashore (21:4)

1. The εμπορ- root having to do with commerce is perhaps the most explicit similarity here. However, we may also see some of the elements of ζητουντι καλους (seeking beautiful (Matt 13:45) in the text's turn to ζηλος (zeal) (John 2:17). Similarly, ευρων δε ενα (and seeking one) (Matt 13:46) appears in ευρεν (found) (John 2:14). If one is willing to engage in a retro-reading, we may see the presence of a string of μαργαριτας (pearls) (Matt 13:45) in John 2:16–17:

   καὶ τοῖς τὰς περιστερὰς πωλοῦιν εἶπεν· Ἄρατε ταῦτα ἐντεῦθεν, μὴ ποιεῖτε τὸν οἶκον τοῦ πατρός μου οἶκον ἐμπορίου. ¹⁷ ἐμνήσθησαν οἱ μαθηταὶ αὐτοῦ ὅτι γεγραμμένον ἐστίν· Ὁ ζῆλος τοῦ οἴκου σου καταφάγεταί με.

   Having read both forward and backwards, we are able to appreciate one aspect of a nearby pronouncement about the wind/Spirit in John 3:8: "You do not know whence it comes or whither it goes."

2. We turn now to the sovereign-reign-God theme closely interwoven in John 6. Jesus anticipates and refuses the crowd's offer to be a king on their terms. This sixth chapter has the most frequent references in John to ουρανος (heaven) (some ten times). This is significant because Matthew's preferred expression for the reign of God is the reign of heaven. The conclusion of John 6 is coordinated with two of the reign-of-God parables in Matt 13:44–50, those concerning the treasure discovered in a field and the finding of the pearl of great price:

- Υπαγει (go away) (Matt 13:44) and υπαγειν (go away) (John 6:67)
- Concomitantly, απελθων (go away) (Matt 13:46) and απελθων (go away) (John 6:66)

Stories

At first glance, this tight linguistic symmetry is of little import, since the *departing* of the figures in the parables happens in order that they might obtain the field or the pearl; the departing in John 6 is about abandoning the following of Jesus. However, remember that Matt 13:44 depicts a θησαυρος (treasure) that is hidden. Hear again John 6:68, in which the word θησαυρος (treasure) is clearly present, though hidden:

ἀπεκρίθη αὐτῷ Σίμων Πέτρος· κύριε, πρὸς τίνα ἀπελευσόμεθα;
ῥήματα ζωῆς αἰωνίου ἔχεις

John 6:67–68 concludes by saying, "You have the words of eternal life." In John 6, his words frame (vv. 60, 68) the question (6:67) of the one who refuses to be the crowd's king on their terms. His words are, as well, the appropriate conclusion to the two other substructures in John 6:

He gave them bread	from heaven	to eat.
vv. 31–40	41–51	52–59
The Word	became flesh	and dwelt among us.
vv. 45	51–59	60–66

3. Finally, Matthean parables supply reign-of-God roots in what happens at the Johannine seashore in John 21. In both cases, there is a catch from the sea, including attention to a net.

There is a discernible progression in chronological focus within and among these three Johannine scenes concerning the marketplace, treasure, and seashore:

- The first concerns Jesus' word in tandem with an explicit recall of past Scripture (John 2:16–17).
- The second explicitly focuses on Jesus' words as presently mediating eternal life (John 6:68).
- The third culminates in a reiterated saying of Jesus that includes attention to his coming (John 21:22–23).

The evangelist's dogged focus on the words of Jesus as *parabolic treasure* distinguish this portion of the Johannine effort from near analogues in more rarefied wisdom, apocalyptic, and gnostic traditions.[13]

BUILDER AND KING (LUKE 14:25–33) AND THE TRIAL BEFORE PILATE (JOHN 18–19)

> Now large crowds were traveling with him; and he turned and said to them, [26] "Whoever comes to me and does not hate father and mother, wife and children, brothers and sisters, yes, and even life itself, cannot be my disciple. [27] Whoever does not carry the cross and follow me cannot be my disciple. [28] For which of you, intending to build a tower, does not first sit down and estimate the cost, to see whether he has enough to complete it? [29] Otherwise, when he has laid a foundation and is not able to finish, all who see it will begin to ridicule him, [30] saying, 'This fellow began to build and was not able to finish.' [31] Or what king, going out to wage war against another king, will not sit down first and consider whether he is able with ten thousand to oppose the one who comes against him with twenty thousand? [32] If he cannot, then, while the other is still far away, he sends a delegation and asks for the terms of peace. [33] So therefore, none of you can become my disciple if you do not give up all your possessions." (Luke 14:25–33 NRSV)

Luke's unique warning against premature discipleship unaware of the attendant cost has distinct ties with the Johannine language of the trial before Pilate. Luke sketches a portrait of a builder who "sits down" and calculates before he builds, lest he be mocked for not "completing" the task. John's Jesus, having "completed" the work the Father gave him to do, nevertheless asks that it may be brought to "completion" in his disciples, and "sits down" in the presence of Pilate in contemplation of what must yet be done to make those statements fully true (John 17:4, 23; 19:13).

In a similar vein, Luke's Jesus asks, "Which king going to war and (being insufficiently marshaled against another king) doesn't sit down, calculate, and sue for peace?" John filters this scenario through the lens of mundane kingship upended, within which Jesus lifted up is cast in the role of victorious king who grants peace. Hence, there is an extended discussion

---

13. See Collins, *Jewish Wisdom*; Reynolds and Stuckenbruck, *Jewish Apocalyptic Tradition*; F. Murphy, *Apocalypticism*; Perkins, *Gnosticism and New Testament*, esp. chs. 8, "Jesus as Word," and 9, "Discourses of the Revealer."

in John 19 of the nature of Jesus' kingship not of this world, as opposed to Caesar's. Jesus' promise to the disciples of a peace the world cannot give (John 14:27, realized in 20:19) is the fruit of his claim that he has conquered the world (John 16:33).

A *MNA* (COIN) IN A *SOUDARION* (SWEAT RAG) (LUKE 19:20; JOHN 20)

Only in John 20:7 do we hear that the burial wrappings of John 19:40 included a *soudarion*. I agree with those who see in this cloth a reflection of the face covering used by Moses in response to the revelation of God's glory.

However, there is more than that at work here. There may well be a dialogue with Luke 19:20, wherein a fearful recipient of a μνα (*mna*) coin (one-sixtieth of a talent) simply wrapped it in a σουδαριον (*soudarion*), buried, and returned it. The Lukan scenario chastises the man for forgetting that his master "takes up [αιρ] what I did not lay down [τιθημι]" (Luke 19:22). That description affords us a venue from which to understand some of what has happened to Jesus in John 20. The Jesus of John 10:17 has described the culmination of the hour as involving his laying down (τιθημι) his life and receiving (λαμβανειν) it again, for which the Father loves him. Mary's exclamation that "we don't know where they have put [τιθημι] him" (John 20:2) suggests that it is the Father who has taken up Jesus, just as anticipated in John 10.

And there is yet more than this in the Johannine context of the cerements, representing a reasoned and creative development beyond that in Luke's narrative. Greek μνα is a loanword from Semitic מ-נ-ה. From a root meaning to count, מ-נ-ה can mean either count/number/reckon or assign. At 3 Kgs 21:25 LXX (1 Kgs 20:25), מ-נ-ה (in the piel) is rendered as αλλαξομεν (ex/change, alter). That αλλασσο, I would suggest, shows up as the stylistic echo we hear in the uniquely Johannine ο αλλος (the other [disciple]) in John 20:3-4, 8. John's αλλος disciple is in part a device by which we attend to Jesus as μνα, the coin of exchange.[14] But what is the nature of this exchange?

14. I think that Luke, who many times and uniquely refers to the μνα (coin), gets special mileage out of it when, for example, he employs the μν in μνεισθαι (remembering) in Luke 24:6, 8 and the μονα (solitary) nature of the burial clothes in Luke 24:12. The implicit recall of μνα in Luke 24 should also be seen, perhaps, against the background of one of the last words of Luke's burial account, *mura* (myrrh), in Luke 23:56. Μυρα is a lexical neighbor of μνα, and the Hebrew homophone of Greek *mura* is מור, which means

I am convinced that John is in part inspired by the discussion in Rom 1:23 wherein we find the apostle diagnosing the basic human predicament as having exchanged (ηλλαζαν) the glory of the one incorruptible God for lesser corruptible phenomena. In that fall, humanity lost the glory of God, something restored in Jesus' transformation.

Jesus lifted up and transformed in the glory of God: that is what we learn from careful attention to the burial clothes at the empty tomb.

THE BLIND LEADING THE BLIND (LUKE 6:39; JOHN 9)

Only Luke calls this a parable. Its parallel in Matt 7 does not do so. John employs this to characterize the Pharisees in John 9:40–41. There is also a broad congruity between the statement in Luke 6:40 that a disciple is not greater than his master and the man in John 9 healed of blindness. That is, the man's expulsion is also Jesus' experience. It is on the outside of the synagogue that Jesus encounters him.

A LAD IN HIS LETTERS (JOHN 6:1–15)

This short story, culminating in Jesus withdrawing from the crowd's attempt to seize him and force him to be king on their terms, unique in the specifics outlined here, proceeds in three parts.

1. The letters of Κοδραντης (penny) are scattered throughout John 6:9–10a, reflecting the two-mite coin of the widow in Mark 12:42. The letters of Κοδραντης are underlined here:

   > Ἔστιν παιδάριον ὧδε ὃς ἔχει πέντε ἄρτους κριθίνους καὶ δύο ὀψάρια· ἀλλὰ ταῦτα τί ἐστιν εἰς τοσούτους; ¹⁰ εἶπεν ὁ Ἰησοῦς· Ποιήσατε τοὺς ἀνθρώπους ἀναπεσεῖν. ἦν δὲ χόρτος πολὺς ἐν τῷ τόπῳ. ἀνέπεσαν οὖν οἱ ἄνδρες τὸν ἀριθμὸν ὡς πεντακισχίλιοι. (John 6:9–10)

   That noun occurs again in the Gospel canon only in Matt 5:26, "pay the last penny." Luke makes no explicit mention of the coin.

   The modest gift of the lad in John 6:9 may serve as complement to that of the modest gift of the widow at the temple in Mark 12:43–44

"ex/change, alter." Lukan remembering is in part riveted on the transformation of Jesus as μνα. John knows this tradition, and goes one better, moving from μνα as "count" to μνα as "ex/change or alter."

and is appropriately placed here after Jesus' engagement with temple personnel in John 5. With both the widow and the lad, an arguably modest gift is, in Jesus' estimation and action, made into something exponentially greater.

2. The intercalated letters of σωμα (body) in John 6:10, anticipating the eucharistic dimension of Jesus feeding the crowds with bread, follows.

εἶπεν ὁ Ἰησοῦς· Ποιήσατε τοὺς ἀνθρώπους ἀναπεσεῖν. ἦν δὲ χόρτος πολὺς ἐν τῷ τόπῳ. ἀνέπεσαν οὖν οἱ ἄνδρες τὸν ἀριθμὸν ὡς πεντακισχίλιοι.

3. In John 6:8 are the scattered letters of the name Ιωσηφ (Joseph).

λέγει αὐτῷ εἷς ἐκ τῶν μαθητῶν αὐτοῦ, Ἀνδρέας ὁ ἀδελφὸς Σίμωνος Πέτρου·

In Gen 37:30 LXX Joseph is the παιδαριον (lad, young man) who will eventually solve the problem of famine in his people's land. The sacred author's task, unique to him among the canonical Gospel accounts of this feeding, also anticipates the fragments of bread in John 6:13. Whereas Gen 37:2 LXX describes Joseph as seventeen years old, the unique phrase describing the fragments in John, "twelve baskets from the five loaves" (John 6:13), is a wink to the reader/hearer that the seventeen-year-old stand-in for Joseph is on the scene. The crowd intends to ἁρπάζειν (seize Jesus) and have him βασιλ (rule) over them (John 6:15). Such only partially reflects the import of the Genesis account of the brothers' violent resistance to Joseph upon hearing his report of the βασιλ (reign) that Yhwh grants him in Gen 37:8. The verb ἁρπάζειν (seize) appears as such in the surmise of Joseph's father in Gen 37:33 LXX that "a beast seized Joseph." There is also a linguistic fact that may assist us in grasping the reason the evangelist turned to Joseph as an implicit assistant in this feeding narrative. The name Joseph is built out of a Hebrew root meaning add/increase.

The evangelist then has retrieved a fragment, a piece of synoptic tradition about a penny, which was not reproduced in lockstep by Matthew and not at all by Luke. Rather, he has incorporated this leftover into a fresh articulation of Jesus feeding a crowd informed by the Joseph tradition in Genesis. With sufficient inspiration, a creative chef can do wonders with leftovers.

BEHOLD THE HUMAN (JOHN 19:5), CAESAR'S COIN (MARK 12), AND JESUS' LITURGY

Where else in John do we have evidence of the evangelist exploring Jesus as a μνα-coin? The uniquely Johannine scene in which Pilate says "Behold [ἰδου] the human" (John 19:5) is a narrativization of the human as image of God. It may be partly derived from the uniquely Markan notice that has Jesus saying, "Let me see [ἰδω] a coin" (Mark 12:15). He then continues, "Whose image and inscription are here?," ending in the saying, "Then give to Caesar what is Caesar's, and to God what is God's." I read that as a call to give back the entire person, the human image of God à la Gen 1, to its proper owner, God, even as one pays the Roman tax. And I judge it not much of a stretch to see Jesus in John 19:5 as the image of God, the new Adam/new Human, who gives his person unreservedly to God.

Is this a parable? The word doesn't occur as such. However, there is a coda to this argument about the coin that reverberates with other echoes of the dispute in Mark 12 over the coin, as well as a text from Jeremiah, both converging in the discussion with Pilate in John 19. The thesis goes like this.

The letters of παροιμια (simile, comparison), here underlined, are sprinkled throughout the introductory questions of Jesus' Markan interlocutors.

> Καὶ ἀποστέλλουσιν πρὸς αὐτόν τινας τῶν Φαρισαίων καὶ τῶν Ἡρωδιανῶν ἵνα αὐτὸν ἀγρεύσωσιν λόγῳ. ¹⁴ καὶ ἐλθόντες λέγουσιν αὐτῷ· Διδάσκαλε, οἴδαμεν ὅτι ἀληθὴς εἶ καὶ οὐ μέλει σοι περὶ οὐδενός, οὐ γὰρ βλέπεις εἰς πρόσωπον ἀνθρώπων, ἀλλ᾽ ἐπ᾽ ἀληθείας τὴν ὁδὸν τοῦ θεοῦ διδάσκεις· ἔξεστιν δοῦναι κῆνσον Καίσαρι ἢ οὔ; δῶμεν ἢ μὴ δῶμεν

> And they sent to him some of the Pharisees and some of the Herodians, to entrap him in his talk. ¹⁴ And they came and said to him, "Teacher, we know that you are true, and care for no man; for you do not regard the position of men but truly teach the way of God. Is it lawful to pay taxes to Caesar, or not? ¹⁵ Should we pay them, or should we not?" (Mark 12:13–15 RSV)

The coin in question is a δηναριον, which Jesus asks to see (ιδω) (Mark 12:15).

A form of the verb "to see" and then the letters of δηναριον appear in the sprinkled diction of John 19:4–5:

Stories

καὶ ἐξῆλθεν πάλιν ἔξω ὁ Πιλᾶτος καὶ λέγει αὐτοῖς· Ἴδε ἄγω ὑμῖν αὐτὸν ἔξω, ἵνα γνῶτε ὅτι οὐδεμίαν αἰτίαν εὑρίσκω ἐν αὐτῷ. ⁵ ἐξῆλθεν οὖν ὁ Ἰησοῦς ἔξω, φορῶν τὸν ἀκάνθινον στέφανον καὶ τὸ πορφυροῦν ἱμάτιον. καὶ λέγει αὐτοῖς· Ἰδοὺ ὁ ἄνθρωπος.

Pilate went out again, and said to them, "Behold, I am bringing him out to you, that you may know that I find no crime in him." ⁵ So Jesus came out, wearing the crown of thorns and the purple robe. Pilate said to them, "Here is the human!"

Note also the Johannine echo of Jer 11:19, the letters of whose αρνιον (lamb) are already present in the letters of δηναριον:

> I was like an [ακακον] innocent [αρνιον] lamb led to the slaughter;
> I did not realize that they had plotted against me, saying,
> "Let us destroy the tree and its fruit;
> let us cut him off from the land of the living,
> that his name be remembered no more." (Jer 11:19)

John probably intends to elicit memory of this passage; the word αρνιον (lamb) is extremely rare in the Septuagint, occurring only four times.[15] And look again at the phrase in John 19:5:

καὶ τὸ πορφυροῦν ἱμάτιον

and the purple garment

While Mark's δηναριον requires a repositioning of the initial letter nu- to spell αρνιον, John has written his scene so that the description of the purple cloak also yields the letters αρνιον in the correct order. (I would say "effortlessly," but that would be to discount the palpably artistic achievement present here.)

In short, while Mark 12 makes a statement about a coin that Jesus transforms into a statement about humanity in God's image, John 19:4–5 conceals the same coin in the description of Jesus before the crowd as vehicle for asserting Jesus as an innocent lamb led to the slaughter.

The Freely Offered Liturgy of Jesus in John

How does Jesus use this coin of the realm that he somehow is? There are several scenes in John that have a financial dimension that speak to each other:

---

15. Ps 113 (114):4, 6; Jer 11:19; 27:45 LXX (Jer 50:45 MT).

John 2	John 12
Objection to the emporium in his Father's house	Objection to a perceived waste of expensive oil, and a call to sell it and give to the poor

The selling of chapter 12 corresponds to the buying and selling of chapter 2. Jesus' retort to Judas's objection focuses on his own person, the care of which does not preclude subsequent care for other poor persons.

John 4	John 10
Paid laborers	Jesus implicitly contrasts those who shepherd the sheep for pay and his giving his own life for the sheep

Again, the latter text highlights Jesus' free self-offering, which implicitly supersedes the paid laborers of the earlier chapter 4.

At the center of this configuration resides chapter 6, whose question about where the disciples might buy enough provisions for the crowd raises echoes of Isaiah and Proverbs concerning the grain and wine offered freely by Yhwh and Wisdom. Eating here in John 6 may provide a counterpoint to the tree of life in John 19.

So, at one level, the evangelist builds a narrative case concerning Jesus giving himself freely as an offering to God for the benefit of humans.

The second major point here concerns the relation of this self-offering to a widely recognized reality in the Hellenistic and Roman world, that of the λειτουργια. Λειτουργια referred to those acts of public beneficence that were imposed by governments on citizens who could afford them. The duties were always somewhat expensive, and often onerous, so much so that we have record of several instances in which a person complains about the cost or its frequency. And in one preserved text, we have someone making the objection on behalf of someone without adequate means, saying that the liturgy was inappropriate in that case.[16]

---

16. See "Leitourgia" entries in *NewDocs*; Bagnall et al., *Encyclopedia of Ancient History*; and the series Supplementum epigraphicum graecum, Zeitschrift für Papyrologie und Epigraphik (SEG). See, e.g., in SEG, Chaniotis, "Hermogenes." For an example of a city's public thanksgiving for these good works in western Asia Minor, see Kern, *Inschriften von Magnesia*, 89, line 51. Another city in western Asia Minor showed its appreciation for such liturgies by erecting an image of benefactors (Gaertringen, *Inschriften von Priene*, 103; *OGIS* 541). Such liturgies were also undertaken by women of considerable financial means (Mantas "Independent Women").

I raise this issue of liturgies in part because I think that they constitute an underappreciated dimension of the Johannine presentation. Think of the several instances of John's Jesus discussing his and his Father's εργα (works). That word is at the linguistic heart of *leitourgia*. These works are to be distinguished from those about which the crowd asks in John 6. Upon hearing their query, "What works shall we do, in order that we might work God's works?," Jesus answers, "Believe in the one [God] sent." Their own greater works that supersede his (14:12) follow on their belief in his work, which is primary.

In short, John's Jesus is engaged in a massive public work, a liturgy unique to him and irreplaceable for the world. While he instantiates the offering of the new human to God, his liturgy also instantiates the utility of his self-offering for the world. That, I believe, is a fuller articulation of Jesus as transforming Caesar's coin.

JOHANNINE PARABOLISM AND THE I AM SAYINGS

These examples of synoptic parables being reshaped to depict some aspect of Jesus as such is a process that we might have anticipated after considering John's I AM sayings. I refer to those sayings that are completed with a predicate, such as bread, light, door, shepherd, resurrection, life, and vine. They are arguably a reflection of themes in the synoptic parables as well.[17] John is very interested in transmuting synoptic parabolic material into more than one sort of description of who Jesus is.

UNTYING KNOTS (DAN 5; JOHN 19:38-42)

Apart from parables, John has transformed a narrative bearing a puzzle at its heart, Dan 5. I conclude this chapter with consideration of that text's role in John's account at the cross and tomb of Jesus.

The burial of Jesus in John, when seen from one perspective, presents Jesus as the central knot in what we may call a puzzle, *an approximation of a parable*. The evangelist here draws on the acclamation of the prophet Daniel in Dan 5:12 LXX as one who, among other things, "unties knots [συνδεσμους]." The Fourth Evangelist reflects that in his unique notice that Jesus' body was bound (εδησαν, from the cognate verb δεω). As the

---

17. See Schweizer, "Johannine 'Parables.'"

narrative unfolds in John 20, it becomes clear that Jesus is also one who unties the knots, in this case, of his burial clothes (John 19:40; 20:6–7). Other characteristics of Dan 5 shared with John include the following: discussion of the status of kingship from a theological point of view, the presence of drinking vessels, explicit attention to the acts of both writing and reading, attention to an illuminated writing about judgment, and the presence of Aramaic transmitted by a Greek text.

We are dealing here with a revelatory reading of a text, explicitly in Daniel and implicitly in John. And this is not the only such reading in the New Testament. For example, Paul renders an interpretation of Exod 34 in 2 Cor 3. However, the knot that Daniel unties in Dan 5:26–28, and with which John is concerned, is writing on a wall—פרסין—תקל—מנא מנא in the Aramaic. In a seminal article on this scene, Al Wolters suggests that Daniel's interpretation offers not one, but three, different vocalizations of the Aramaic consonants constituting three different statements that God has weighed on the scale, by which he has taken a reading and actively judged the kingdom of Belshazzar; and finding it wanting, handed over that kingdom to Persia. Herein I reproduce the chart that presents those three readings of the Aramaic:[18]

	Level A	Level B	Level C

Dan 5:26 — דְּנָה פְּשַׁר־מִלְּתָא מְנֵא מְנָה־אֱלָהָא מַלְכוּתָךְ וְהַשְׁלְמַהּ׃

Menē	mnh 'lh' mlkwth [mĕnā']	wšlmh [mĕnā']
Mina	Reckoned has God your kingdom	and paid it out

v. 27 — תְּקֵל תְּקִילְתָּה בְמֹאזַנְיָא וְהִשְׁתְּכַחַתְּ חַסִּיר׃

Teqēl	tqlyth bm'zny' [tĕqal]	Wškht hsyr [tiqqal]
Shekel	Weighed have you been in the scales	and found too light

v. 28 — פְּרֵס פְּרִיסַת מַלְכוּתָךְ וִיהִיבַת לְמָדַי וּפָרָס׃

Perēs	pryst mlkwtk [peras]	wyhbt lmdy wprs [pāras]
Half-Mina	Assessed has been your kingdom	and given to the Medes and Persians

18. Wolters, "Riddle of the Scales," 176. Reproduced by permission of Hebrew Union College Press.

The first level A reads the Aramaic as markers of weight, the second level B vocalizes the consonants to express statements of God's taking the measure of what has been placed on the scale, and the third level C vocalizes the Aramaic consonants to produce different statements about God's acting on that assessment, i.e., acting to judge Belshazzar's reign. At the center of the Danielic puzzle is the image of the scales, represented in Babylonian astrology by the constellation Libra. Wolters emphasizes the presence of the scales because he is inclined to date the fall of Babylon to the fall of 539 BCE. This coheres with the autumn conquest by Cyrus of the Babylonian kingdom in 539 BCE, a date attested in inscriptions of the period and already noted by R. H. Charles in his commentary on Daniel.[19] The autumnal conquest inspired Dan 5's literary rendition of the constellation Libra, says Wolters. That seems plausible to me.

Both Daniel and John emphasize the act of writing. There is writing on a wall in Dan 5:5, and in John 19:22, we have Pilate ploddingly emphasizing the fact that what he has written, he has written. I suggest that the Fourth Evangelist exercises a variant of the Danielic puzzle by replicating the word תקל as it appeared in Theodotian's first-century Greek rendering of Daniel's Aramaic.[20] That is, the Greek transliteration θεκελ in Dan 5:27 LXX is replicated in John 19:39–40, as seen in this presentation of John's Greek that underlines the letters of the word in question:

λιτρας εκατον	καθως εθος
One hundred liters	As is the custom

The word θεκελ is present as one reads in the direction of the Aramaic script, from right to left. There is little that is arbitrary in this selection of highlighted letters. They all occur at the beginning of their respective words, when considering the Greek. However, it is especially interesting that they occur at the end of the words in which they are embedded when

19. Charles, *Book of Daniel*, 137.

20. John follows the Theodotionic Greek of Dan 5, the one that postdated the Old Greek (OG) rendition of the Aramaic and one that follows the Aramaic more closely than did the OG. Theodotionic Daniel was available to the early church of the first century. The Theodotionic text is longer than the OG, giving us vv. 6, 14, 15, 24, 26–28. Noteworthy characteristics of the Theodotionic text include attention to the loosening of the king's loins (συνδεσμοι), the presence of σοφια in Daniel, Daniel's charge that the king has not "glorified God" who gives him breath, and the seer's assertion that the writing on the wall was sent (απεσταλη) from God.

reading in the usual Aramaic direction, right to left. So where are they, at the end or the beginning? The ambiguity of this burial preceding resurrection employs wordplay that delights the scribal heart and has a precedent in Ps 34 of the Hebrew Bible.[21] Moreover, the hidden quality of this word within words has already been adumbrated at the beginning of the burial account when we are told that Joseph of Ari*mathaia* was a secret *mathētēs* of Jesus. The vowels e-e in the Johannine θεκελ replicate exactly those in the Greek transliteration θεκελ of Theodotion. And in between "one hundred liters" in John 19:39b and "as is the custom" in John 19:40b occurs the εδησαν (they bound) (John 19:40a), which links the Johannine text with the foundational description of Daniel as one who unties knots (συνδεσμους).[22]

Just as important is the fact that John's text has variants of the other two words in Daniel's puzzle. In John 19:39 we read of the σμυρνης (fragrant) oil. Compare that with the מְנֵא of Aramaic and Greek Dan 5:26:

| Σμυρνης (smyrnēs) | מְנֵא (menē) |

And John 19:42 discusses the feast of Παρασκευειν (Preparation) for Pesach/Passover.[23] Compare the Aramaic puzzle word as rendered in Wolters's level C reading of Aramaic Dan 5:28, *pāras*:

| paraskeuein | פְּרֵס (pāras) |

All this Mediterranean divination is merely preparation for the dialogue of Jesus and Mary in John 20:16: "She said to him, Ἑβραϊστι (in Hebrew) Ραββουνι, which means Teacher." In Ἑβραϊστι, b-a-r-s is present, and the requisite omicron of b-a-r-o-s (weight) comes from Ραββουνι. This

21. The twenty-two verses (excluding the superscription) of Ps 34 mirror the number of letters in the Hebrew alphabet. The consonants that begin the first, middle, and final verses of the psalm are א-ל-ף. (As a composite, these letters equal aleph, the first letter of the alphabet.) Therefore, as one approaches the conclusion of the psalm, one has arrived at the point where, in a sense, one begins. See R. Murphy, *Tree of Life*, 10. This instance of ending-as-beginning is especially pertinent to John because Ps 34 has often been understood as one of the allusions behind John 19:36, "Not a bone of it will be broken."

22. Hints of engagement with Aramaic Daniel abound in this part of John. The letters of the name Daniel are present within the latter half of John 19:38: Ιουδαιων ... ηλθεν. And Aramaic itself is hinted at in the place name Αριμαθαια. Indeed, the uniquely Johannine notice at 18:1 concerning the Valley of *Kedron* presents the letters קדרון that are lexical neighbor to Hebrew קתר (knots).

23. While the name *Paraskeuēs* (Preparation) is not unique to John's burial account, λιτρας εκατον and καθως εθος, as well as σμυρνης, are.

occurrence of Ραββουνι is singular in the Gospel. The usual mode of this address in the text is simply Ραββι. And βαρος is also present if one begins with consideration of Ραββουνι (supplying the *b-a-r-o*) and then moves to Εβραιστι (supplying the *s*).

He<u>brai</u>sti Rabb<u>ou</u>ni
Hebrai<u>sti</u> <u>Rabb</u>ouni

I read this *Hebraisti Rabbouni* as a deliberate juxtaposition that not only alludes to Greek βαρος (weight), but in the two-directional toggled reading of βαρος also depicts the movement of the scales themselves. In casting the terms of his address in this way, the evangelist would be alluding to the Pauline teaching about the weight of glory that Jesus now enjoys and will impart to others (see 2 Cor 4:17). Indeed, the unique diction of John 20:12 reinforces this vision of glory enveloping the body of Jesus on the scales: "She saw two angels clad in white, one at the head and one at the feet, where the body of Jesus lay."

In short, in a text notorious for its frequent incorporation of future apocalyptic expectations into the presentation of Jesus' person, we have a concomitant narrative reminder that *present revelation* is also an active category at work in the person of Jesus. And this statement about present revelation is expressed in John 1 and John 20 through the trope of the scales, borrowed from Dan 5.[24] (More on John 1 below.)

At the very least, the Fourth Evangelist is intimating that, just as Daniel's interpretation of the puzzle was untied to render a statement about a change in kingdoms, so Jesus' burial in the evangelist's rendering has proleptically announced a shift in reign of a related but higher order, the definitive inauguration of the reign of God discussed in John 3 (something *seen* as described in John 3:3). Though Jesus' reign, now in its inaugural phase, is "not of this world," I read that as referring to its lack of restriction to coordinates of time and space. And the effects of Jesus' reign have begun to be felt. For example,

---

24. There are remote parallels to this exercise of intertextuality in the scribal culture of the millennium that preceded it. The cuneiform tablets of Asshurbanipal's library, now in the British Museum, attest to dynamics such as *extispicy*, in which an unfavorable reading of entrails may be reversed, depending on whether one reads right to left or in the opposite direction. Moreover, in these cuneiform tablets we find scribes who, for example, comment on a medical/magical text with a reference to the Epic of Gilgamesh. This is intertextuality in a much earlier instantiation of scribal culture, a tradition in which John stands. See the catalog of cuneiforms in the Cuneiform Commentaries Project, administered by Eckart Frahm and a colleague at Yale University.

"the prince of this world is cast out," even though the evangelist is careful not to equate that prince with any single temporal ruler.

John explores the *judgment* theme in this burial, suggesting that Jesus is the instrument whereby God ends the reign of the world's prince. Is *light* present as well in John's transformation of Dan 5:26–28? A case can be made to that effect, one that depends on attention to the number of syllables at work. Wolters points out that in the Masoretic rendering of his level A, we have a total of six syllables. And in his level B, he counts twenty-one syllables.[25] The sum of six plus twenty-one equals twenty-seven. We know from a reference to the second psalm in Acts 13:33 that there was some attention to the numbered ordering of the psalms. And Ps 27 begins, "The Sovereign is my light and my salvation." The evangelist's engagement with the Danielic puzzle words in Dan 5:26–28 incorporates an allusion to twenty-seven and, obliquely, to Yhwh as light. Within this burial account, John has concentrated the elements of light and judgment that were so characteristic of Jesus' discourse in John 3, 8, and 12, and thereby suggested the proper context for his earlier insistence on these themes. It also seems worth observing that there are twenty-seven syllables in the Greek words that separate the major components of θεκελ, highlighted above. This is indirect confirmation that indeed the Fourth Evangelist is engaging the puzzle of Dan 5 at its Aramaic level, and not only at the Greek.[26]

Just as significantly, perhaps, when we see this dynamic in John, we are also, I would suggest, witnessing an epitome of a leitmotif that has been persistent, and persistently puzzling, in John 3, 8, and 12. When Jesus' interlocutors engage him with various questions in John 3, 8, and 12, he invariably answers with statements that seem to have little to do with the

---

25. Wolters suggests that the words in his column C may be pronounced in such a way as to render twenty-one syllables as well ("Riddle of the Scales," 177).

26. There may already be a pre-Johannine tradition that associates numeric quantity and binding. "I will lead you [εν αριθμω] in number" (Ezek 20:37 LXX) is an epitomization of "I will bring you into the discipline [בְּמָסֹרֶת] of the covenant" (Ezek 20:37 Heb.). The Hebrew is derived from עָסַר (to bind) and anticipates the eventual work of the Masoretes, who meticulously preserved in writing the proper reading of the consonantal text they received. See Danker, *Multipurpose Tools*, 46–48. Presumably the arithmetic note struck by the LXX reading alludes to assertions concerning the doubling of individual letters, words, or phrases or to the short versus long forms of vowels such as *e* or *ē* that help to establish the proper reading of the Hebrew. From this point of view, the evangelist's reference to "binding" the body of Jesus in John 19:40, surrounded as it is by the twenty-seven syllables in Aramaic Dan 5:26–28 as recounted above, allude to Jesus as the Word (of the covenant) being bound or fixed.

question asked. But his answers just as invariably combine the themes of judgment and light. I propose that this is related to Dan 5, where we have a candlestick by which the writing about judgment is read.

Moreover, the dynamics of John 19–20 have an analogue in the Gospel's opening eighteen verses, the Prologue. The puzzle words of Dan 5 are intimated, but in a slightly different way from that in the burial.

M-n-ē: The fortieth word of the Johannine Prologue is ἠν (was). I emphasize its fortieth position because forty is the numerical equivalent of the letter mu. Here we have the letters of *m-n-ē*. By itself this would mean nothing. However, in John 1:13 we have arguably not one, but two, allusions to θεκελ—*ek thelematos . . . ek thelematos*.

And what of *p-r-s*? Both John 1:14 and 1:18 discuss the Father in the genitive case: *patros . . . patros*.

And even this would not mean much if there were not an allusion to the name Daniel here. But at the center of the Johannine Prologue of about 250 words, right after the 125th word in 1:11, we have ιδια ηλθεν.

This broad congruity between the elements of Dan 5's writing and its employment in John 1 and John 19–20 is best understood in its unity by holding fast to the image of the scales themselves. The elements of the handwriting concern three issues—*counting of weights, placing something in the scales for weighing, and action based on the comparative weights*. In Wolters's chart above, level A has to do with a simple numerical counting, level B concerns the act of placing something in the scales, and level C concerns the subsequent comparison of the weights on the two sides of the scales and subsequent paying out because of that comparison. Reading the Prologue of John 1 from this vantage point, we have the act of counting to forty (level A), followed by a focus on the incarnation of the Word (level B), and then a comparison of this event with John the Baptizer and Moses (level C). Note also the proximity of the two θεκελ phrases in John 1:13, as well as the fact that the two *p-r-s* occurrences (1:14, 18) are widely disparate from each other and serve to frame the act of the Word's exegesis of the Father. This concentration of one theme (*th-k-l*) and disparate placement of another (*p-r-s*) is a literarily pictorial evocation of the scales. What do we see in John 19? Reading the burial in John 19 from this vantage point brings us first to a *counting* of liters (level A), then to a focus on the treatment of the crucified corpse of Jesus. *He placed himself on the cross as on a scale*, and his corpse is the (partial) result of that act (level B). The final anticipated component, that of *comparing and giving out* (level C) is presented, as we have seen, on the other side of the scale when Jesus encounters Mary Magdalene. In that conversation, we have the other "weight" (βαρος) against which the deposited corpse may be compared.

Incidentally, two other tales of Jewish life at a gentile court may help to craft John's text and give a particular slant to its interpretation. Joseph in Gen 41 is, like Daniel, offered a gold chain of authority. The name Joseph of Arimathea in John 19 may in part be a deliberate echo of the Aramaic figure like Joseph in Dan 5. The name Nicodemus of John 19 may in part be a deliberate echo of the three youths of 1 Esd 3–4 who engage in a contest issuing in a clear victory (νικη) of one of them (1 Esd 4:59) and the return of their δημος (people) from Babylonian exile (1 Esd 9:53).[27]

In conclusion, a Danielic reading of the cross and tomb in John offers us at least the following theological themes for our consideration:

- God's sovereignty
- The displacement of the world's prince
- Scribal assistance to a government's self-understanding
- Jewish wit concerning the power that shapes history toward freedom and shalom
- A reiteration that what has been handed down concerning Jesus is "according to the Scriptures"

And perhaps most poignantly,

- God's writing is done in Jesus' flesh lifted up.

Jesus, who loosens the bonds of his burial cloths (19:40; 20:6–7), is presaged by Daniel, who loosens the knots of riddles. And Jesus, who was sent by the Father (20:21), is an event anticipated by the hand that was *sent* to write in Dan 5.[28] Indeed, when Jesus asserts his sent-ness in John 20:21, he uses the same word as is used of the hand being sent in Dan 5:24 LXX (αποστελλ-). This stands in contradistinction to the sending (πεμπ-) of the disciples.[29] Remember that this discussion of sent-ness occurs in a scene in which Jesus is displaying his hands and side.

---

27. See Gruen, *Heritage and Hellenism*, 160–67.

28. Jordaens's *The Four Evangelists*, painted ca. 1620 and now in the Louvre, depicts John at the far right of the composition, both reading and writing. This is true only of that figure.

29. I also judge it likely that 8:1–11, a later addition to the gospel, which depicts Jesus

CONCLUSION

While John eschews the word "parable" (παραβολη), he presents Jesus in ways that mimic the content of several synoptic parables and one Danielic knot. The glorified Jesus continues in the Fourth Gospel to teach in parables, but it is his own parabolic nature that comprises the focus of this part of the evangelist's agenda.

---

writing on the ground with his finger (John 8:6), thereby shows in part its awareness of the Danielic theme of the "fingers as of a human hand" that write (Dan 5:5 LXX).

Chapter Five

Seeing

ALTHOUGH ONE MAY HEAR *but not see the similarity among Greek* basileia *(reign) and Hebrew* בָּשֹׂר *(bāsor, good news) and* בָּשָׂר *(bāsār, flesh), the evangelist expends considerable effort in depicting God's reign operative in the flesh of the parabolic Jesus. Employing the poetic device of Hellenistic puzzle poems, John physically arranges blocs of material to depict Jesus as king of Israel lifted up on the cross into glory. A related visual representation of the mother of Jesus is interwoven throughout John in tandem with the infancy narratives that proclaim Jesus as God with us, king of Israel, and Lord.*

SEEING THE REIGN OF GOD IN MARK AND JOHN

καὶ ἔλεγεν αὐτοῖς· Ὑμῖν τὸ μυστήριον δέδοται τῆς βασιλείας τοῦ θεοῦ· ἐκείνοις δὲ τοῖς ἔξω ἐν παραβολαῖς τὰ πάντα γίνεται, ¹²ἵνα βλέποντες βλέπωσι καὶ μὴ ἴδωσιν, καὶ ἀκούοντες ἀκούωσι καὶ μὴ συνιῶσιν, μήποτε ἐπιστρέψωσιν καὶ ἀφεθῇ αὐτοῖς.

And he said to them, "To you has been given the secret of the kingdom of God, but for those outside, everything comes in parables; ¹² in order that
'they may indeed look, but not perceive,
and may indeed listen, but not understand;
so that they may not turn again and be forgiven.'" (Mark 4:11–12)

Seeing

Markan commentators are agreed that at the heart of the mystery of the reign of God resides the person of Jesus. So, we look again at Mark 4:11 but with a lens trained on the underlined letters of *Iesous*:

καὶ ἔλεγεν αὐτοῖς· Ὑμῖν τὸ μυστήριον δέδοται τῆς βα<u>σι</u>λείας τ<u>οῦ</u> θεοῦ· ἐκείνοις δὲ τοῖς ἔξω ἐν παραβολαῖς τὰ πάντα γίνεται

We do the same with those verses dealing with the reign of God in John. Look again at the reign-of-God language in John 3:3, 5 for the name Jesus:

ἀπεκρίθη Ἰησοῦς καὶ εἶπεν αὐτῷ· Ἀμὴν ἀμὴν λέγω σο<u>ι</u>, ἐὰν μή τις γεννηθῇ ἄνωθεν, <u>οὐ</u> δύναται ἰδεῖν τὴν βα<u>σι</u>λείαν τοῦ θεοῦ.

ἀπεκρίθη Ἰησοῦς· Ἀμὴν ἀμὴν λέγω σο<u>ι</u>, ἐὰν μή τις γεννηθῇ ἐξ ὕδατ<u>ος</u> καὶ πνεύματος, οὐ δύναται εἰσελθεῖν εἰς τὴν βασιλείαν τοῦ θεοῦ.

Note that in two of the three verses, the letters of the name of Jesus intersect with βασιλεια, the word for reign.

The same phenomenon occurs in John 12:40, though the differences depicted by Mark and John in what happens to people in the presence of God's reign are formidable:[1]

Τετύφλωκεν αὐτῶν τοὺς ὀφθαλμοὺς καὶ ἐπώρωσεν αὐτῶν τὴν καρδίαν, ἵνα μὴ ἴδ<u>ω</u>σιν τοῖς ὀφθαλμοῖς καὶ νοήσωσιν τῇ καρδίᾳ καὶ στραφῶσιν, καὶ ἰάσομαι αὐτ<u>ούς</u>.

He has blinded their eyes
and hardened their heart,
so that they might not look with their eyes,
and understand with their heart and turn—
and I would heal them.

For all their differences, Mark's reign of God and John's reign of God bespeak *Jesus*.

ἵνα βλέποντες βλέπωσι καὶ μὴ ἴδ<u>ω</u>σιν, καὶ ἀκ<u>ού</u>οντες ἀκούωσι καὶ μὴ συνιῶσιν, μήποτε ἐπιστρέψωσιν καὶ ἀφεθῇ αὐτοῖς.

in order that

---

1. Two prominent text-critical studies of recent decades engage in highly refined analyses of the changes wrought by John 12:40. They opt for different primary influences to explain the changes. Appealing to a combination of the Hebrew text and LXX is the study of Menken, *Old Testament Quotations*, 99–122. Opting for the Old Greek is that of Schuchard, *Scripture Within Scripture*, 91–106.

Jesus and the Reign of God in John

> "They may indeed look, but not perceive,
> and may indeed listen, but not understand;
> so that they may not turn again and be forgiven." (Mark 4:12)

One way of understanding the difference is that John has retained the emphasis on Jesus as such, honoring the Markan base, but has placed it differently, among the anthropological effects of God's reign.

Yet more may be said. For within the Isaian base with which both Mark and John are in dialogue resides the figure of Sophia, who also mediates the reign of God. She appears in John 12:40 in these words:

Τετύφλωκεν αὐτῶν τοὺς ὀφθαλμοὺς καὶ ἐπώρωσεν αὐτῶν τὴν καρδίαν, ἵνα μὴ ἴδωσιν τοῖς ὀφθαλμοῖς καὶ νοήσωσιν τῇ καρδίᾳ καὶ στραφῶσιν, καὶ ἰάσομαι αὐτούς.

In John 12:38 (as we saw in ch. 2 of this study), the evangelist draws upon God's sovereignty as seen in the Servant Poem of Isa 53. In John 12:40, just noted, the Johannine author also draws upon the central figure of Sophia, whom we have come to know in her mediation of God's reign in the Wisdom of Solomon (and as explored in ch. 3 of this study).

While God's reign in the world is accompanied in the Johannine narrative by a blindness and hardness permitted by the sovereign will, the reign of God is also made available to disciples of Jesus/Sophia as the sovereign wills.

What then are the other terms and conditions of this recondite vision in the text? To that task we now turn.

This chapter examines John's rendition of the visual rationale for Jesus' parabolic actions. The rationale that concerns us says, "That looking, they may not see" (Mark 4:12a). Part of the challenge embodied in this chapter resides in attending to the placement, the physical position, of certain themes in the text in relation to one another. Here we think about seeing in John, what it is and accomplishes, and what it is not.

The descriptions of God's reign in John 3:3, 5 involves seeing and entering. I read that primarily in the context of the lifting up of Jesus. One sees the reign (βασιλεια, *basileia*) when the Word in flesh (בָּשָׂר, *bāsār*) is lifted under the banner proclaiming him king of the Jews. One enters the reign when one enters the empty tomb aware of Jesus, who has provided life-giving water from his side in John 19 and who will communicate Spirit in John 20. Jesus reigns in the flesh, *basileia* in *bāsār*, preeminently in his being *lifted up*. However, that is only part of what is to be seen regarding the parabolic Jesus' instantiation of God's reign.

Seeing

What is visible in John? John 8:28 asserts that, when Jesus is lifted up, they will know that I AM. To what extent does the look of the text assist in explicating that reality? What do we see?

I begin with this hors d'oeuvre: In John 12:20, some Greeks arrive and "want to see Jesus." Consider this event in dialogue with the inscription in the Second Temple:

ΜΗΘΕΝΑ ΑΛΛΟΓΕΝΗ ΕΙΣΠΟΡΕΥΕΣΘΑΙ ΕΝΤΟΣ ΤΟΥ ΠΕΡΙ ΤΟ ΙΕΡΟΝ ΤΡΥΦΑΚΤΟΥ ΚΑΙ ΠΕΡΙΒΟΛΟΥ· ΟΣ Δ᾽ ΑΝ ΛΗΦΘΗ, ΕΑΥΤΩΙ ΑΙΤΙΟΣ ΕΣΤΑΙ ΔΙΑ ΤΟ ΕΞΑΚΟΛΟΥΘΕΙΝ ΘΑΝΑΤΟΝ.

> Let no foreigner enter within the partition and enclosure around the sanctuary. Whoever is caught will himself be responsible for the death ensuing.[2]

This inscription was written on multiple signs, in both Greek and Latin, though no Latin examples are extant. And it was intended to warn non-Jews against approaching the inner courtyard and its proximity to the holy of holies.

It is no accident for John, precisely at this point, to discuss the following themes:

- Warning to the one who does not receive (*lambanein*; same root word as in the ΛΗΦΘΗ/caught in the... inscription) my words (John 12:48)
- Sign of Jesus' ensuing death in his "lifting up" saying (John 12:33). Its focus on Jesus lifted up, thereby drawing all to himself, is directly antithetical to the spirit of the temple signs.
- Casting out of the prince of this world (John 12:31)

Most commentators recognize that John is transforming temple symbolism in this Gospel. This motif is apparent as early as John 2:19, 21: "'Destroy this temple and I will raise it in three days.'... He spoke of the Temple of his body." A further note is in order about the interplay of these images and John's abstention from the word προσευχη. That word functioned to indicate not only prayer, but also a place of prayer.[3] It is probably accurate to

---

2. "Temple Warning Inscription"; author's translation. See also Bickerman, "Warning Inscriptions."

3. For Ptolemaic Egypt, see *NewDocs* 201.

see the evangelist's diction promoting Jesus as the primary locus in whom the divine-human conversation occurs. And among those to whom that offer of Jesus-as-place is addressed are both those deprived of temple but also those ensconced in the houses of prayer.

Now, how important is seeing in John?

The Relative Importance of Seeing (John 4, 13–21)

The sweep of John 4 is an epitome of "the hour" of chapters 13–21. From the perfect noontime believer's seeing to the slightly deficient 1 PM search for signs, believing in which a father's son gets new life, this couplet prepares us for "Blessed those who do not see but who believe" (John 20:29).

Having said that, however, I am about to make a case that John exhibits a concentrated visual focus on the act of Jesus lifted up. I would suggest that this is in part derived from Gal 3:1 in which Paul declaims about his having displayed Christ crucified before your very eyes. Paul's cruciform sensibility is a driving force in his thought, as at Phil 2:8 where he adds the phrase "even death on a cross" to a hymn otherwise exhibiting traits of Sophia's descent into the world.[4] What does this lifting up look like in John? It is the cross, but not just the cross.

New Creation and Reconciliation (2 Cor 5) Visible in John 19:16—20:18

Jesus is lifted up on the cross, into the Father's glory, from "handed over" to "Mary Magdalene went and told." Read the following chart as three vertical columns:

	Pilate (19:31)	
Scripture tunic (19:24)	Scripture bone (19:36)	Scripture rise from dead (20:9)
	Pilate (19:38)	

---

4. For further reading on this Pauline theme, see Gorman, *Cruciformity*.

Seeing

This alignment seems to be intentional. Follow the letter prompts in the following two charts:

	C 19:31–33	
A 19:20–22		E 20:4
B 19:25–27		F 20:15
	D 19:38–42	

A–C	plans of the Jews	E–C	legs/running
B–D	public/private witness	F–D	garden(er)

And the entire composition is framed:

G 19:16–19		I 20:1–2
H 19:28–30		J 20:18

G–H		I–J	
handed over		Mary Magdalene went and told	

There are some precedents for this painting with words in the so-called *technopaigneia* (puzzle poems) of Hellenism. These poems discuss but also portray inter alia the wings of a bird in flight, an axe, an egg, altars, and shepherds' pipes.[5] The reader will perhaps recognize that the *techn-* component of *technopaigneia* is also present in the τεχνιτις (craftsperson) used of Sophia in Wis 8:6. (See the discussion in ch. 3 of this study, "Sophia.")

THE CROSS THROUGHOUT JOHN?

This lifting up occurs, according to John J. Gerhard, throughout John.[6] Gerhard's hypothesis is that a five-point figure is present in five major sections of the Gospel. The sections of the text as identified by Gerhard are 1:19—4:3; 4:4—6:15; [6:16–21]; 6:22—12:11; 13:1—17:26; 12:12—21:25. Such a configuration is congruent with the five occurrences of υψοω (lifted up) in the text (although there are six such units, if one also counts 6:16–21). Each large section contains a smaller groups of phrases that display similarities to one another, and they display this pattern:

$$1-3 \quad 1-5 \quad 2-4$$
$$2-5 \quad 3-4$$

That pattern is writ large when three of the large sections are lined up horizontally and two sections placed under them, forming a figure with arms extended and two legs under the head. The point of this word puzzle is to depict not only at text's end but throughout the text the ongoing divine self-revelation in Jesus lifted up.

Why this five-point configuration? I would read the occurrences of δοξαζ- (glorify) as offering one avenue of understanding. How so? We know from John 8:28 that Jesus declared, "When you have lifted up the Son of Man, then you will know that I AM." δοξαζ- occurs in a cluster of five occurrences within the hour, in John 13:31 (2x) and 13:32 (3x) (focused on love) and again in John 17:1 (2x), 4, 5, and 10 (focused on the Son and Father and immediately preceding that chapter's focus on the name). To the extent that the five occurrences limn the five wounds (in feet, hands, and side), they also function at the same time as reminder of the five-letter word ονομα (name). Jesus lifted up is a revelation of God who is Love.[7]

5. Trypanis, "Technopaigneia." See also Fowler, *Hellenistic Poetry*, 313.
6. Gerhard, *Miraculous Parallelisms of John*.
7. This is congruent with the thesis thoroughly explored for the entire text by Moloney, *Love in John*, esp. 73–82.

Seeing

More detailed sketches of the arrangements in John are available. John Paul Heil has given us a close reading of John 18–21. He identifies five major units within these chapters. They are John 18:1–27; 18:28—19:11; 19:12–42; 20:1–31; 21:1–25. Within each of the first four, he suggests that there are "six alternating scenes that function together as a dynamic progression of four narrative intercalations or sandwiches while the fifth section contains three scenes that function as one sandwich."[8] What he intends with this sandwich image may be seen in the following chart:

1. 18:1–14: A1 (18:1–9)—B1 (18:10–11)—A2 (18:12–14)
2. 18:10–18: B1 (18:10–11)—A2 (18:12–14)—B2 (18:15–18)
3. 18:12–24: A2 (18:12–14)—B2 (18:15–18)—A3 (18:19–24)
4. 18:15–27: B2 (18:15–18)—A3 (18:19–24)—B3 (18:25–27)

His observations about the segments and their analogies are carefully and closely argued.

I would add that the inner-Johannine dialogue that he traces is complemented by the dialogue carried on by these chapters with Gen 3, especially verses 1–7, detailing the rupture of the relationship between Yhwh and the human couple.

Gen 3		John 18–21
3:1–3 Did he say?		18:1–27 Asked about his teaching (18:18–19)
3:4–5, 7	Die, know good and evil	18:28—19:11 (18:30–32; 19:4)
3:6	See, take (eat)	19:12–42 (19:14, 16)
3:4–5	Eyes opened, he ... she	20:18
3:6–7	Naked, know, eat	21:1–25 (21:7, 12)[9]

SEEING JESUS LIFTED UP IN JOHN'S CHOICE OF PSALMS

Here we attend to some of the psalms quoted by John and inquire as to their value in the literary seeing of Jesus.

Appreciating this first point requires a grasp of the five collections of prayers within the Psalter:

8. Heil, *Blood and Water*, 4.
9. See also Schaser, "Inverting Eden."

Book	Psalms
1	1–41
2	42–72
3	73–89
4	90–106
5	107–50

In John 1–12, the evangelist quotes, within a range of approximately fifty psalms, three psalms not exceeding the Psalter's *third* book. *Set 1* of John's quoted psalms involves Pss 69, 78, and 82, plus 118. They are cited in emerging canonical order. *Set 2*, in John 13–21, has John quoting within a range of about twenty psalms, not exceeding the Psalter's *second* book. They are Pss 41, 35/69, 22, and 34. They are quoted out of sync with the emerging canonical order. John's use of Ps 69 occurs in the two sets of psalms as just described, quoting the zeal (John 2:17) and hatred (John 15:25) of Ps 69.

I would suggest that the psalms quoted track the 3–2 configuration in John's lifted-up schema:

.		.		.	John 1–12 quotes three psalms within first three books of Psalter
		.		.	John 13–21 quotes psalms within first two books of Psalter

In set 1, the first letter of three of the four quoted is ה (Pss 69, 78, 118). In set 2, the first letter of three of the four quoted is א (Pss 41, 22, 34). הא as a word means "behold." Greek *idou* (behold) occurs five times throughout John. In set 2, the total complement of the first letters yields רְאָה, which as a word means "see."

It seems plausible to assert that the visual picture of Jesus lifted up has played a role in the choice of psalms quoted. Part of the psalms' function is to support the agenda of seeing Jesus.

SEEING

DESCENT AND ASCENT

We have then a five-part portrait of Jesus lifted up.[10] But understanding the portraiture of the evangelist is not complete until one has seen, interwoven with the figure of Christ crucified, the schema of Jesus glorified. The figure below that also unifies the text involves a series of correspondences between the beginning and ending chapters, as well as between the middle chapters. It begins with visible descent from Jerusalem. The definitive upward movement begins with his raised eyes, arrest, and cross, beginning in chapter 17.

					GOSPEL OF JOHN					
1–2					New creation					21
	3				Spirit				20	
		4			Woman—royal official—son			19		
			5		Jesus' actions and teachings disputed		18			
				6	Division and unity of disciples	17				
				7	To Jerusalem and Greeks	12				
				8	Commandment(s)—(new)	13				
				9	(Dis)place(ment)	14				
				10	Two metaphors and opposition	15				
				11	Sorrow/joy World goes after Jesus Jesus' conquest of world	16				

∼

The correspondence between chs. 1–6 and 17–21 is patent, as is the correspondence between chs. 7–11 and 12–16. The "range" of 1–6 and 17–21, on the outer perimeters of the text, sits atop and is greater than the range of 7–11 and 12–16 between them. The repeated downward vertical movement repeated in chapters 7–11 and 12–16 *complements* the down and upward movement happening within chapters 1–6 and 17–21. The top segment's two phalanges are closest together at chapters 6 and 17, and furthest apart

---

10. The schema reflects in part the structure of Lamentations, whose five parts consist of chapters containing, respectively, twenty-two, twenty-two, sixty-six, twenty-two, and twenty-two verses. Lamentations is wholly taken up with the city of Jerusalem. John is also persistently attentive to Jerusalem, placing Jesus there, unlike the Synoptic Gospels, on three separate occasions.

at chapters 1 and 21.[11] As a whole, this is a formal portrait of a standing figure with arms upraised. And in that regard, it mimics the portrait of Luke's risen Jesus imparting his blessing in Luke 24:50. This figure is superimposed on the 3–2 cross, already examined, that also structures the entire text.[12]

Moreover, that down and upward sweep of chapters 1–6 and 17–21 supplies the visual equivalent of a *parabola*. Remember that in geometry, a parabola consists of a plane curve trajectory whose coordinates are equidistant from a shared point of reference. In chapter 4 of this study, I have pointed out ways in which John seems to have transmuted parables from the synoptic tradition. Here I simply point out the visual parabolic trajectory in which those materials are set.[13]

The dialogue between themes on either side of the figure is not limited to those listed above. For example, authority in John 5:27 finds its narrative partner in the clear indication in John 18 that Jesus is handing himself over at the event that would otherwise be termed an arrest.[14] Truth in John 8:32, 40, 44–46 finds its narrative partner in John 13:38. Peter has just claimed that he will follow Jesus even at the cost of laying down his life. Jesus simply asks about that claim and offers the accurate counterclaim that his fidelity won't last the night.

We have then a text containing a schematic reminder of Jesus lifted up, on the cross and into the glory of the Father. But I would suggest a caveat from the perspective of systematic theology about this sketch of Jesus-lifted up. The head of the sketch is not visible. One might read the figure as

11. For an analysis of (new) creation as bookending John, see Brown, "Creation's Renewal in John."

12. This schematic portrait of Jesus lifted up functions as a *symbol* of Jesus' presence to the community. John 20–21 in particular embody several aspects of the word *symbolon* in Greek literature: something that allows inference, marks on the body, a pledge or token of more to come, even an agreement between parties. See the insightful exploration by Schneiders, "Symbolism in Fourth Gospel."

13. This is not said to deny John's arrangement of some parabolic materials in other places. For instance, the sayings about walking in the light (11:9–10; 12:35) do not occur on the same horizontal level as those listed in the chart above. Yet even this example makes the reader jump from ch. 11 below to ch. 12 above it, thus emphasizing the unity between the two sides of the trope. See the still-useful discussion by Sturch, "Jeremias and John."

14. The word for authority (εξουσια) is intercalated in the uniquely Johannine 18:20:
ἀπεκρίθη αὐτῷ Ἰησοῦς· Ἐγὼ παρρησίᾳ λελάληκα τῷ κόσμῳ· ἐγὼ πάντοτε ἐδίδαξα ἐν συναγωγῇ καὶ ἐν τῷ ἱερῷ, ὅπου πάντες οἱ Ἰουδαῖοι συνέρχονται, καὶ ἐν κρυπτῷ ἐλάλησα οὐδέν·

SEEING

a portrait of Jesus in the act of ascending to the Father, much as we have in John 20. But that would curtail our grasp of the early church's widespread awareness that Jesus in his full humanity has *already* been subsumed into the glory of God. Jesus lifted up in this sketch is only properly appreciated when the invisible head is understood as visual *metonym*, the part referring to the wholly human Jesus reigning in glory and expected to come again. The visible figure with arms upraised is then the saving effect currently wrought by the fully glorified Jesus. Such a sensibility respects our inability at present to see all dimensions of the reality of Jesus. And such a sensibility respects the future role of Jesus as coming judge and leaves open the precariousness of present participation in the body of Christ, still subject, like their Master, to persecution and death.[15]

JESUS LIFTED UP IN JOHN: THE "MARIAN" DIMENSION

The same outline of Jesus lifted up, which suggests Jesus standing/risen (ἀνεστη) with arms upraised and head invisible to the world, is patient of an extended interpretation that places the mother of Jesus to the fore. In what follows, I list those aspects of both the Matthean and Lukan infancy narratives that permeate the Johannine text. By lifting the *legs* and joining them to the *hands*, the sketch resembles the letter *M*.

				John					
	1–2							21	
7		3					20		12
8			4			19			13
9				5		18			14
10				6	17				15
11									16

In a text that never mentions the name Mariam for the mother of Jesus, her *m* structures the text from start to finish. The geography at the top of the following configuration concerns going to Jerusalem and leaving Jerusalem. That is, chapter 7 is about going to Jerusalem, and chapter 1 to which it is adjacent in this configuration has people coming down from

---

15. Farrow, *Ascension and Ecclesia*, 272–73. There is a stone carving of the Ascension congenial with this interpretation in the Church of Santo Domingo de Silos in Spain.

Jerusalem. After Jesus has manifested himself in Jerusalem in chapter 20, the scene proceeds to Galilee in chapter 21 (i.e., Jesus proceeds from Jerusalem), and chapter 12 is about going to Jerusalem. Even the theme of *division and unity* (John 6 and 17) occurs precisely at the center of the *M*, which is both the point of division between the two halves of the *M* and the beginning of the other half of the one letter. Seen from this vantage point, this is theologically historicized poetic prose, which we might already have known from the Prologue. In what immediately follows, we examine the *arms* in the shape of a *v* in the center of the letter *M* against the backdrop of Marian material in Matt 1–4 and Luke 1–4.

The Johannine chapter numbers below and centrally listed themes in plain type refer to the chapters of the Fourth Gospel. The intercalated themes in **bold** refer to Matt 1–4 on the left and to Luke 1–4 on the right. So, for example, the first level in what follows reads, "The *new creation* of John 1–2 and 21 is partly informed by infancy narrative themes in Matthew *gen* (begat) and Luke *archē* (from the beginning)."

	John	
John 1–2	New creation	John 21
Matt 1–2 **Matt 1:1**	*Gen, archē*	**Luke 1:21–22** **Luke 1:2**

∼

John 3	Spirit	John 20
Conceived in Spirit **(Matt 1:20)**		**Spirit will overshadow you** **(Luke 1:35)**

∼

Seeing

John 4	Woman—royal official—son, to home	John 19
Mary—Herod—son (Matt 2:7-12)		Mary blessed among women (Luke 1:42), Quirinius—son (Luke 2:12)
House (Matt 2:12)		To home (Luke 2:20)

∼

John 5	Name given	John 18
Matt 1:21		Luke 1:31

∼

John 6	Divided and one	John 17
	Divided	
Magoi, proclaiming Jesus king, go home (east) (Matt 2:12)		Parents of Jesus walk ahead without the youth (Luke 2:43)
Joseph/Mary, knowing Jesus as conceived in Holy Spirit, go to Nazareth (north) (Matt 2:23)		
	One	
Angels, Jewish family, *magoi* (Matt 1-2)		Jewish family, angels, shepherds, temple personnel, Father (Luke 1-2)

This complex in John 6 and 17 draws from the infancy narratives of Matthew and Luke, sources that begin in division of opinion *about* Jesus, move to separation *from* Jesus, and climax in unity *with* Jesus Christ. The journey of the Matthean *magoi* out of country (to the east) and the journey of the family up country (to the north) engrave the movements necessary to see the *M* that John does: in the Johannine sketch of Jesus lifted up, the *legs* are brought *up* to join the *hands*, thus creating the shape of the letter *M*.

Themes shared at the juncture of arm and leg, i.e., at John 1, 2, and 7, include:

(< Matt 1–2)

Galilee/Jerusalem	
Mosaic law	
Spirit	

Themes shared at the juncture of arm and leg at John 12 and 21 include:

(< Luke 1–2)

	Prophecy and age
	Luke 2:33–36

Here we continue to compare the material in the *legs* with one another, and do so against the backdrop of Marian material in the infancy narratives of Matt 1–2 and Luke 1–2:

John 7	In Jerusalem, seeking Jesus	John 12
Searching eastern *magoi* to Jerusalem (Matt 2:1)		Mary and Joseph in Jerusalem (Luke 2:48)

∼

John 8	Commandment(s)—new	John 13
Not wanting to put her away . . . Take Mary your wife, take the child and his mother (Matt 1:20; 2:20)		No kin by name of John . . . according to the command (Luke 1:61, 63)

∼

John 9	(Dis)place(ment)	John 14
Travel to Egypt (Matt 2:13)		**Go to census** (Luke 2:2-3)

∼

John 10	Development of two metaphors— gate, shepherd; vine, gardener— and opposition	John 15
King *and* Nazarean < *nzr*, crown (Matt 2:2, 23)		**Light of revelation to the gentiles *and* glory to your people Israel** (Luke 2:32)
Order to slay Bethlehem's infants (Matt 2:16)		**A sign opposed** (Luke 2:34)

∼

John 11	Sorrow/joy World goes after Jesus Jesus' conquest of world	John 16
Rachel's cry—King Herod fails to kill the king of the Jews (Matt 2:18)		**Tidings of great joy**—(a riff on imperial propaganda)—**to all the people** (Luke 2:10) **Why have you been such a pain to us?** (Luke 2:48)

What we have in this Marian dimension of John's Jesus confirms our previous observation about the proximate ecclesiological dimension in the sketch of Jesus lifted up. The Johannine tradition at the point of this text's creation announces the formative role exercised by the church's preeminent disciple in mediating Jesus to the world; announces that Jesus is Word of the Father, yes, but also his mother's Son.

These very dimensions, discipleship and Mary as ideal disciple, are emphases characteristic of Matthew and Luke. And the Fourth Gospel subtly gestures toward each of these evangelists. John 6:45 (μαθων) and 7:15 (μεμαθηκως) concentrate that learning/discipleship (μαθετε/μαθητης) in the verbal forms chosen and gesture toward Matthaios (Matthew). John 13:10 rings changes on the tradition, pointing toward Loukas.

> λέγει αὐτῷ ὁ Ἰησοῦς· Ὁ λε<u>λ</u>ουμένος <u>οὐκ</u> ἔχει χρείαν εἰ μὴ τοὺς πό<u>δας</u> νίψασθαι, ἀλλ' ἔστιν καθαρὸς ὅλος· καὶ ὑμεῖς καθαροί ἐστε, ἀλλ' οὐχὶ πάντες.

John changes his preferred verb of washing from *nipso* to *louo* in a sentence that proceeds to mention *ouk* and *podas*: *Loukas*.

Matthew on the left of the *M*, Luke on the right.

SEEING THE REIGN OF GOD IN JOHN 17

There is another manifestation of the reign of God inherent in the symmetries of John 6 and 17, concerning the disciples' receiving of Jesus (Jesus' words) and the divine perfection revealed thereby.

In John 6:15, we have Jesus literally distancing himself from the type of kingship (βασιλεια) offered by the crowds. Soon thereafter, they want to take (λαβειν) him who walks on water into the boat (6:21). In John 17:8, we see the intercalation of the letters of βασιλεια (reign) amid the disciple's receiving ελαβον the words of Jesus.

> ὅτι τὰ ῥήματα ἃ ἔδωκάς μοι δέδωκα αὐτοῖς, καὶ αὐτοὶ ἔλαβον κ<u>αὶ</u> ἔγνω<u>σα</u>ν ἀληθῶς ὅτ<u>ι</u> παρὰ σοῦ ἐξῆλθον, καὶ <u>ἐπίστευσαν</u> ὅτι σύ με ἀπέστειλας.

In that same verse Jesus makes explicit mention of receiving.

> ὅτι τὰ ῥήματα ἃ ἔδωκάς μοι δέδωκα αὐτοῖς, καὶ αὐτοὶ <u>ἔλαβον</u> καὶ ἔγνωσαν ἀληθῶς ὅτι παρὰ σοῦ ἐξῆλθον, καὶ ἐπίστευσαν ὅτι σύ με ἀπέστειλας.

> Because the words that you have given me I gave them, and they *received* and know truly that I have come from you, and they believe that you sent me.

The perfection on offer in chapter 17 is signaled in part by the τελ- root in verse 23.

> I in them and you in me, that they may be *perfected* as one.

Seeing

Both here in 17:23 and in 17:8, the verb of sending, αποστειλας, limns the *tel-* root concerning perfection, completion.

At issue is the reign of God. The shape of *theta* (θ), the first letter of θεος (God) (John 17:3) is a circle divided at the middle, which provides a visual context for understanding the scope of the chapter's variegated language. We might well imagine a circle on whose circumference are situated the letters Π for Πατηρ (Father) and Δ for δοξα (glory), with Υ for Υιος (Son) visible along the diameter of the circle.

If Father and Son are explicit here, perhaps glory implicitly gestures toward Spirit (who had not yet been given by ch. 17). That is not to deny that glory is shared by Father and Son. The letters πνευμα (Spirit) are intercalated in the very verse speaking of the primordial gift of glory from Father to Son.

> πάτερ, ὃ δέδωκάς μοι, θέλω ἵνα ὅπου εἰμὶ ἐγὼ κἀκεῖνοι ὦσιν μετ' ἐμοῦ, ἵνα θεωρῶσιν τὴν δόξαν τὴν ἐμὴν ἣν δέδωκάς μοι, ὅτι ἠγάπησάς με πρὸ καταβολῆς κόσμου.
>
> Father, [regarding] what you gave me, I want that where I am, they may be with me, that they may see my glory which you gave me because you loved me, before the creation of the cosmos. (John 17:24)

Glory is cited eight times; Father six times; Son twice, with a dozen instances of self-reference by Jesus, in εγω (*ego*, I).

I think that the eight glory references also concern the quaternity of the name Yhwh. The six Father references concern rungs of ascent made by the Son from the median toward the circumference of the circle, preeminently by the historically raised pole joining Father references in north and south. Joining the Father references in the northeast and west, and then the Father references in the east and southwest, establishes those rungs of the ladder. The two Son references bespeak Jesus' activity commanded by the Father and animated in the Spirit. And the sum of two Son references and twelve εγω statements equals fourteen. The resultant total picture is the relationship of the circle to its diameter, what today we name as the value of pi, 3.14. . . . The Arabic system of computation was not then available, but the ratio 22/7 was used with sufficient care that building was possible using line and circle. The diction of the seventeenth chapter is also replete with words bearing the initial letter delta, which in majuscule lettering is three sided.

A summary of the numerical dynamics in the diction of John 17 yields a worthwhile result:

Frequency of Occurrence	Word
2	Ὑιος (Son)
12	Εγω (I)
6	Πατηρ (Father)
8	Δοξα (glory)
28	

Twenty-eight is a so-called perfect number. That is, it is the sum of the preceding whole integers that divide evenly into twenty-eight. They are one, two, four, seven, and fourteen. The ideological value of considering the kingdom's perfection rests on the authority (17:2), life (17:3), and truth (17:17) revealed thereby, presented in this thought experiment focused on the circular form having neither beginning nor end.

ΜΥΕΩ

What do we see when we consider all three of these macro-dynamics together? That is, what may be seen within the context of the five-point lifting up, the standing figure with arms upraised, and the letter *M*?

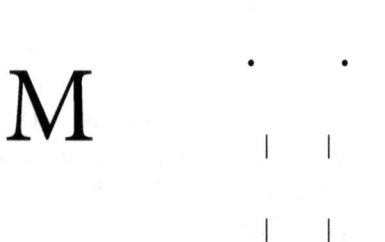

We see *M*, the shape of components of the first letter of the verb μυεω, meaning "to initiate into mysteries/teach." And we see the shape of the uncial letter upsilon, the second letter of the verb ΜΥΕΩ.

Together, these advert to one of the functions of the text, to lead the addressees to an ever-deepening encounter with the *mystery of Christ among us*. True, the term μυστηριον does not occur in John. However, as used in the Greco-Roman milieu in which the text was crafted, μυστηριον included an appreciation of silence. One might see the evangelist emphasizing the notion that what happens through God in Christ escapes full articulation in words.

PUSHING THINGS UP TO THEIR FIRST PRINCIPLES

The evangelist's reaching into the infancy narratives is arguably congruent with the principle stated in John 6:12, "that nothing be lost." Commentators have also regularly referred to the opening of John in which the language of Gen 1 is present as another kind of retrieval, namely, reaching up to the ἀρχη, the very beginning of creation, God the First Principle.

Let us consider the infancy narratives themselves as reaching up to a first principle as well, one pertinent to the reign of God that informs this study. Consider also some of the first consonants of Mark 1:15, Jesus' inaugural announcement of the reign of God, as a principle to which both Matthew and Luke looked to inform their infancy narratives. The Greek of Mark 1:15 reads:

> καὶ λέγων ὅτι Πεπλήρωται ὁ καιρὸς καὶ ἤγγικεν ἡ βασιλεία τοῦ θεοῦ· μετανοεῖτε καὶ πιστεύετε ἐν τῷ εὐαγγελίῳ.

Matthew is widely recognized as engaging in midrash. In fact, one may readily trace the only four occurrences of *haggadah* in the Hebrew Bible as assisting in shaping themes in Matt 1 and 2.[16] Within that framework, two terms in Mark 1:15, *kairos* and *basileia*, lend their first letters, *k* and *b*, to a prominent theme in Matt 2, that of the *k-k-b*, the star followed by the *magoi*. The first letters of Mark 1:15's λέγων καιρὸς βασιλεία μετανοεῖτε stand out in the Greek of Matt 4:17, though in a different order:

> Ἀπὸ τότε ἤρξατο ὁ Ἰησοῦς κηρύσσειν καὶ λέγειν· Μετανοεῖτε, ἤγγικεν γὰρ ἡ βασιλεία τῶν οὐρανῶν.

Following the Matthean letters *b-m-l-k* right to left, as one reads Hebrew, we have a stylistic support for the content of the verse in that the reader is invited to an experience of *b-m-l-k*. That is, one is being asked to

---

16. Haggadah—A bunch of hyssop in context of "salvation in a house" (Exod 12:22); a unit of militia in context of "burial in Bethlehem" (2 Sam 2:25); undo heavy burdens in context of the sins of house of Jacob (Isa 58:6); strata on the "earth" in context of a discussion of the "heavens" and the name of the Lord (Amos 9:6).

consider anew the change of mind involved in responding to Jesus' speaking and preaching; it involves a focus on the king.

I would also point to *metanoeite*, *kairos*, and *basileia* in Mark 1:15 as lending their first letters, *m-k-b*, to the shaping of Luke's Benedictus and Magnificat in the spirit of the Maccabean texts. Well over a half century ago, Paul Winter argued for a Maccabean substratum to the two Lukan hymns.[17] What we have just seen can function as an additional rationale for Winter's thesis.

One might also consider the letters *k-p-l* in καιρος, πεπληρωται, λεγων as gesturing toward Hebrew *k-p-l* (double). Matthew 3:2 and 4:17 place identical and brief announcements in the mouths of John the Baptist and Jesus:

> Repent, for the kingdom of heaven has drawn near.

The broad-stroke similarities between John the Baptist and Jesus in Luke 1–2 may be seen as that evangelist's exploration of the *k-p-l* component in Mark 1:15, though in his case the *Parallel Lives* of Plutarch offers a Greek language parallel as well.

Even as John moves back beyond children to the issue of birth and ultimately to the First Principle (αρχη), so too Matthew and Luke's infancy narratives look to combinations of the first letters in the inaugural announcement of the reign of God in Mark 1:15. Each one of them in various ways is pushing things up to their first principles.

---

17. Winter, "Magnificat and Benedictus."

Bibliography

Adamson, Peter. *Philosophy in the Hellenistic and Roman Worlds.* Vol. 2 of *A History of Philosophy Without Any Gaps.* Oxford: Oxford University Press, 2015.
Anderson, Bernhard W. *Understanding the Old Testament.* 3rd ed. Englewood, NJ: Prentice Hall, 1975.
Anderson, Paul N. *The Riddles of the Fourth Gospel: An Introduction to John.* Minneapolis: Fortress, 2011.
Ando, Clifford. *Law, Language, and Empire in the Roman Tradition.* Empire and After. Philadelphia: University of Pennsylvania Press, 2011.
Aratus. *Phenomena.* Edited by Douglas Kidd. CCTC. Cambridge: Cambridge University Press, 1997.
Arendt, Hannah. "What Is Authority?" In *The Portable Hannah Arendt*, edited by Peter Baehr, 462–507. Penguin Classics. New York: Penguin, 2000.
———. *The Portable Hannah Arendt.* Edited by Peter Baehr. Penguin Classics. New York: Penguin, 2000.
Aristotle. *Metaphysics.* Translated by Hugh Tredennick. Vol. 1. LCL 271. Cambridge, MA: Harvard University Press, 1933.
Attridge, Harold W. "Trinitarian Theology and the Fourth Gospel." In *The Bible and Early Trinitarian Theology*, edited by Christopher A. Beeley and Mark E. Weedman, 71–83. Washington, DC: Catholic University of America Press, 2018.
Bagnall, Roger S., et al., eds. *The Encyclopedia of Ancient History.* 13 vols. Oxford, Wiley-Blackwell, 2012.
Barrett, C. K. *The Gospel According to St. John: An Introduction with Commentary and Notes on the Greek Text.* 2nd ed. Philadelphia: Westminster, 1978.
Beaulieu, Stéphane. *"Behold My Servant": An Exegetical and Theological Study of the Identity and Role of the Servant in Isaiah 42:1–9.* Piscataway, NJ: Gorgias, 2015.
Berlin, Adele, and Marc Zvi Brettler, eds. *The Jewish Study Bible.* 2nd ed. Oxford: Jewish Publication Society, 2014.
Bickerman, Elias J. "The Warning Inscriptions of Herod's Temple." In *Studies in Jewish and Christian History*, 1:483–96. Ancient Judaism and Early Christianity 68. Leiden: Brill, 2007.
Blenkinsopp, Joseph. *Isaiah 40–55: A New Translation with Introduction and Commentary.* AB 19a. New York: Doubleday, 2000. 184–86.

Bibliography

Breyer, Stephen. *Reading the Constitution: Why I Chose Pragmatism, Not Textualism.* New York: Simon and Schuster, 2024.

Brown, Jeannine K. "Creation's Renewal in the Gospel of John." *CBQ* 72 (2010) 275–90.

Caragounis, Chrys C., ed. *The Development of Greek and the New Testament: Morphology, Syntax, Phonology, and Textual Transmission.* Grand Rapids: Baker Academic, 2004.

———. "The Kingdom of God: Common and Distinct Elements Between John and the Synoptics." In *Jesus in Johannine Tradition*, edited by Robert T. Fortna and Tom Thatcher, 125–34. Louisville, KY: Westminster John Knox, 2001.

Carter, Warren. *John and Empire: Initial Explorations.* New York: Clark, 2008.

———. *John: Storyteller, Interpreter, Evangelist.* Peabody, MA: Hendrickson, 2006.

Cassin, Barbara. "Sophists." Translated by Elizabeth Rawlings and Jeannine Pucci. In *Greek Thought: A Guide to Classical Knowledge*, edited by Jacques Brunschwig and Geoffrey E. R. Lloyd, translated under direction of Catherine Porter, 957–76. Harvard University Press Reference Library. Cambridge, MA: Belknap, 2000.

Chaniotis, A. M. "Hermogenes (Aphrodisias), Posthumous Honorific Decree." SEG 54 (2004) 359–60.

Charles, R. H. *A Critical and Exegetical Commentary on the Book of Daniel.* Repr., Eugene, OR: Wipf & Stock, 2006.

Chennattu, Rekha M. *Johannine Discipleship as a Covenant Relationship.* Peabody, MA: Hendrickson, 2006.

Collins, John J. *Jewish Wisdom in the Hellenistic Age.* OTL. Louisville, KY: Westminster John Knox, 1997.

Coloe, Mary L. *John 1–10.* Edited by Barbara E. Reid. Wisdom Commentary. Collegeville, MN: Liturgical, 2021.

———. *John 11–21.* Edited by Barbara E. Reid. Wisdom Commentary. Collegeville, MN: Liturgical, 2021.

Copleston, Frederick. *A History of Philosophy.* 9 vols. New York: Doubleday/Image, 1993.

Cotton, Hannah M., et al., eds. *Jerusalem.* Vol. 1 of *Corpus Inscriptionum Iudaeae/Palaestinae.* Berlin: de Gruyter, 2010.

Couturier, Guy P. "Jeremiah." In *The New Jerome Biblical Commentary*, edited by Raymond E. Brown et al., Article 18:265–97. Englewood Cliffs, NJ: Prentice, 1990.

Culpepper, R. Alan. "Jesus' Sayings in the Johannine Discourses: A Proposal." In *Glimpses of Jesus Through the Johannine Lens*, edited by Paul N. Anderson et al., 353–82. Vol. 3 of *John, Jesus, and History.* ECL. Atlanta: SBL, 2016.

Cuneiform Commentaries Project. http://ccp.yale.edu.

Danker, Frederick W. *Multipurpose Tools for Bible Study.* Rev. ed. Minneapolis: Fortress, 1993.

Davies, W. D., and Dale C. Allison Jr. *The Gospel According to Saint Matthew.* 3 vols. Edinburgh: Clark, 1991.

Delebecque, E. "Autour de verbe *eimi*, 'je suis' dans le quatrième évangile." *RThom* 86 (1986) 83–89.

Digital Dead Sea Scrolls, The. http://dss.collections.imj.org.il.

DiLella, Alexander. "Fear of the Lord and Belief and Hope in the Lord amid Trials: Sirach 2:1–18." In *Wisdom, You Are My Sister: Studies in Honor of Roland E. Murphy, O. Carm. on the Occasion of His Eightieth Birthday*, edited by Michael L. Barré, 188–204. CBQMS 29. Washington, DC: Catholic Biblical Association, 1997.

Donahue, John R. *The Gospel in Parable: Metaphor, Narrative, and Theology in the Synoptic Gospels.* Philadelphia: Fortress, 1988.

Bibliography

Donfried, Karl P. "The Allegory of the Ten Virgins as a Summary of Matthean Theology." *JBL* 93 (1974) 415-29.

Duckworth, George E. *Patterns and Proportions in Vergil's "Aeneid": A Study in Mathematical Composition.* Ann Arbor: University of Michigan, 1962.

Farrow, Douglas. *Ascension and Ecclesia: On the Significance of the Doctrine of the Ascension for Ecclesiology and Christian Cosmology.* Grand Rapids: Eerdmans, 1999.

Fowler, Barbara Hughes. *Hellenistic Poetry.* Madison: University of Wisconsin, 1990.

Funk, Robert W., et al. *The Five Gospels: The Search for the Authentic Words of Jesus.* New York: Macmillan, 1993.

Gaertringen, Friedrich Hiller von. *Inschriften von Priene.* Berlin: Reimer, 1906.

Gerhard, John J. *The Miraculous Parallelisms of John: A Golden Mold of Symmetric Patterns.* 2nd ed. Tangerine, FL: Orlando Truth, 2008.

Glicksman, Andrew T. *Wisdom of Solomon 10: A Jewish Hellenistic Reinterpretation of Early Israelite History as Seen Through Sapiential Lenses.* DCLS. Berlin: de Gruyter, 2011.

Gooch, Paul W. *Reflections on Jesus and Socrates: Word and Silence.* New Haven, CT: Yale, 1996.

Gorman, Michael J. *Cruciformity: Paul's Narrative Spirituality of the Cross.* Grand Rapids: Eerdmans, 2001.

Greene, William Chase. *Moira: Fate, Good & Evil in Greek Thought.* New York: Harper, 1944.

Gruen, Erich S. *Heritage and Hellenism: The Reinvention of Jewish Tradition.* Hellenistic Culture and Society. Berkeley: University of California, 1998.

Heil, John Paul. *Blood and Water: The Death and Resurrection of Jesus in John 18-21.* CBQMS 27. Washington, DC: Catholic Biblical Association of America, 1995.

Howatson, M. C. "Plato." In *The Oxford Companion to Classical Literature*, 442-44. 2nd ed. Oxford: Oxford University Press, 1989.

Josephus. *The Jewish War.* Translated by G. A. Williamson. Penguin Classics 90. New York: Penguin, 1972.

Kalimi, Isaac. *Metathesis in the Hebrew Bible.* Peabody, MA: Hendrickson, 2018.

Keener, Craig. *The Gospel of John: A Commentary.* 2 vols. Peabody, MA: Hendrickson, 2003.

Kern, Otto. *Die Inschriften von Magnesia am Maeander.* Berlin: Spemann, 1900.

Kiley, Mark C. "The Beloved Disciple, Judas Iscariot." In *Reading Between the Letters of the Gospels*, 88-134. Eugene, OR: Wipf and Stock, 2024.

———. "The Exegesis of God: Jesus' Signs in John 1-11." In *Society of Biblical Literature: 1988 Seminar Papers*, edited by David J. Lull, 555-69. SBLSP 27. Atlanta: Scholars, 1988.

———. "Marcan Love, *Sotto Voce.*" *BTB* 39 (2009) 71-76.

———. "Yhwh in the Servant Poems of Isaiah and in Matthew 4-12." In *Reading Between the Letters of the Gospels*, 4-12. Eugene, OR: Wipf and Stock, 2024.

Korpel, M. C. A., and Johannes deMoor. *The Structure of Classical Hebrew Poetry: Isaiah 40-55.* OtSt 41. Leiden: Brill, 1998.

Levine, Amy-Jill. *Short Stories by Jesus: The Enigmatic Parables of a Controversial Rabbi.* New York: Harper Collins, 2014.

Livy. *History of Rome: Books 3-4.* Translated by B. O. Foster. Vol. 2 of *History of Rome.* LCL 115. Repr., Cambridge, MA: Harvard University Press, 2013.

Bibliography

Mantas, Konstantinos. "Independent Women in the Roman East: Widows, Benefactresses, Patronesses, Office-Holders." *Eirene* 33 (1997) 81–95.

Meier, John P. *Probing the Authenticity of the Parables*. Vol. 5 of *A Marginal Jew: Rethinking the Historical Jesus*. AYBRL. New Haven, CT: Yale University Press, 2016.

Menken, Maarten J. J. *Old Testament Quotations in the Fourth Gospel: Studies in Textual Form*. CBET 15. Kampen, Neth.: Kok Pharos 1996.

Mettinger, Tryggve N. D. *A Farewell to the Servant Songs*. Scripta Minora Societatis Humaniorum Litterarum Lundensis 3. Lund, Swed.: Gleerup, 1983.

———. "In Search of the Hidden Structure: YHWH as King in Isaiah 40–55." In *Writing and Reading the Scroll of Isaiah: Studies of an Interpretive Tradition*, edited by Craig C. Broyles and Craig A. Evans, 1:143–54. VTSup. Leiden: Brill, 1997.

Moloney, Francis J. *Love in the Gospel of John: An Exegetical, Theological, and Literary Study*. Grand Rapids: Baker Academic, 2013.

Murphy, Frederick J. *Apocalypticism in the Bible and Its World: A Comprehensive Introduction*. Grand Rapids: Baker Academic, 2012.

Murphy, Roland E. *The Tree of Life: An Exploration of Biblical Wisdom Literature*. New York: Doubleday, 1990.

Natali, Carlo. "Schools and Sites of Learning." Translated by Catherine Porter and Jeannine Pucci. In *Greek Thought: A Guide to Classical Knowledge*, edited by Jacques Brunschwig and Geoffrey E. R. Lloyd, translated under direction of Catherine Porter, 200–202. Harvard University Press Reference Library. Cambridge, MA: Belknap, 2000.

Neusner, Jacob. *The Mishnah: A New Translation*. New Haven, CT: Yale University Press, 1988.

———. *Rabbinic Literature: An Essential Guide*. Abingdon Essential Guides. Nashville: Abingdon, 2005.

Neyrey, Jerome H. "'Are You Greater Than Our Father Jacob?' Jesus and Jacob in John 1:52 and 4:4–26." In *The Gospel of John in Cultural and Rhetorical Perspective*, 87–122. Grand Rapids: Eerdmans, 2009.

O'Connor, Michael. *Hebrew Verse Structure*. Winona Lake, IN: Eisenbrauns, 1997.

Paul, Shalom M. *Isaiah 40–66: Translation and Commentary*. Grand Rapids: Eerdmans, 2012.

Perkins, Pheme. *Gnosticism and the New Testament*. Minneapolis: Fortress, 1993.

Plato. *Cratylus. Parmenides. Greater Hippias. Lesser Hippias*. Translated by Harold North Fowler. LCL 167. Cambridge, MA: Harvard University Press, 1926.

Pontifical Biblical Commission. "On the Historical Truth of the Gospels." Catholic Resources, Apr. 21, 1964. https://catholic-resources.org/ChurchDocs/PBC_HistTruth Gosp.htm.

Poster, Carol. "The Idea(s) of Order of Platonic Dialogues and Their Hermeneutic Consequences." *Phoenix* 52 (1998) 282–98.

Rad, Gerhard von. *Deuteronomy: A Commentary*. OTL. Philadelphia: Westminster, 1966.

Reynolds, Benjamin E., and Loren T. Stuckenbruck, eds. *The Jewish Apocalyptic Tradition and the Shaping of New Testament Thought*. Minneapolis: Fortress, 2017.

Richey, Lance Byron. *Roman Imperial Ideology and the Gospel of John*. CBQMS 43. Washington, DC: Catholic Biblical Association of America, 2007.

Robinette, Brian D. "Christology—Who Do You Say That I AM?" In *Theological Foundations: Concepts and Methods for Understanding Christian Faith*, edited by J. J. Mueller et al., 105–30. Winona, MN: Anselm Academic, Christian Brothers, 2011.

Bibliography

Ross, David O., Jr. *Backgrounds to Augustan Poetry: Gallus, Elegy and Rome*. Cambridge: Cambridge University Press, 1975.
Ruprecht, Eberhard. " Die Auslegungsgeschichte zu den sogenannfen Gotresknechtslieder im Buch Deuterojesaiu unter methodischen Gesichtspunkren bis zu Bernhard Duhm." PhD diss., Ruprecht-Karls-Universität-Heidelberg, 1972.
Ryan, Alan. *On Politics: A History of Political Thought from Herodotus to the Present*. New York: Liveright, 2012.
Schaser, Nicholas J. "Inverting Eden: The Reversal of Genesis 1–3 in John's Passion Narrative." *WW* 40 (2020) 263–70.
Schnackenburg, Rudolf. *The Gospel According to St John*. Translated by Cecily Hastings et al. 3 vols. New York: Crossroad, 1987.
Schneiders, Sandra M. "Symbolism in the Fourth Gospel." In *Written That You May Believe: Encountering Jesus in the Fourth Gospel*, 63–77. New York: Herder, 1999.
Scholem, Gershom. "The Name of God and the Linguistic Theory of the Kabbala." Translated by Simon Pleasance. *Diogenes* 79 (1972) 59–80; *Diogenes* 80 (1972) 164–94.
Schroeder, Frederic M. "Friendship in Aristotle and Some Peripatetic Philosophers." In *Greco-Roman Perspectives on Friendship*, edited by John T. Fitzgerald, 35–57. SFSHJ. SBL Resources for Biblical Scholars 34. Atlanta: Scholars, 1997.
Schuchard, Bruce G. *Scripture Within Scripture: The Interrelationship of Form and Function in the Explicit Old Testament Citations in the Gospel of John*. SBLDS 133. Atlanta: Scholars, 1992.
Schweizer, Eduard. "What About the Johannine 'Parables'?" In *Exploring the Gospel of John: In Honor of D. Moody Smith*, edited by R. Alan Culpepper and C. Clifton Black, 208–19. Louisville, KY: Westminster John Knox, 1996.
Snodgrass, Klyne R. *Stories with Intent: A Comprehensive Guide to the Parables of Jesus*. Grand Rapids: Eerdmans, 2008.
Sturch, R. L. "Jeremias and John: Parables in the Fourth Gospel." *ExpTim* 89 (1978) 235–39.
"Temple Warning Inscription." Wikipedia, last edited May 17, 2025. https://en.wikipedia.org/wiki/Temple_Warning_inscription.
Theobald, Michael. "Johannine Dominical Sayings as Metatexts of Synoptic Sayings of Jesus: Reflections on a New Category Within Reception History." In *Glimpses of Jesus Through the Johannine Lens*, edited by Paul N. Anderson et al., 383–405. Vol. 3 of *John, Jesus, and History*. ECL. Atlanta: SBL, 2016.
Trypanis, C. A. "Technopaigneia." In *Greek Poetry: From Homer to Seferis*, 341–42. Chicago: University of Chicago Press, 1981.
Van Tilborg, Sjef. *Imaginative Love in John*. BibInt 2. Leiden: Brill, 1993.
Viladeseau, Richard. *Theological Aesthetics: God in Imagination, Beauty, and Art*. Oxford: Oxford University Press, 1999.
Virgil. *Georgics*. In *Eclogues. Georgics. Aeneid, Books 1–6*, translated by H. Rushton Fairclough, 128–287. Rev. ed. LCL 63. Cambridge, MA: Harvard University Press, 1935.
Wilkinson, Robert J. *Tetragrammaton: Christians and the Name of God; From the Beginnings to the Seventeenth Century*. Studies in the History of Christian Traditions 179. Leiden: Brill, 2015.
Williams, Jenni. *The Kingdom of Our God: A Theological Commentary on Isaiah*. London: SCM, 2019.

Bibliography

Winter, Paul. "Magnificat and Benedictus—Maccabean Psalms?" *Bulletin of the John Rylands Library* 37 (1954–55) 328–47.

Wolters, Al. "The Riddle of the Scales in Daniel 5." *HUCA* 62 (1991) 155–77.

Wright, Addison G. "The Structure of the Book of Wisdom." *Bib* 48 (1967) 165–84.

———. "Wisdom." In *Jerome Biblical Commentary*, edited by Raymond E. Brown et al., 558. Englewood Cliffs, NJ: Prentice-Hall, 1968.

Zimmermann, Ruben. *Puzzling the Parables of Jesus: Methods and Interpretation.* Minneapolis: Fortress, 2015.

Ancient Document Index

OLD TESTAMENT

Genesis

1	66–67, 68, 90, 130, 161
1:1	66, 67
1:1a	42
1:26	66–67
3:1–3	149
3:1–7	149
3:4–5	149
3:6	149
3:6–7	149
3:7	149
3:15	80
28	73, 86
28:16	87
37:2 LXX	129
37:8 LXX	129
37:30 LXX	129
37:33 LXX	129
41	140

Exodus

2:11	84
3	24, 27–28n12
3:2–3	27
3:3	27
3:5	27
3:6 LXX	35–36n15
3:14	27, 39
3:14 LXX	35, 35–36n15, 36, 37, 39, 77n6, 85
3:18–19	27
4:1	55–56
12:22	161n16
17	70
20	70
34	134

Deuteronomy

5	70
6:1–3	70
6:4	13
6:17	70
22:6	107
22:6–7	107–8
22:7	108
30:11	60n20

1 Samuel

8	104
8–12	103–4
9	104
10	104
11	104
12	104

2 Samuel

2:25	161n16

Ancient Document Index

1 Kings (3 Kings LXX)

3	65
3:1	65
20:25	127
21	3
21:17	3
21:25 LXX	127

Job

28:21	67n4

Psalms

1:2	71
1–41	150
2	60
12:2b	58
22	150
23	24, 57–58
23:1	57
23:2a	58
23:3a	58
23:4a	57
23:4b	58
23:5a	58
23:5c	57
27	24, 57–58, 138
27:1	58
27:10	58
34	136, 136n21, 150
35	150
41	150
42–72	150
62:5 LXX	87, 89
69	150
73–89	150
78	150
82	150
84:4	106
90–106	150
107–50	150
113:4 LXX	131n15
113:6 LXX	131n15
114:4	131n15
114:4 LXX	131n15
114:6	131n15
114:6 LXX	131n15
118	58, 150
118:24	120
119:47	71

Proverbs

	132

Song of Solomon

2:13	87n11

Wisdom of Solomon

	64, 87–88, 90, 91
1:1—6:21	88
1–4	72
5–9	72
6	64
6–10	64
6:17	87
6:17–20	86–87
6:17–21	89
6:18	87
6:19	86
6:20	86
6:22—9:18	88
7:8	82
7:11	82
7:13	72
7:13–14	82
7:24b	99
7:24d	84
7:27c–d	99
8	6, 64, 85
8:1	81–82
8:5	80, 81n8, 87n11
8:5–8	79–80, 85–86
8:6	80, 82, 86, 148
8:7	80, 83, 84, 86
8:8	80, 84–85, 86
8:9	82n9
9	72
9:11	77n7
10	6, 64, 74–79
10:1	78
10:2	78
10:4	77, 78

10:4a	77
10:6	78
10:8	77, 78
10:9	77, 78
10:10	1, 64, 71, 72, 73–74, 77, 78, 82, 86, 89
10:13	78
10:15	78
10:16–17a	79
10–19	72
10:20	77
10:21	78
11:1–14	72
11:2–16	88
12:23–27	88
13	72
13:5	72
15	72
15:18—16:29	88
16:1–4	72
16:5–14	72
16:15–29	72
17:1—18:4	72
17:1—19:22	88
18:5–25	72
19:1–17	72
19:18a	82
19:22	72

Sirach

Prologue	66
27–29	68
1	64, 66
1:1–30	66–69
1:2	87
1:3	67
1:4	67
1:5	67
1:8	66, 67
1:9	66, 67, 87
1:11	67, 68
1:12	67, 68
1:13	68
1:14	68
1:16	66, 68
1:18	67, 68
1:19	87
1:20	68
1:25	67
1:26	68
1:27	68
1:28	68
1:30	68

Isaiah

	17, 132
40:9	55
40:9–10	80
40:10	40, 54
42	6, 41, 43, 54
42:1	56
42:1–4	41, 43, 44
42:1–9	41
42:3	42
42:5–9	41
42–53	40
49	6, 41, 42, 43, 54
49:1–4	41
49:1–6	41, 43, 43–44, 45–46
49:4	48
49:5	56
49:6	42, 56
49–50	42
50	6, 41, 43, 51–52, 54
50:4	56
50:4–9	41, 43, 44, 48–49
50:5	49
50:6	51
50:6–8	56
50:7	42, 49, 49n9, 52
50:9	51
52:13—53:12	41, 43, 44, 52–54
52:15	56
52–53	6, 41, 43, 54
53	59, 89, 90, 144
53:1	58
53:4	60
53:5	56
53:9	54, 59
53:12	42
58:6	161n16

Jeremiah

11:19 LXX	131, 131n15
23	60n20
23:1–8	59, 60
23–24	59
23:33	60, 60n18
23:33 LXX	60
23:33–40	60
23:39	60
24:1–10	60
27:45 LXX	131n15
50:45	131n15

Lamentations

	151n10

Ezekiel

	49n9
20:37	138n26
20:37 LXX	138n26

Daniel

	135n20
5	6, 103, 133–40
5:5	135
5:5 LXX	140–41n29
5:6	135n20
5:12 LXX	133
5:14	135n20
5:15	135n20
5:24	135n20
5:24 LXX	140
5:26	134, 136
5:26–28	134–35, 135n20, 138n26
5:27	134
5:27 LXX	135
5:28	134, 136

Amos

8:1–3	60
9:6	161n16

DEUTEROCANONICAL BOOKS

1 Esdras

3–4	140
4:59	140
9:53	140

PSEUDEPIGRAPHA (OLD TESTAMENT)

Psalms of Solomon

17	59
17.1	59
17.16	59
17.25	59
17.27	59n17
17.32	59
17.40	59
17.46	59

DEAD SEA SCROLLS

1QIsa^a	49, 49n9

ANCIENT JEWISH WRITERS

Josephus
Jewish War

7.129	63

RABBINIC WORKS

Mishnah
Zera'im

Berakhoth	107

Mo'ed

	107

Kodashim

Hullin	107

NEW TESTAMENT

Matthew

1	161
1:1	154
1–2	154, 155, 156
1–4	154
1:20	154, 156
1:21	155
2	161
2:1	156
2:2	157
2:7–12	155
2:12	155
2:13	157
2:16	157
2:18	157
2:20	156
2:23	155, 157
3:2	162
4	57
4:17	162
5:6	25
5:10	24
5:20	28, 104
5:26	128
6:9–13	24n8
6:21	10
6:22–23	22
6:22–24	21–22
6:22c	23
6:31	21
6:33	23, 24n8
6:33–34	20
6:34	21
7	128
7:6	23
7:7	32
7:8	32
7:8–9	32
7:9	32
7:21	104
8	57
9	57
11:2	71
11:4	71
11:5	71
11:12	25, 26n9, 27n11, 71
11:16–19	71
11:22	71
11:25–27	71
11:28	71
11:29–30	71
12	57
13:24–30	111n8
13:31–32	122n11
13:33	117
13:35	112
13:36–43	122–23
13:39	122
13:44	9, 108–9, 109, 124, 125
13:44–50	123–25
13:45	124
13:46	111, 124
13:48	124
16:19	30
18:3	28
18:13	104
19:23–24	28
21:33–43	122n11
22:1–14	122n11
22:2–14	118
24:11–12	32n13
24:18	107
24:45–51	112
25	119
25:1–13	119
25:6	120
25:14–30	122n11

Mark

	60n19
1:15	14, 15, 16, 17, 31, 103, 104, 161–62
4:11	143
4:11–12	142
4:12	143–44
4:12a	144

Mark (cont.)

4:13–20	105
4:17	161
4:24	111
4:26–29	110
4:30–32	122n11
4:32	106
8	104
8:22—9:13	39n17
8:27–30	39n17
8:31	11
9	104
9:1	39n17
9:30	11
9:47	28
10	104
10:23–25	28, 104
10:32	11
11	104
12	104, 131
12:1–11	122n11
12:13–15	130
12:15	130
12:34	29
12:43–44	128–29
14:25	31
14:65	13

Luke

1	89, 90
1:2	154
1–2	40, 56–57, 155, 156, 162
1–4	154
1:21–22	154
1:31	155
1:35	56, 154
1:38	56
1:42	155
1:48	56
1:53	82n10
1:61	156
1:63	156
1:72	56
1:78	56
2:2–3	157
2:10	157
2:12	155
2:20	155
2:26	56
2:32	157
2:33–36	156
2:34	56, 157
2:36	56
2:43	155
2:47	56
2:48	157
2:51	56
4:16–30	17–19
4:20–22	17
4:35	20
6:39	128
6:40	128
9:27	28
10:25–37	113–14
11:5–8	120
11:7	121
11:9–13	32
11:13	121
12:13–21	121
12:35–38	112
12:41	112
12:48	156
13	122
13:6–9	112
13:18–19	122
13:21	117
14:16–24	122n11
14:25–33	126
15:11–32	111
16:8	122
16:16	25
16:19–31	117–18
16:31	118
17:37	107
18:1–8	115–16
18:9–14	116
18:24–25	28
19:11–27	122n11
19:20	127
19:22	127
20:9–18	122n11
22:15	87n11

23:56	127n14	2:1–2	15
24:6	127n14	2:1–11	21, 57–58n15, 80–82, 114
24:8	127n14	2:1–12	16, 42, 66, 81n8
24:12	127n14	2:3	57
24:50	152	2:4	80
24:52	123	2:5	80–81
		2:6	45, 57, 117
		2:9	81

John

1	59, 97, 137, 152, 153–54, 156	2:10	57, 81
		2:11	57–58n15
1:1	11, 58	2:13	11, 24
1:1–4	35–36n15	2:13—3:21	20, 21, 23–24
1:1–18	111, 112, 139	2:13–14	77
1–2	151, 153, 154	2:13–22	62
1:3	1	2:14	124
1–6	151, 152	2:14–15	22, 77
1:10	1	2:15	23, 34
1:11	139	2:15–18	23n7
1–11	24, 57–58	2:16	22, 124
1:12	2, 28, 58	2:16–17	124, 125
1–12	72, 107, 150	2:17	37, 124, 150
1:13	139	2:18	77
1:14	3, 139	2:19	65n2
1:18	35–36n15, 139	2:21	23, 77n7
1:19	114	2:23	77
1:19—4:3	148	2:23–25	77n6
1:19–37	14n5	2:24	77n7
1:29	21, 66	3	9, 11, 33, 39n17, 94, 112, 120, 137, 138–39, 151, 153, 154
1:29–51	20		
1:30	21		
1:32	68, 122		
1:35	21, 66	3:1–2	23n7
1:36	102	3:2	23
1:36–39	20–21	3:3	1, 7, 10, 13, 14, 27, 28, 29, 33, 38, 39, 72, 86, 93, 104, 117, 137, 143, 144
1:38	62		
1:43	21, 66		
1:46–48	72		
1:47–51	59, 60	3:4	13
1:49	15, 36, 57, 60, 66	3:5	1, 7, 10, 14, 27, 29, 33, 38, 39, 72, 86, 93, 104, 117, 143, 144
1:49b	66		
1:51	36, 37, 38, 68, 86		
2	2, 6, 9, 40, 42, 44–45, 57, 62, 72, 82n9, 85, 106, 112, 132, 156		
		3:8	124
		3:11	39
2:1	15, 57–58n15, 66	3:11–13	23n7
		3:14	11, 29, 68, 98

John (cont.)

3:15	14
3:16–21	22–23
3:17	35
3:18	39
3:20–21	93
3:22–30	14n5
3:25	93
3:28	35
3:29	119
3:29–30	93
3:30	13, 14, 14n5
3:31–35	14n5
3:36	28
3:39–42	100
4	6, 9, 40, 42, 46–48, 72, 85, 99, 101n30, 104, 106, 119, 132, 146, 151, 153, 155
4:1–3	83
4:1–42	82
4:4	48, 82
4:4—6:15	148
4:5	101
4–5	72
4:5–6	83
4:7	14
4:10	82
4:12	48, 83
4:20–27	99, 100
4:26	78
4:29	100
4:31	52
4:33	80, 82
4:34	82
4:35	99, 100
4:36–38	79
4:37	99
4:42	100
4:44	100
4:47	57
4:48	79
4:49	57
4:51	57
5	9, 62, 68, 70, 71, 94n20, 112, 120, 129, 151, 153
5:4	89
5:5	69
5:6	69
5:7	58
5:8	69
5:9	58
5–10	100
5:14	69
5:16	70
5:17	70
5:18	69, 70
5:19	70
5:20	4
5:21	3
5:27	121, 152
5:27–28	4
5:35	119
5:43	69, 70
5:44	69, 70
6	21, 59, 71, 72, 112, 132, 133, 151, 153, 154, 155, 158
6:1–15	128–29
6:4	11
6:8	129
6:9	128
6:9–10	128
6:10	129
6:10–11	58
6:12	161
6:13	129
6:15	25, 26, 26n10, 129, 158
6:15–21	9n1
6:16–21	148
6:19	28
6:20	26n10, 34, 58
6:21	158
6:22—12:11	148
6:26	34
6:30	28
6:31	37
6:31–40	125
6:32	34
6:40	14
6:41–51	125
6:45	125, 158

6:47	34	9:35–41	28
6:51–59	125	9:39	116, 121
6:52–59	125	9:40–41	128
6:53	34	10	14n5, 70, 94n20, 98, 110, 127, 132, 151, 153, 157
6:53–54	31, 31–32		
6:53–58	34		
6:54	31	10:3	32
6:60	125	10:6	96
6:60–66	125	10:7	3
6:62	28	10:8	32, 114
6:66	124	10:8–10	69, 70
6:66–70	118	10:9	32
6:67	124, 125	10–11	72
6:67–68	125	10:12	25, 26, 26n10
6:68	9, 59, 109, 124, 125	10:14	32n13
7	70, 71, 94, 151, 153, 156	10:14–15	110, 111n8
		10:17	127
7–11	151	10:17–18	110–11, 111n8
7:15	158	10:18	3, 71
7:19	70	10:22	9n1
7:22–24	70	10:27–30	26–27
7:38	71	10:28	26n10, 32
8	70, 71, 94, 138–39, 151, 153, 156	10:29	26n10
		10:30	96
8:1–11	89, 90, 140–41n29	10:34	37
8:6	140–41n29	10:40	14n5, 83–84
8–9	72	10:40–42	9n1
8:13	98	10:41	14n5
8:13–14	70	11	6, 40, 42, 49–52, 58, 85, 94, 102, 106, 118, 119, 151, 152n13, 153, 157
8:15	121		
8:17	69		
8:28	145, 148		
8:31–38	71	11:1–6	51–52
8:32	152	11:1–44	83–84
8:35	70	11:3	83
8:38	11	11:5	80, 83
8:40	69, 70, 152	11:6–7	80
8:41	69, 70	11:7–8	84
8:44	69, 70	11:8	52
8:44–46	152	11:9	120
8:48	114–15	11:9–10	152n13
8:49	69, 70	11–12	42
8:58	35–36n15	11–13	120
9	24, 58, 59, 94, 128, 151, 153, 157	11:15	52
		11:20	83
9:23–24	21	11:25	14, 80, 85
9:35	116	11:26	84

John (cont.)

11:28	52, 83, 84
11:31	83
11:34	114
11:37	96
11:40	84
11:41	42
11:42	11
11:42–43	80
11:44	84
11:45	28
11:49	120
12	6, 24, 54, 85, 90, 95, 96, 106, 119, 132, 138–39, 151, 152n13, 153, 154, 156
12:1–8	85, 98
12:3	80, 84
12:4–8	85
12:8	98–99
12:10	96
12:12—21:25	148
12:13	37, 38, 58
12:13b	36, 120
12:14–15	37
12–16	151
12:18	85
12:20	38, 145
12:24	123
12:27–28	11, 96, 97
12:31	145
12:32	11, 98
12:33	145
12:35	152n13
12:36	122
12:38	54, 58, 90, 144
12:40	143, 143n1, 144
12:48	145
13	10, 62, 92, 97, 112, 113, 120, 151, 153, 156
13:1	11, 110
13:1–2	12
13:1—17:26	148
13:2	122
13:4–5	112
13:5	10
13:7	120
13:10	158
13:11	10
13:13	10
13:15	114
13:17	97, 112
13–17	34, 86–87, 95–96
13–19	72
13–21	24, 92, 146, 150
13:25	109
13:28	120
13:29	109
13:31	148
13:32	148
13:33	87
13:34a–b	100
13:38	152
14	92, 94n20, 151, 153, 157
14:1	116
14:2	97
14:4	27n12
14:5	87, 120
14:6	13
14:7	27
14:8	74
14:12	28, 74, 133
14–15	87n11
14:21	27, 87
14:22	27–28n12
14:23	27–28n12, 64
14:23–24	91
14:26	34, 74, 97
14:27	34, 127
14:30	27
14:31b	87
15	92, 112, 151, 153, 157
15:2	74
15:5	122
15:6	74
15:12	87, 100
15:14	87
15:16	118
15:17	87, 100
15:18—16:33	116

15:25	38n16, 150	18:26	102
16	72, 82n9, 92, 151, 153, 157	18:28—19:11	149
		18:29	101
16:2	86	18:30–32	149
16:8	28, 34	18:35	102
16:10	28	18:36	10–11, 34
16:20	34	19	14, 55, 61, 65n2, 92, 103, 127, 132, 139–40, 144, 151, 153, 155
16:33	35, 86, 127		
17	27–28n12, 61, 72, 92, 151, 153, 154, 155, 158–60		
		19:3	13
17:1	148	19:4	149
17:2	2, 86, 160	19:4–5	130–31, 131
17:3	78, 86, 159, 160	19:5	130, 131
17:4	126, 148	19:6—20:18	146
17:5	148	19:9	42, 61
17:6	78	19:10–11	35
17:8	158, 159	19:12–42	149
17:10	148	19:13	61, 62, 126
17:11	78	19:14	149
17:12	78	19:16	35, 149
17:17	2, 3, 160	19:16–19	147
17–21	151, 152	19:19	37, 38, 38n16
17:23	126, 158–59	19:19–22	13
17:24	159	19:20	2, 13, 27n12
17:26	78	19–20	139
18	11, 101–2, 151, 152, 153	19:20–22	147
		19–21	95
18:1	136n22	19:22	135
18:1–9	149	19:24	106, 146
18:1–14	149	19:25	65, 106
18:1–27	149	19:25–27	147
18:3	102	19:26–27	65, 91, 114
18:10	102	19:27	82n9
18:10–11	149	19:28–30	24, 147
18:12–14	149	19:30	33
18:13	102	19:30–35	33
18:15	102	19:31	33–34, 146
18:15–18	149	19:31–32	24–25
18:16	102	19:31–33	147
18:19	102	19:31–35	33
18:19–24	149	19:34	29
18:20	152–53n14	19:36	136n21, 146
18–21	72, 149	19:38	136n22, 146
18:22	13, 102	19:38–42	97, 108, 147
18:24	102	19:39	110, 111, 136
18:25–27	149	19:39–40	110, 135

John (cont.)

19:39–42	29
19:39b	136
19:40	127, 134, 138n26, 140
19:40a	136
19:40b	136
19:42	136
20	97, 103, 113, 122, 127, 137, 144, 151, 153, 154
20:1–2	147
20:1–31	149
20:2	127
20:3–4	127
20:4	147
20:6–7	134, 140
20:7	127
20:8	29, 127
20:9	146
20:12	137
20:15	147
20:16	136
20:18	147, 149
20:19	20, 121, 127
20:19–23	19–20
20:19c–20a	16
20:20	73
20:21	140
20–21	90, 120–21, 152n12
20:21–22	121
20:21–23	17
20:22	14, 122
20:24	56
20:24–29	55–56
20:25	56
20:26	90
20:27	73
20:27–28	73
20:28	56
20:29	113, 146
21	60–61, 63, 72, 90, 102, 151, 152, 153, 154, 156
21:1	61
21:1–25	149
21:4	124
21:5	120
21:7	98, 113, 149
21:7–11	14
21:8	29
21:12	29, 113, 149
21:12–14	63n23
21:13	121
21:13–15	25
21:14	113
21:15–19	9, 30–31
21:18	113
21:22–23	125
21:23	95, 114
25:1–13	120
27–30	25

Acts

12:10	110
13:33	138

Romans

1:23	128
14:17	34

1 Corinthians

4:20	33
6:9	24
6:10	24
15:24	33
15:50	24, 34

2 Corinthians

3	134
4:17	137
5	146

Galatians

1	95
3:1	146
5:21	24

Philippians

2:8	146

Hebrews

1:8	34
11:33	34

EARLY CHRISTIAN WRITINGS

Augustine of Hippo

	90

GREEK AND ROMAN LITERATURE

Antiphon

	29

Aratus
Phaenomena

783–87	8–9, 9n1
833	9n1
977–81	9n1

Aristotle

	101–2

Metaphysics

3.4.1001 a 29	106n2

Homer
Odyssey

19.100–104	61
19.105	61
19.107–14	61

Livy
History of Rome

3.34	100–101

Plato
Hippias Maior

	95–97
281D	95
283E	97
285E	97
291E	97
301C	96
302B	96
304B	97
304D	96

Laches

	92

Laws

	92

Lysis

	92

Meno

	92
81B	95
82E	95
83E	95

Parmenides

	92

Phaedo

	92

Phaedrus

	92

Ancient Document Index

Republic

	92–94
5.473D	93
5.473E	93
5.475C	93
5.475D	93
5.475E	93
7	94

Socrates

91–92, 95, 96, 97

Virgil

89

Georgics

1.429–30   9

www.ingramcontent.com/pod-product-compliance
Lightning Source LLC
Chambersburg PA
CBHW051744230426
43670CB00012B/2153